INTERPERSONAL
PSYCHOTHERAPY

INTERPERSONAL PSYCHOTHERAPY

ARTHUR BURTON

PRENTICE-HALL, INC.

Englewood Cliffs, New Jersey

PRENTICE-HALL SERIES IN PERSONALITY, CLINICAL AND SOCIAL PSYCHOLOGY,
Richard S. Lazarus, Editor

Current printing (last number):

10 9 8 7 6 5 4 3 2 1

13–475046–2

Library of Congress Catalog Card Number:
78–163393

Printed in the United States of America

Prentice-Hall International, Inc., *London*
Prentice-Hall of Australia, Pty. Inc., *Sydney*
Prentice-Hall of Canada, Ltd., *Toronto*
Prentice-Hall of India Private Limited, *New Delhi*
Prentice-Hall of Japan, Inc., *Tokyo*

To MARTHA

Other books by the same author—

MODERN HUMANISTIC PSYCHOTHERAPY

**ENCOUNTER: THE THEORY AND PRACTICE
OF ENCOUNTER GROUPS**

THE SELF-ACTUALIZATION OF THE THERAPIST

PREFACE

Psychotherapy is the principle of civilization carried to its modal point. It is the way humanism finds expression as the ministration of one feeling person to another. And it is the identification of man with the inevitable pain and suffering of being man, and the expectation of its relief by still other men.

Above all, psychotherapy is the scientific way man applies rational procedures to irrational data, in a framework which dispenses with lunar, stanic, totemic and similar causative theories of the past. It has proved its social efficacy in a century of application—and there is the consensual testimony of at least a million clients. But its results are not limited to testimony alone, for statistical evidence—that mensuration which the process makes possible—supports it as well. Society validates that which is useful to its preservation, and psychotherapy is not only *not* in any danger of extinction but has become a flourishing modern entity. Indeed, this is the Age of the Therapeutic Man, and not only are there more applicants for its healing benefits, but also more people than ever who want to be psychotherapists.

Psychoanalysis was appropriate to its time. But Freud could not have been expected to find that universal anodyne which would perpetually endure and precisely in a world changing as radically as this one has. Even endogenous metahealing, that anthropological verity of every single culture of record, alters as the shaman gives rise to the psychiatrist.

The corrections today are all in the direction of the ego, and of course its interpersonal transactions, for Freud was primarily fascinated by the id. Nothing, in my opinion, militates against the basic discoveries of the unconscious determinants of behavior, the id and the superego, dream analysis, transference, resistance, pregenital character formation, the Oedipal and castration complexes, and so forth. They still apply in certain ways. But today we tend more to find the healing dynamic of psychotherapy in the interpersonal relationship—between a psychotherapist and his client—and less in the structural formulations of the therapist and the indigenous insight which accompanies its evolution. That is, every psychotherapy is interpersonal, has always been interpersonal, and will always be interpersonal. What differs in this book is the emphasis placed on the phenomenology and quality of the therapeutic encounter.

Process does not of course come without substance; but to emphasize one over the other has tremendous facilitative effects, and sometimes changes the nature of the psychotherapy as well. Do I then dare call this book *Interpersonal Psychotherapy*? I believe so, because my conception and style of psychotherapy has exactly this intention of stressing the meaning of the interpersonal equation rather than the images, symbols, wishes, and ideas in the mind of the client. I came to this point almost reluctantly over many years of practice, and possibly there is a message in it for the newcomer. All of the basics of psychotherapy are here: How to begin it; how to maintain it; and how to conclude it. But the emphasis is interpersonal, for this seems to me the most theoretically profitable of all modern approaches.

Quite obviously psychotherapy is not to be learned from books. But books on psychotherapy do make possible the anticipation of the problems which lie ahead, and give the beginner the needed confidence—sometimes false, to be sure—without which he might never approach the client. That is why this book, designed for the learner, makes no assumptions regarding previous therapeutic work, and even spells out many of the pragmatic and housekeeping tasks of psychotherapy which are uniformly omitted from such books. My experience has been that even sophisticated therapists are always casting about to find new and better ways of employing the telephone, taking vacations, making and receiving referrals, setting fees and collecting them, using written and other communications, opening and terminating therapy, and so forth. The trained psychotherapist may agree or disagree with what I say but I believe he will want the opportunity to consider it.

Interpersonal Psychotherapy has been written for the counselor as well as the psychotherapist. The exclusive use of the latter term throughout the book derives more from the need for consistency and economy than from differences of substance. There *is* a difference between counseling and psychotherapy; but I see it rather as a difference in level and intensity of therapeutic encounter and nothing more. Two persons who meet for the purpose of ameliorating and being ameliorated can call the process anything they wish, but the operations involved in the transaction tend to be the same, and the outcome similar, regardless of what we call it.

I want to acknowledge with gratitude the forebearance and understanding of my class in Basic Psychotherapy which listened to and commented upon these lectures. My thanks, also, to Dave Krebs, Ph.D., Don L. Lunde, M.D., Bruce B. Peck, Ph.D., Edward Rudin, M.D., Bernard Steinzor, Ph.D., William U. Snyder, Ph.D., and John Warkentin, M.D., Ph.D., who read some of the chapters.

The case incidents used as illustrative material in this book are fictional and should not be misidentified.

ACKNOWLEDGMENTS

1. To Van Nostrand Reinhold Company for a quotation from Carl Rogers in I. G. Sarason (ed.), *Contemporary Research in Personality*, 1969.
2. To Jay Haley and Grune & Stratton for a quotation from *The Strategies of Psychotherapy*, Grune and Stratton, 1963.

3. To the *American Journal of Psychiatry* and Ivan Gendzel for a quotation from Ivan B. Gendzel, 1970, Vol. 127.
4. To Allen B. Wheelis for a quotation from *The Illusionless Man*, W. W. Norton, 1966.
5. To Marshall Edelson for a quotation from *The Termination of Intensive Psychotherapy*, Charles C Thomas, Publishers, 1963.
6. To Marianne H. Eckhardt and *Contemporary Psychoanalysis* for a quotation from an article of hers, 1969, *6*, 1–12.
7. To Doubleday and Company for a quote from Theodore Roszak's *The Making of a Counter Culture*, 1969.
8. To Doubleday and Company for a quotation from C. G. Jung, *Man and His Symbols*, 1964.
9. To the *Archives of General Psychiatry* for a quotation from P. H. Knapp, "Image, Symbol, and Person," 1969, *21*, 392–406.
10. To McGraw-Hill Book Company for a quote from B. B. Wolman (ed.), *Handbook of Clinical Psychology* in J. G. Watkins, "Psychotherapeutic Methods," 1965.
11. To *Family Process* for a quotation from N. W. Bell, 1962, *1*, 175–193.
12. To the William Alanson White Foundation for a quote in *Psychiatry* from an article by Mackinnon and Michels, 1970, *33*, 82–93.
13. To Basic Books, Inc. for a quotation from the *Collected Works of Sigmund Freud*, Vol. 5, 1959.
14. To the *Australian Psychologist* for a quote from White and Sarfaty, 1970, *5*, 184–190.
15. To Science and Behavior Books for a quotation from N. W. Ackerman, in B. H. Zuk and I. Boszormenyi-Nagy (eds.) *Family Therapy and Disturbed Families*, 1967.
16. To M. Bush and the *Journal of the American Psychoanalytic Association* for a quotation from an article, 1969, *17*, 136–190.

Arthur Burton

Davis, California

CONTENTS

CHAPTER

VIII   Instrumental Problems   103

IX   Adjunctive Healing Procedures   116

THE CONCEPT
OF PSYCHOTHERAPY

I

Psychotherapy is one way modern man seeks relief from psychic pain and hopes to find self-fulfillment. Of course, he often finds little of either. But the fact that psychotherapy is purchased by millions, and practiced by so many others is some evidence of its social value. The task of psychotherapeutic science is to clarify just what psychotherapy is, and then to specify the circumstances under which it can be most effectively applied.

Deep down everyone believes he is a counselor and counsel is given freely in our society. But the therapeutic situation does not involve counsel of this sort. Therapy involves a formally structured interpersonal relationship, governed by an intricate and complex set of rules and forms, which brings the client a special experience he cannot obtain elsewhere. These procedures have been winnowed and culled over almost a century of therapeutic practice and offer increased assurance of success. They are disregarded at the client's peril, and the learner is often only dimly aware of how pertinent they are. Becoming a qualified therapist involves internalizing certain theories, methods, and ethics so that they automatically come into play in an integrated way in treatment. In critical moments of stress, such training comes to the fore. The professional's confidence is based on knowing what to do and when to do it without thinking.

REDUCTION OF SYMPTOMS

Psychotherapy is more than reduction of symptoms. To make the client more comfortable, less anxious, more productive, and more at home with himself are certainly necessary goals. But today fewer clients will settle for just this, and behavioral therapists tend to ignore the subjective needs of their clients. They fail to emphasize a positive or ontic thrust toward a more meaningful, creative, and useful life, and the classical presentation of neurotic symptoms is only a part of the treatment process. Reduction of a person's anxiety is no longer a feat by itself. Clients expect their therapy to lead them in a new life-growth direction, to open vistas for them, and they count the therapy an essential failure if it fails to do so. It may well be that in the future, therapists will delegate the amelioration of specific psychic symptoms

1

to behavioral, hypnotic, organic and similar therapies, while psychotherapy as such will uniformly reach into the philosophy of life and core of the client. Many clients may, indeed, come to seek both forms of therapy. My concept of therapy involves ever-evolving mental structures on the way from birth to death and their consequent meaning and use for the client at various stages of life.

Maslow[1] says mental health and normality call for feeling good subjectively, for periods of peak and plateau experience, for the ability to do and to achieve, for occasional ecstasy, for humor and meaning in life, and for ability to appreciate truth, goodness, and beauty. Neurotics, by definition, are incapable of this. In the past we have unfortunately assumed that once a client was freed from his disease, from an anxiety or a phobia, these special states of being would spring forth by themselves. Nothing is further from the truth. Positive mental health rarely results from negatives. Fulfillment comes only from interpersonal experiences, which become naturally joyous and attitudinal, because they offer the client love, hope, meaning, and faith in some way.

Psychotherapy can be viewed not only as a corrective medicine, but as an important interpersonal experience to rival any known to man. We have deliberately refused to recognize this because medicine has historically been short-term and aloof, and the doctor could not be involved in a relationship which mattered to him emotionally. The refusal of the classical analyst to allow the patient to look at him illustrates this attitude.

METHODOLOGY OR ENCOUNTERING

There is a tendency today in psychotherapy to play down therapeutic method and emphasize the actual encounter of the participants themselves. I have myself written on the importance of freedom to encounter.[2] Many therapists feel some "natural" or phenomenological method of experiencing will take over the therapeutic situation if only the client and the therapist are left free to come honestly to know each other. The basic encounter group and sensitivity training depend on this philosophical approach.

There is much truth in this; but my experience has been that only someone who is technically accomplished in a certain healing method feels free to disregard or abridge that method. Carl Rogers and Rollo May, for example, being masters of the technique of psychotherapy, are now free to allow their phenomenological selves total openness in treatment and they can safely proceed on the basis of intuition and empathy when someone else might come to grief with the same client. The authentic therapist encapsulates, abridges, and symbolizes the preliminary stages of therapy. Having been over them so many times, he need not, in every case, rehearse in detail the individual stepping stones to emotional growth. This is learning with much of the trial and error anticipated. For this reason, it is often painful for the professional to supervise the learner therapist who must "touch every base"

---

[1] A. Maslow, *Motivation and Personality*, 2nd ed. (New York: Harper & Row, 1970).
[2] A. Burton (ed.), *Encounter, The Theory and Practice of Encounter Groups* (San Francisco: Jossey-Bass Publishing Co., 1969).

in treating his client. This "inner knowledge" and training assurance is precisely what distinguishes the friend who freely gives well-meaning counsel from the professional who bides his time with his advice. It takes information, theory, technical skill, and personal courage not to jump in. Knowing when not to counsel is the most difficult thing of all to learn.

But no book on psychotherapeutic technique, not even this one, can make a therapist of someone who does not have that bedrock of humanity—which is the regard for people in distress. To be continuously involved—as a vocation—with emotionally sick or troubled people calls for a commitment of more than just intellect. It is a "calling," and the calling must reinforce itself every single day with every client. It certainly has something to do with the therapist's own personality structure and the way he has attempted to realize himself. (This subject is treated in more detail later on in this book.) Still, there is no aptitude test for identifying a therapist and it is necessary to test oneself "under fire" before the best and worst is known. This book may then offer the prologue to just such experiencing and learning situations with people in trouble.

Most of us now accept the concept that the thing which essentially heals in psychotherapy is the scientific meta-encounter between two people, one needing a certain form of help and the other offering to help in that particular way. All research interpreting healing systems confirms this. Even medicative and somatic approaches are not exempt from these influences as placebo studies have so interestingly revealed.[3] The placebo's effectiveness is often proportional to the client's faith in the one who prescribes it, and also to the way the client interprets the placebo. But charisma or saintliness is apparently not enough. The greatest Yogi or guru does not heal with regularity because he cannot systematically interpret the analytic data involved in the causality of personality events. Science makes this possible. Psychotherapy as a formal scientific method increases the possibility of improvement, which is why we learn systematically to be therapists.

Many psychopathological states are self-limiting, and others are aided by supportive help from family, friends, teachers, relatives, etc. Sometimes an unusual change of life circumstances produces the necessary relief or growth. But it is foolish, and perhaps even dangerous, to wait for such improbable events, and I consider the old medical cliché, "he will grow out of it," pernicious. Psychotherapeutic science improves the odds of finding health, authenticity, and fulfillment and it is a wise and courageous client who applies for it early and sticks with it. Therapy is not the only way one can be healed, but it is the most certain way in the present state of man's knowledge.

DIAGNOSIS

In this book I am very little concerned with diagnostic rubrics even though my own training was heavily diagnostic. I once firmly believed that

---

[3] J. D. Frank, "Role of Hope in Psychotherapy," *Int. J. Psychiat.*, 1968, *5*, 383–395. Also D. Rosenthal, and J. D. Frank, "Psychotherapy and the Placebo Effect," *Psych. Bull.*, 1956, *53*, 294–302.

no psychologist could begin doing therapy until he had administered one thousand Wechslers and five hundred Rorschachs—to first gain fundamental insight into the personality. I now believe this was a misdirected ideal. There seems to be a very small correlation between the conventional psychiatric pigeonholes and the possibility of successful therapy. Even schizophrenia, that supposedly dread and always regressive disease, has turned out not to be that at all. We now recognize that we were too glib in diagnosing schizophrenia and considering it fatal because we were perhaps overimpressed by the early ideas of Kraeplin, Bleuler, Freud, and Jung. Even psychopaths now respond to special forms of group therapy in prison settings; chronic alcoholics to the Alcoholics Anonymous program; heroin addicts to Synanon; delinquent children to reality therapy; and so forth. Many psychotics, formerly considered incurable, now have a favorable prognosis under the new medicine, possibly even more favorable than the outlook for some neurotics.

What seems to count more than the client's diagnosis is his ontic or life thrust to become authentic—to become and exist. Some mild neurotics never make it because they don't have enough of this life thrust, and some psychotics find a more profitable life because they will not compromise by living on a lower or more vegetative level of existence. The main deficiency of the mental hospital is that it says to the patient that he must not opt for much. A diagnostic category says nothing about ontic thrust, risk taking, or the client's need to be authenticated. What's more, the average psychiatric diagnosis is highly suspect and appears to have little reliability as well as a poor validity for treatment and living purposes. It is most often made on a scanning basis, under the most limiting of circumstances, and rarely involves long term follow-up to test its adequacy. It gives the diagnoser a sense of satisfaction he hasn't earned! Such a diagnosis may serve legal, social, and sometimes personal requirements, but strong dependence on diagnosis is defensive, and it usually indicates a true lack of insight into the personality of the person studied.

PSYCHOLOGICAL TESTING

The interpersonal psychotherapist will use psychological tests sparingly. He will not allow test scores to prejudice his observations and intuitions about his client, and he will rarely reject a client because of test scores which go against his clinical judgement. Of course, it takes time to build such judgement, which is why tests are usually over-employed by the learner. Tests have stopped being a fetish, a way of impressing the client, and have found a more valuative and trustworthy position in psychotherapy. In my experience, the better trained the therapist, the less he uses psychological tests. Their proper use in therapy is beyond the scope of this book; but I must say that therapy often provides a new diagnostic dimension for their use, and a proper field of application for them.

THERAPISTS AS HUMANE FORCES

The fact that the therapist uses his humanity as much as his clinical techniques to help people has often been overlooked. If truth, freedom, justice, and beauty are more frequent in health than disease, as Maslow claims, where then do they come from in the treatment of a client? Does one discover beauty by himself because his phobia has gone or is it because he has discovered something about being a person? Therapists are often embarrassed about their very human sentiments and their fundamental decency. But as a class they are a sensitive and devoted group of people, and their values are such that the feelings of people and their fulfillment count most in life. They have a furious intolerance for sickness, degradation, regression, despondency, dependency, and sloth. They work for the reinstatement of animal spirits and the vital life in people and not just for the lowering of anxiety. This is what they constantly struggle for in themselves. And this provides the humanizing model which is the beacon for self-fulfillment in therapy.

The therapist's underlying attitude becomes a unified and consistent philosophy about the client and his possibilities, even if it is never completely stated, or, in fact, cannot be put into words. The client has a right to know what his psychotherapist's conception of man is, even if he never asks it directly. This, more than anything, determines how good a model the therapist will be for him. Behavioral therapy, because of its mechanistic and objective outlook, has little of these values to offer, and even denies their importance. If a man is merely a bundle of firing neurons, neurons which fire together under certain associational or conditional possibilities, what is the imaginative value of a Renoir or Chagall? Interpersonal psychotherapists are above all human in the sense that they accept the arts as important products of culture, and are not afraid to quote poetry or to admire paintings in therapy. They recognize and accept themselves as artists as well as scientists. They do not strive for scientific ideals so unrelated to the realities of life as to be a form of dissociation—ideals which in the present century may yet be proven to be an erroneous approach to the problems of man. The best therapists I know are cultured and learned men, not only in psychology and psychiatry, but in literature, painting, sculpture, and drama. They bring all of man's knowledge to bear on their clients' problems. They are alert to their clients' suffering as a part of all mankind's suffering, and can place it in a proper social perspective. Therapy means socializing the asocial person and the student must first be socialized himself before he can be a therapist.

LEANING ON THE THERAPIST

One of my schizophrenic clients talks about her need to "lean on me." I have difficulty with this particular metaphor, but I understand that her Self needs to remain temporarily close to mine until she can stand alone as she needs and wants to. Psychotherapy is a leaning proposition. The "child" in each client requires an authentic adult to "be with" until certain corrective growth experiences help the child to become himself an authentic adult, making it possible for others to lean on him. But "leaning on" by itself does not help. Otherwise mothers and wives, brothers and sisters, teachers and professors, would make excellent therapists. The therapeutic situation is certainly a vigorous dependency in the service of the ego; but the resolution of that dependency, that is, freedom from it, starts the first moment therapy begins. This is not true of other dependencies. They go on and on being dependencies without ever resolving the life, or the symbolic, situation.

THE POWER STRUGGLE

Psychotherapy is a replay of the "power struggle" inherent in the original mother-child relationship—the first and possibly most important attachment in a person's life. No one really recalls that such a struggle took place, and everyone resists finding out about it. Adler was the first to truly sense the power politics of growing up in the family. But "bad" and murderous feelings are more common in mothers than our repressions let us remember as several recent books have pointed out.[4] But the therapeutic struggle differs from the maternal struggle in that it does not involve emotional aggrandizement. Otherwise forces such as sexuality, the accumulation of riches, and emotional bondage would play a greater part in therapy than they do. Therapy is better described as the struggle of one Self helping another be It-Self, to accept the full freedom of being—the most frightening thing of all to man. It is no-mother being mother in quite a different way from before. Therapy is passionate, yet dispassionate, attention to an inner life secretly and arbitrarily imposed upon. This requires therapeutic intervention within a special healing context to change the image of growth, power, and life.

Intervention is almost a reproachful term today, but the client always resists precisely that realization and understanding he wants most. Furthermore he resists in a way he does not understand and cannot understand until much later. This is why Ouspensky[5] defines psychology as the "study of lies." While the goals of the client's life are his and not the therapist's, interventions are a way of maintaining the client's immersion in a process he does not fully comprehend and in which he, at first, has only a very limited faith. More people are lost to the benefits of therapy by technical errors at this stage than in any other single way for the client at first interprets the technique as the healer himself. He drops out and, sometimes forever, loses faith in this form of healing procedure because he sees the intervention as interfering and not helpful. Unfortunately, the genuineness or charisma of the therapist does not always compensate for such initial bumbling.

Development "power struggles," even the most benevolent forms, require technical ability, tact, insight, and courage for their resolution. These are not qualities the therapist is necessarily born with. They develop through the therapist's own suffering, growth, and experience. Learning why to intervene—and when and how to intervene—is a basic part of reorganizing the client's thoughts and feelings in therapy. This gives him new possibilities and choices in his life. In therapy, the power dynamics which the double-bind

---

[4] J. C. Rheingold, *The Mother, Anxiety, and Death* (Boston: Little, Brown & Co., 1967), among others.
[5] P. D. Ouspensky, *The Psychology of Man's Possible Evolution* (New York: Bantam Books, 1968).

and social "games" represent become first absurd, then a matter of humor—grim, but nevertheless humor, and then action. At this point, double-binds and "games" can no longer be destructive to the personality in the old way.

LOVE AND HATE

Love and good will are not enough in therapy. It is also necessary to be able to hate meaningfully. A therapist who cannot feel hate is, himself, probably a repressed person. Love for parents is always a matter of love *and* hate, and love without hate leads eventually to guilt. Obviously, the feelings of the client for his parents will sooner or later be a part of his feelings for the therapist. This is called transference. Most authentic therapists acknowledge their aggressions and put them to use in creative psychotherapy. Hating is caring! And psychotherapy is love and hate in the service of growth. Most learners are led to believe that they must never have aggressive feelings toward their clients. Interpersonal psychotherapy teaches, on the other hand, that any feeling is proper if it is acknowledged. Synanon is, in my opinion, based upon unadulterated venom; but it works, and, historically, saints have not made outstanding psychotherapists.

WHO IS THE CLIENT?

Who is the client? Paradoxically, the best definition is that a client is a person who applies for help. But the "real" client may not be that person but his mother or his spouse who seems to be normal and who applies for him or pushes him into therapy. Do we then not treat the identified client but ask to see the mother or spouse instead? Recent evidence suggests that the family rather than the person may be the unit of authentication, and that a kind of family homeostasis exists of which we have been only dimly aware. Treating the client sometimes involves authentication of his family as well, and this brings troublesome problems into dyadic therapy. But interpersonal psychotherapy fully acknowledges that therapy never stops with just the client. Even if only the client can be treated, the effects always reach beyond him. It is not unusual to treat one member of a family and then have several others ask to come too. Interpersonal therapy maintains this wider social posture and does not necessarily see the family as an interference, or something to be put off until the client is well. The client is always part of a larger world.

WHO IS THE THERAPIST?

Who is the therapist? Various licensing and certification procedures define this legally and set a minimum qualification floor. But such laws do not serve to distinguish the gifted and motivated therapist from the borderline, lukewarm one. The personality and authenticity of the therapist is so intimately involved in what he does that we might say that therapy is what a therapist does. But the essence of what the therapist does cannot be licensed, nor even yet scientifically defined, and this is probably more true of the therapeutic profession than of any other. Faith, artistry, and charisma still play too much of a part in therapeutic work, and while they should not be demeaned, it would be a happier thing if we could select therapists as efficiently as we choose life insurance salesmen. Since we haven't reached this stage yet, therapy becomes what the psychotherapist is emotionally prepared to do for his client, within certain limits, and with certain controls.

THE NATURE OF PSYCHOTHERAPY

Growth requires an environment which even if it does not encourage growth, at least does nothing to covertly discourage it. Children all grow up, but their pattern of growth depends on a very complex and exquisite maternal feedback mechanism which, if it goes awry, leaves a child with a haunting sense of incompleteness and loneliness. Such children become charged with a life-long mission to search for their missing experience or Self. Psychotherapy has been described as a process of mutual loneliness because the therapist shares his alienation with his client and in this way helps him find a way out of his "search."[6]

Carl Rogers has probably had more to say about the concept of psychotherapy than most others. He describes it this way:

> I mean any change in the personality structure, and in the behavior of the individual, which clinicians would agree implies greater integration, less internal conflict, more energy utilizable for effective living. I mean a change in behaviors away from those generally regarded as immature and toward those generally regarded as mature, responsible, and socialized.[7]

To attain this, he says the therapist must provide:

1. Unconditional positive regard.
2. Congruence.
3. Empathic-understanding.
4. Be perceived as genuine.

I would amplify these findings in the following way. Therapy involves:

1. Putting oneself at the disposal of the client without sham or dishonesty and with a deep desire to help.
2. Helping to put the unintegrated Self of the client back together.
3. Making the "inhuman" impulse and desire more human.
4. Making temporal and spacial binds more open.
5. Making new values possible or old ones more appropriate.
6. Helping to recognize *change* and *experience* as values in themselves.

---

[6]H. Stierlin, *Conflict and Reconciliation* (New York: Doubleday Anchor, 1968).
[7]C. R. Rogers, "The Therapeutic Relationship: Recent Theory and Research," in P. G. Sarason (ed.), *Contemporary Research in Personality* (2nd ed.) (Princeton: D. Van Nostrand Co., Inc., 1969), p. 294.

7. Freeing the client from separation anxiety and the guilt of the perception of a wasted life.

8. Freeing the creative imagination, and making the continuity of Self and world evident and workable.

To attain this, the following operations are required:

1. A continuation in symbolic fashion of the unconfirmed or disconfirmed child-mother relationship.

2. Deferring sexuality in treatment so as to bring all energies to bear on the healing task and as proof of existential sincerity.

3. An "involved detachment" in which both participants realize themselves through the joys and despairs of therapy.

4. A movement from self-reproach and other-reproach to freedom-to-be.

5. An opportunity to openly think about the forbidden and to experience approval for intimacy.

6. A new "philosophy" of existence, less past- or future-oriented, which gives greater weight to being present *now*.

Psychotherapy, in summation, must be considered the application of available scientific knowledge to a humanistic framework of altering styles of being and living, so that they provide a greater satisfaction to the client.

THE AIMS
OF PSYCHOTHERAPY

II

There are no generally agreed upon aims in psychotherapy. Watkins classifies the various aims propounded into the following four categories: "(1) Those which view the relief of the patient from symptoms, anxiety, and conflict as the chief objective of psychotherapy; (2) those which perceive the objective as establishing a feeling of adequacy of the Self, self-integration, and personal maturity; (3) those in which the aim is the improvement of interpersonal relationships, including the ability to give and receive love; and (4) those which seek to achieve an adjustment to society and culture."[1] As a basis for the consideration of the aims of psychotherapy I studied the literature and abstracted 40 different aims cited there. They are:

1. To find oneself
2. To become self-realized
3. To will what one is
4. To accept oneself
5. To be less guilty or anxious
6. To be more socially productive
7. To be more creative
8. To be a happier person
9. To be a better person
10. To become individuated
11. To become mature
12. To be a genital adult
13. To somatize less
14. To get more out of sexuality
15. To be at peace with oneself

[1] J. G. Watkins, "Psychotherapeutic Methods," in B. B. Wolman (ed.), *Handbook of Clinical Psychology* (New York: McGraw-Hill Book Co., 1965), p. 1143.

16. To be at one with the cosmos
17. To be more fully masculine (feminine)
18. To be able to love
19. To be authentic
20. To be closer to God
21. To be less compulsive
22. To be less paranoid
23. To have fewer mood swings
24. To have more pleasure
25. To make more friends
26. To be a more sensitive person
27. To be more self-integrated
28. To feel less inferior
29. To be better adjusted
30. To have a better sublimation
31. To be able to work and play
32. To have a reorganized self-concept
33. To become self-actualized
34. To find autonomy and freedom
35. To experience previously denied attitudes
36. To be fully functioning
37. To be responsible
38. To develop an integral locus of evaluation
39. To be more human
40. To do good works

These aims of psychotherapy are considered more or less specific to the following psychological conditions, all of which have been treated by psychotherapy:

1. Making a vocational choice
2. Phobias and obsessions
3. Impotence and frigidity
4. Inferiority feelings
5. Schizophrenia
6. Voyeurism
7. Homosexuality
8. Multiple personality
9. Somnambulism
10. Stuttering

11. Obesity
12. Ulcers, asthma, hypertension, etc.
13. Tics
14. Sociopathic personality
15. Addictions
16. Marital problems
17. Hysteria
18. Depression
19. Anxiety and panic reaction
20. Study habits
21. Shyness
22. Nailbiting and thumbsucking
23. Bed-wetting
24. Exhibitionism
25. Kleptomania
26. Delusions and hallucinations
27. Paranoia
28. Amnesia
29. Accident proneness
30. Suicidal tendencies

It must be obvious that any technique which is used for as wide a range of conditions as this, and which has so many different goals, is a non-specific technique with a wide-angled lens designed to cover a great deal. But Watkins is incorrect when he says only a symptom can be treated as such, or that psychotherapy can opt merely for the growth of self without, at the same time, touching the symptoms which then trouble the personality. Even the primary medication, such as phenothiazines, which are employed in psychiatry are not as specific as tetracycline or penicillin. They seem only to change nervous thresholds in the mid-brain. The pathogen in functional behavior is not a microbe or bacterium but sensory deposits, percepts, images, feelings, attitudes, habits, and styles. These do not necessarily have point-to-point sequential relationships but are imbedded in complex matrices which facilitate and inhibit each other. Simple behavioral sequences, and their anxious accompaniment, can be altered, reduced, and reformed, but higher-order emotional behavior does not as yet conform to such simple schemes. There is considerable precedent in medicine for the administration of healing agents without actual knowledge of their action or structure, as long as experience shows they work. Psychotherapy is something of this sort.

But it begs the question to say that the client determines his own goals. Clients come with cover complaints and test carefully to see if they can venture further. Many of them don't know what they are seeking except that they want their discomfort and ineffectiveness changed. The people they are dissatisfied with often turn out not to be the people who are damaging them most. And sex, that great focal complaint, is frequently only the carrier wave of even greater underlying dissatisfactions and inhibitions. Of course, the client determines the aims of therapy, just as he sets the aims of his life, but only through the experiences of his therapist. To refer it all to him, to give him the total responsibility for choosing in a process he fears, resents, and knows little about, is to deny our obligation. Clients bring complaints, and maintain them, which they preconsciously know will keep them in therapy. Only when they have a certain therapeutic security can they really formulate their intrinsic aims.

Psychotherapists should be modest about what psychotherapy can do. It does not give anyone a new personality. Clients after therapy are still defective persons, but they are viable and they have better interpersonal satisfactions. Freud knew best of all how really little psychoanalysis could accomplish. A tremendous effort is involved for small gains, and at times the whole process seems remarkably inefficient. The true aims of psychotherapy appear only much later in treatment and it was Freud who said that they only became finally clear in the last hour.

To compound the problem, fewer clients come today with specific complaints. Instead they offer a lack of meaning and purpose in their lives, a sense of loneliness, and a feeling that nothing is worthwhile. This has been called the existential neurosis and Frankl claims that 60% to 70% of the neuroses are of this sort. Such factors as our society's growing affluence, with accompanying improvements in people's wellbeing and general level of education, the absence of heros, the diminishing power of organized religion, the generation gap, and the computer have all served to heighten our sense of alienation from history and tradition. In desperation, sensing their illness, people have been turning from this vacuum to psychotherapy.

In contrast to neurosis, the problems of existence are always deep and tied to Thanatos. The thrust of this set of problems is to provide positive, humanistic models for changing feelings and attitudes rather than to alleviate symptoms. The Self is the symptom. The Self finds no joy in its preoccupations. This shows up clinically as depression and guilt.

To treat a part of the person while treating all of him at the same time is a perfectly legitimate operation. Increased sexual efficiency, a job promotion, more friends, a wider and less inhibited milieu, are all necessary goals of psychotherapy. One must respect the client who wants only to succeed in one of these areas without penetrating more deeply into his psyche. While the psychotherapist may regret such minimal goals, setting goals is the client's responsibility. The therapist may be comforted by the uneasy fact that most people live miserable lives. Phenothiazines are thus the biggest money makers of all in the pharmaceutical world! It is the fundamental arrogance of the missionary to insist on what the client doesn't, at the moment, want.

Psychotherapy has concentric aims—all of them valid. These aims go from the outer perimeter to the inner core, and the final aims at the center would be Jung's individuation, Freud's genital man, or Binswanger's authentic one. But the center itself is presumably only a construct and relevant only to the individual life under discussion. Very few people ever hit the jackpot.

Perhaps the primary drive toward authenticity, and not its obtainment, is the goal itself. We give our clients ontic-thrust and they then seem to go forth and tackle untackleable problems. They learn to disregard molehills and focus on mountains. They get a better sense of proportion. Not even the authentic man, let alone the creative artist, is ever free of problems. But he does his work despite them. It has always seemed to me that the psychotherapy of schizophrenia involves primarily the job of convincing the client to give up his coding, autism, and nihilism while shifting his attention to the problems of life. Both schizophrenia and depression imply that a certain appreciation of beauty has been lost from life.

Someone has said that we help substitute more dynamic problems for boring or outworn ones. Even by itself, this would be a worthwhile goal. The effective person makes a motor out of his problems and uses them for his self-expression. Clients tell us that after treatment is concluded they still have some of their obsessional thinking but they "don't pay any attention to it." Anxiety may be the wrong road to knowledge, but only the dead have no anxiety.

The conventional ways to describe client status is to talk about failure of ego, deficiency in self-concept, the presence of mental conflicts, or even the absence of a sufficient quantum of pleasure. We can also say that the client's Self is fixated on an infantile or pregenital level, that he plays games with non-rewarding payoffs, that he is fundamentally a masochist and only mental suffering rewards him, or that he cannot take risks, make choices, and accept responsibility for behavior. These linguistic and conceptual formulations all amount to the same thing: the client cannot effectively live the life he has made for himself. The neurotic life always involves an overabundance of anxiety and an underabundance of living.

Most of us today agree that the search for a single overriding trauma is doomed to failure. Such a trauma may be found, but finding it does not, by itself, reduce the client's discomfort or inhibition. It seems more profitable to look at current psychopathology from the point of view of a basic disaffirmation in the input (which can occur under imprinting contact theory or on a psychological or learning structure theory) and which continues through the developmental years with disordered goals, habit, and communication. Being human calls for basic trust. When it is absent, we must postulate interpersonal damage which denies straight-forward thought, being, and action. The pathogen is, for me, a disordered maternal or care-taking environment rather than any specific trauma as such. Even hunger, that most basic of innate needs, is now known to operate effectively only in the presence of proper learning opportunities.[2]

To go from the general to the more specific, the following are some of

2H. Bruch, "Hunger and instinct," *J. Nerv. ment. Dis.*, (1969), *149*, 91–114.

the sub-goals of psychotherapy which appear as a regular aspect of treatment. None of them necessarily correlate perfectly with psychic growth, but all of them are more or less present in successful psychotherapy.

INFLUENCE OF THE PAST

The life-historical past is a drag on the present and sets severe limits on the client's future. All clients overestimate the influence the past has had on them. A client of mine spends hours, in therapy and out, railing against a brother who has now been dead twenty years. What a waste! His brother can no longer hurt or even influence him, and yet he has circumscribed his life with his deceased brother. As therapy proceeds he talks less and less about him, and I hope the brother will soon resubmerge into the limbo of the client's life where he belongs, and not influence current choices. Psycho-analysis has somewhat oversold the traumas of infancy and childhood; but it is certainly true that our clients' major successes have been in the past, and they seek to reinstate them as only regression can force them to do. Inter-personal psychotherapy sets limits on this rehearsal of the past by making the present more real, more pleasurable, and by offering a future which previously seemed absolutely impossible. I call this psychotherapeutic func-tion, "defusing the past."

BEING RESPONSIBLE

Most of our clients are socially aresponsible people—even if they seem at times to be over-responsible. This has forced Mowrer, for example, to de-velop an entire system of healing around the point of responsibility and restitution.[3] Responsibility calls for making choices—popular and unpopular —painful and pleasurable ones—and then accepting the consequences flow-ing from the choice. Neurotics do make such choices, but simultaneously and ingeniously negate them while choosing. They cannot accept ultimate responsibility for fear of being judged, isolated, and condemned. Therapy reverses all this. For example, when the client can first be responsible for his hostile or loving behavior to the therapist, he has taken the first step towards acting responsibly with another person . . . and another . . . and another. One client, a lady, consistently gives me bad checks. She is totally indifferent to the analytic and moral meaning of the fraud she perpetrates. As therapy con-tinues, however, bad checks become less frequent. They have now stopped for months, and finally she has been able to analyze their meaning. She is aghast at her own lack of responsible financial behavior and has changed several things in her total life space at the same time.

People in therapy unclog their minds, so to speak, just as a commercial additive may unclog motors. Complexes, obsessions, phobias, compulsions, and dissociations all serve to limit knowledge and awareness so that the effective intelligence quotient is reduced. Also, psychological problems seem to involve a kind of emotional blunting, perhaps we should call it a childish-

[3]O. H. Mowrer, *The New Group Therapy* (Princeton: D. Van Nostrand, 1964). Also, "Too little and too late," *Int. J. Psychiat.*, (1967), 7, 536–556.

ness, which obliterates those depths and nuances of the personality which make the individual a socially interesting person. Neurotics complain that they receive few social invitations, but they are basically poor party material. They are often so inner-directed that they don't have any affect for others. Therapy not only frees the intelligence quotient but returns that sweet complexity to the personality which makes for interpersonal mutation and attraction. Clients in therapy become particularly open to parties, romance and marriage, which is probably why Freud wanted to protect them from such new ventures when they undertook them too early.

THERAPY AS FRIENDSHIP

While I don't agree with Schofield[4] that therapy is the purchase of friendship, therapy certainly does offer the client friendship. Most clients feel extreme loneliness, and have abandonment feelings by the time they come to therapy. They have either been unable to make friends, or to hold them having made them, or they are totally estranged from family members. And they are usually scared out of their wits by any opportunity for intimacy which may casually come their way. An ongoing therapeutic relationship offers a dialogue model for friendship, for testing it, for altering the mythologies interfering with intimacy, for putting the body in proper perspective. But this is not a friendship as such. If it were, psychotherapists would be the most popular people in the world—which they obviously are not. The friendship of therapy is genuine but illusory, because essential friendships are not helping ones but sharing relationships.

When the client stops defeating himself socially, he no longer needs the therapist as a friend and an estrangement process sets in. It is significant that while clients rarely forget their therapists after termination, they rarely have their therapists as friends. When Jung, Rank, and Freud did this, the friendships were not particularly outstanding, except perhaps with former clients who later became therapists. Even when termination is hostile, clients have an affectionate tone to their recollections. A man I met recently, who had been in therapy for three years, could not recall the name of his therapist under any form of inducement I could offer him. I interpreted this to mean that he was grateful for the health he had found through the process but he didn't want his therapist around as a personal friend.

SECRETS

Secrets are a part of everyone's life. But if the secrets are too numerous, if they are felt to be inhuman, and if they are a cause of shame, they become a burden on the psyche. Secrets use up needed energy and come to represent one's personal demon. Even before Freud discovered catharsis, it was known that to be able to unburden oneself to a non-judgmental person was curative, and institutional channels were available for such unburdening. The problem today, however, is that no one wants to listen. Everybody is busy himself, talking or acting. In modern marriage, particularly, husbands and wives do

[4]W. Schofield, *The Purchase of Friendship* (New York: Harper & Row, 1968).

not listen to each other. Ministers and priests are busy writing books, chang-ing society, or they are involved with their own or theological problems rather than listening. Even God seems too busy to listen! Psychotherapy is elementally purgative, and purgatives do help some conditions. Interpersonal psychotherapy sets up a climate of trust in which the unspoken and un-speakable can be spoken. After a secret is shared it can no longer be the same to one who sheltered it. This particular aim of therapy, while it seems glib, should not be demeaned for it may indeed be the heart of our work.

INSIGHT AS THERAPY

The evolvement of insight is now down the scale as an aim of therapy. For more than half a century it was the absolute foundation of psycho-analytic technique, but it has now somewhat fallen from grace. All of us have had the experience of clients who arrive at magnificent and overriding insights about themselves but who are unable to do a thing about their neurotic behavior. Freud more or less assumed that insight always carried with it the keys to changing behavior, and that behavior always would change if the case were handled correctly. Alas, action appears to be a separate and distinct step from insight. Nevertheless, it is still true that knowledge and information can provide freedom, but not by themselves. Only insight which is discovered in a matrix of experience and suffering can contribute to the active growth of the neurotic. Without this, the client may shelve his insight as a contingency, or may even use it to reinforce his symptoms and hold fast to them. Neurotics unfortunately use their good intellect to remain sick as well as to grow and be fulfilled.

BUYING COMFORT

Clients in therapy do buy comfort. Disease is *dis-ease*, and anxiety, de-pression, and guilt are painful conditions. A state of unrelieved anxiety or guilt—sometimes over a lifetime—is serious cause for concern on anyone's part. Any therapy which helps the client but still leaves him personally un-comfortable must be deemed a failure. The client is buying something in therapy and he wants his money's worth. It seems trite to include comfort as an aim of therapy, but I believe we too often forget the fact that pain and discomfort bring the client to begin with and his comfort must be considered a valid need. Therapists usually have deluxe offices, at least those in private practice do, and we have them not only for our own comfort but for our clients' comfort as well. One client recently asked me "If I validated parking." By this she meant was I going to provide the necessary modicum of comfort in her regularly coming to see me. But we will see later, it can be a mistake to ease pain and discomfort too quickly, or to make comfort the central focus of therapy. Overly comfortable clients do not go anywhere! Tranquil-izers, in my opinion, fail mostly because they ease anxiety without regard to the part anxiety plays in the person's dynamics. They offer comfort without regard to context. They also disregard the proper sequence of steps to growth, which are after all, the building blocks of the healing process, and which anxiety fuels.

RETURNING PASSION TO THE CLIENT

The problem of therapy is how to return passion to the client's life. I use passion here in the same sense as Malone[5] who employs this term to describe the highest degree of involvement he feels with people on certain days of his life. Even if the therapy question involved something as relatively simple as, "I can't decide between being a doctor or lawyer," or, "My mother doesn't understand me," or, "I don't know whether or not I should accept that promotion," passion in the Malone sense is involved. In the old Christian sense, passion meant involvement, and signified that part of life which offered the greatest essence. Human events in our life which become noteworthy and of more than momentary interest, are therefore passionate events. Neurotics live in a world of dryness and dissociation, and anxiety is in a sense developed to give it some flavor.

But, of course, one doesn't tell a client to become passionate because he doesn't understand what that means. Continual badgering on this score brings anger, retreat, and retaliation. Passion evolves out of successful therapy; but sometimes the therapist lacks it himself. This makes healing difficult for he cannot give what he doesn't have. I am frequently asked to refer people to other therapists. I only refer to those psychotherapists whom I know from personal encounter, have a zest for life. More can often be told about a therapist by what he does outside his office than by what he does in it. His technical personality is always a matter of presentation in the Goffman sense[6] and not his real or fulfilled self. One of the great rewards of being a therapist is to watch this involvement with passion grow as therapy proceeds. When it is maximized, the client probably doesn't need the therapist any more. No one, I might add, is as unqualified to do therapy as a jaded psychotherapist, at least while he remains jaded.

ESTRANGEMENT FROM NATURE

Clients have a disturbing estrangement from nature. People close to nature seem to fall into fewer psychological quagmires. By nature I mean not only the physical world but the Self as a biological organism. If, for example, one can accept the fact that he has a body, that it has orifices which give pleasure, that a tree or a river has phenomenological beauty, that a mountain or a seashore is perfection, then the inroads of the civilized life seem less. If an inventory were taken, our clients would reveal much less motor activity than non-clients. They ski, swim, walk, box, wrestle, and dance less. This is true even aside from the factors of social withdrawal and inhibited energy. Therapy serves in a way to return the person to fundamentals, and away from rarified abstractions which Zen Buddhism sees as the primary evil. Indeed, clients who respond to therapy for the first time begin to notice trees, birds, mountains, seascapes, etc., and become more

---

[5]T. Malone, "Encountering and Groups," in A. Burton (ed.), *Encounter, The Theory and Practice of Encounter Groups* (San Francisco: Jossey-Bass Publishing Co., 1969).
[6]E. Goffman, *The Presentation of Self in Everyday Life* (New York: Doubleday, 1959).

energetic. Some of the current interest in the problems of ecology stems from the fear that nature may be permanently closed off as a way to the Self.

Clients would like to make better use of their bodies. Most neurotics are disembodied. This is part of the Judaeo-Christian heritage in which they were raised. Psychological problems are bodily problems, but these are not necessarily the problems Freud described as sexual. The body actually has little to do with the quality of sexual response. Neurotics act as though their bodies were not a part of their Self, but paradoxically they seem to require more sensuality than others. (Inhibition has its counterpart in an excess of drive.) Thus their body images, as measured, for example, through the Draw-a-Person Test, invariably shows distortions not only in body structure but in function.

Anxiety finds a ready outlook in the organs of the body, singly and collectively. Today the head—migraine—and digestive tract—ulcer, colitis,—are particularly fine sources of focus, but any system of the body can be seized upon. Clients report more than average discomfort with their bodies—and often a free floating discomfort—and they rarely feel a positive thrust from it or a real honest-to-goodness sexual urge.

There are, no doubt, neurotic sport champions, but I have yet to see one. Becoming a champion calls for a certain attitude towards one's body and all of its delivery systems. This goes counter to the inferiority feelings which Adler said are part of every neurosis. Men of strength and size seem to me less inclined toward neuroses, but they certainly have no immunity from psychosis.

Therapy calls for reestablishing the body ego and integrating it into the psyche. Many clients first find their bodies in therapy. This is a difficult task for therapy sets rigid limits to touching, stroking, feeling, and manipulating the body. Most clients want to touch their therapists, and they want, similarly, to be touched. This is how they locate themselves and most often this is merely to reassure themselves that two bodies are actually involved. One should shake hands with some clients, as needed, or lightly touch the arm, or even ask to hold their hand for an instant for this purpose.

The problems connected with such procedures I have described elsewhere.[7] At any rate, as the instinctive forces are freed from their repressions, the body becomes more active internally and externally. In the first instance tonus, facial color, stance, and gait all appear to improve. Later, clients begin to swim, play tennis, bicycle, hike, sail, and do things they never could before. The body exerts and expresses itself, and success on this level comes to represent success on the psychic level as well. Bodily pain comes more and more to be passed over for engrossing activity and bodily complaints become rarer and rarer. Interpersonal psychotherapy makes frequent use of medical support and attempts to improve body functioning through physical medicine as well as through psychotherapy.

[7]A. Burton, *Modern Humanistic Psychotherapy* (San Francisco: Jossey-Bass Publishing Co., 1967).

RETURNING POWER TO THE CLIENT

Psychotherapy returns power to the client. Clients, by definition, are powerless people who cannot act—or even think—in the direction they want to and therapy leaves them more forceful and powerful. The crippled, so to speak, diminish the limits on their ability as they move through therapy. This is always one of the gratifying achievements of therapy, and many times clients become vastly more successful than if they had never had a psychic handicap to begin with.

DEPRESSED AFFECT

By the time most clients reach a therapist they have depressed affect. This simply means they do not have their customary life energy; their mood is grey and pessimistic. They react with hostility instead of beauty and contentment. Their energy, furthermore, is turned inward toward the Self and their world becomes an inner world of guilt in place of muscular joy. The resulting passivity and helplessness then produces the secondary guilt of inauthenticity, in addition to already present neurotic guilt and anxiety. Therapy once again gives the client hope and a proper object to bring his frustration and hate to. The passivity circle is temporarily broken in this way and constructive forces go to work directing energy once again toward appropriate objects. Clients most often do not realize the burden of their depression until they begin to have suicidal thoughts.

SHORT-TERM GOALS

Clients do come to therapists because they want to stop smoking, to lose weight, to be more sexually efficient, to eliminate a specific or limited phobia, to leave an old job and accept a new one, to get over a girl friend who has left. While these problems can also mirror longer-term situations, some of them can be helped by information giving, deconditioning and re-learning procedures, emotional support, persuasion, and sometimes even by the placebo effect. A great deal of therapy today is of the one or two or three interview kind, and not all of it is done by psychotherapists. The problem to be solved may call for a limited solution for practical reasons. The client may set limits to his participation, or he may not be open to a transferential relationship, or he may want to personally struggle some more in his world with just a crutch. Frankl, for example, believes that all neurotic problems can be treated in less than six interviews, an extreme point of view.

The principle of parsimony of course applies in therapy just as it does in any branch of science; the client should not be seen more than is absolutely necessary. It is easy to rationalize further office visits, as is generally done in medicine where the client is often "kept on the hook," possibly for a lifetime as allergists and dermatologists sometimes do. But the basic principles of therapy apply regardless of the number of visits and no client can be expected to come until he finds a perfect life. If the therapist is properly trained for involved and complex psychological problems, the more limited ones fall easily into place.

The following statements represent 20 short-term therapy goals announced by clients.

1. To get along with my mother.
2. To have a better erection.
3. To be able to love my husband.
4. To accept my homosexuality better.
5. To have my ulcer quiet down.
6. To be able to finish my book.
7. To be able to drive my car.
8. To be more aggressive on dates.
9. To tell my boss off.
10. To be invited to office parties.
11. To find a new wife.
12. To get rid of these awful migraines.
13. To stop writing bad checks.
14. To stop exhibiting myself.
15. To make better grades.
16. To decide about a profession.
17. To stop stuttering.
18. To say "no" to her.
19. To stop smoking.
20. To be able to cross the street to go to work.

Of course, these are not all so short-term but they can be focused on as central problems.

THE MEANING OF CURE

Cure as an aim of psychotherapy is a confusing matter. The term has a ring of finality which is strangely out of place in the practice of psychotherapy. In the realm of the psyche, the return of mental objects is the rule and nothing is ever cured. Therefore, there is nothing to cure as such. Because of therapy the client can now do what he could not previously do, does it with less dissatisfaction, and satisfies more people with his behavior than before. Is this a cure? The question of cure only comes up when the client feels totally out of life and before therapy begins. As soon as movement takes place, he never mentions the word cure again. In the dynamics of life, only death is the final cure. The philosophical concept of care implies that only so long as we are involved in caring, do we live fully, and cure somehow implies removal from the scene of care turbulence. In psychotherapy it is perhaps better to speak in terms of being helped, improved, or the degrees of authentification attained. Any terminated clients are liable to need further treatment, and a great many do come back. This is not necessarily because therapy has failed but because new life circumstances bring with them newer problems; because new creative advances are made in the personality from time to time; and because old learning needs occasional reinforcement from its source. No client is ever finally treated just as no one is ever completely analyzed.

In the course of a recent study on self-realization, I sent a questionnaire to (and often interviewed) well-known psychotherapists and pastoral counselors, and used bartenders who do a form of "psychotherapy" as a control group. Here are the replies of two psychotherapists to the question on therapeutic aims:

> The end-point of a psychotherapeutic experience is frequently a varied if not nebulous thing. When is a person fully analyzed or treated? Assuming that you participate in setting individual therapeutic goals, what do you opt for in your clients both practically and idealistically? Do your clients tend to break off before the maximal goal of realization is reached? Do you tend to settle for more and they for less?

> RESPONDENT I

> Reply: The answer to this question can only be given in terms of the particular patient and his personality. For those with severely damaged Egos and deprivations in their background, the goal must of necessity be flexible. For those who are stronger, we may have higher expectations.

> I never set goals in the beginning. It takes quite a while to get to know the person, to understand his dynamics, his strengths and weaknesses. Thus, diagnosis is ongoing and never complete until termination. We try to help them to become stronger, to work through their dependency, to grow and individuate, to check their impulses and to adapt both to what their goals are and the reality framework they are living in. Through the therapeutic relationship we have a chance to "undo" and "make better"; we can also experiment with how many steps they can take each time. I found the main ingredient to be patience.

> Some patients are satisfied with modified goals. They resist strongly any personality modification. If, after trying, they persist, I either recommend a different therapist or tell them to try it out for a while. Some do settle for less—they don't know different.

> RESPONDENT II

> Reply: If a patient wants to stop, I assume it's his decision, absolutely. I do, however, tell him whatever I have left, or feel, for example "Whatever happened to those phantasies (or whatever) which you said you'd work on some time...", or "Is it really good, now, or are you pulling out for some other reason?" or whatever I do feel. I assume that the process is his, the decision his, that there are lots of other therapists around, and other ways of growing than therapy; I do not try to hold someone, ever. I do like a process of some kind, even a few minutes, on anything I have left, unresolved in me. I feel that I cannot let him walk away as long as I have in my own pocket some of the pieces of his puzzle, which he gave me to hold. I need to give these back to him.

> I feel that the process of therapy or growth is a felt, bodily, pre-conceptual one, and therefore it doesn't matter at all, what the patient's specific goals are, nor what mine are for him. The process will, in its own right, be thicker and will in a bodily way resolve many "problems" while he may work on one, or toward the solution of one. I do assume that whatever he needs resolved must resolve or alter, before we have done.

So it seems the aims of psychotherapy are as dynamic as the process itself and that they evolve as that process evolves. The opening aims represent the staging for the aim-evolvement to come later.

THE PROSPECTING
INTERVIEW

III

The first formal meeting between therapist and client is called the prospecting interview. This is a most important meeting. It may determine whether or not the two will have an extended therapeutic relationship and receive the benefits of the healing encounter. It is the sole opportunity for the therapist to evaluate the client's diagnosis, prognosis, and general growth possibilities; but it also gives the client-applicant the opportunity to make his assessment as well. It is a time-limited evaluation process—rarely more than one or two hours, and its impact on the treatment as a whole is probably greater than any single hour in the total process. It is possible, for example, to make a serious technical mistake in later therapeutic hours, and the self-correcting, indigenous healing mechanisms of therapy adjust for them, or the therapist may, through his own efforts, improve the situation. But comparable errors in the prospecting hour are invariably fatal. Even if the therapy does go on, one pays heavily for the mistake in the middle course or the end of therapy.

No sure-fire method for handling a prospecting interview has yet been found and none appears on the horizon. After many years, I still get a prickly feeling when the phone rings announcing a client-applicant. My expectancies focus and my cognitive-perceptual processes sharpen. It seems that the great riddle of the personality, perhaps the meaning of life, is once again to be offered for solution, and the therapist will be a participant in solving that riddle. Furthermore, I am seeking that rare "ideal" client, as do all therapists, through whom something vital may be attained. Perhaps the ideal client will permanently quiet the "riddle of the sphinx," which is the creative drive of every scientist. Ideal clients, insofar as studies have described them, are women, not over 40 and not below 20 years of age, highly intelligent, creative, introspective, verbalizers, attractive, hurting, dependent, upper-middle class in social background, having attended Radcliffe, Mills College or equivalent, and with more or less unlimited finances. We might say she is the kind of woman Mary McCarthy described in her novel, "The Group."

But the client also has his ideal healer in mind. As far as it is possible to sample, he would be a 30- to 50-year-old male, with the following qualities:

1. Individuated
2. Supreme technical skill
3. Charismatic
4. Animal attraction
5. High capacity for nurturance
6. High bedside manner
7. High self-assuredness
8. Superb linguistic facility
9. An office setting of taste and culture
10. Several unconscious (and undisclosed) X-factors

A student sees his ideal therapist this way:

> I would want to see a mature man in his middle age that has lived a life truthful to his values and who is concerned about others and acts that way in his personal dealings with others. I would want the man to have a belief, if one must be categorized, as existentialist belief, and to carry this way of viewing life into his therapy, as this is my system of viewing life. The therapist would also have to [be] up on the latest theories [and] styles of life and would give some consideration to sociological circumstances, also. I would want him to show a genuine understanding and concern for my particular problems. And in summary, he must be living a life that contains happiness for him, a life that is genuine, that shows that he will go against public belief if necessary in standing for his beliefs, and a life full of concern for others. I feel that this is the type of person that I want to see because he will be, through his style of life, showing me into that type of life, and this is the type of life I would want most to be. Married—yes; religion—none in particular; education—a lot of education [and] good quality.

These factors are of course weighted differently in each client's therapist-ideal, and any of the unconscious X-factors may easily override all of the conscious ones. Like falling in love, finding an ideal therapist is largely a below-the-awareness process, for which the conscious awareness merely provides the social and personal credibility. At minimum, the therapist must not have any of the negative qualities which inhibit the unconscious from identifying with him.

Of course, every client finally becomes a therapeutic-ideal compromise, and every therapist represents a similar coming to terms with reality. But every therapist, like every noble professor, requires one or two ideal pupils to keep his Muse and motivation going in science. Whether a therapist gets an ideal client or two depends considerably on his public and professional image, the referrals he gets, and his openness to the rarified ideal.

It is interesting, even a bit strange, that Freud in his letters to Arnold Zweig[1] shows considerable concern, even agitation, about the lack of early

---

[1] E. L. Freud, (ed.) *Letters of Sigmund Freud and Arnold Zweig* (New York: Harcourt Brace Jovanovich, Inc., 1970).

treatment referrals from his colleagues, and his mood goes up when on a certain day he does get such a referral. Why was he so concerned? Because referrals represent our social and professional ego—the way in which our scholarship and work are accepted by people we seek acceptance from. We select our clients, and they select us from a referral pool. This pool usually includes the following sources:

1. Former clients
2. Physicians, attorneys, ministers, etc.
3. Other medical and non-medical psychotherapists
4. Social welfare agencies
5. Legal agencies
6. Schools and colleges
7. The telephone directory
8. Walk-ins (from signs, cards, etc.)
9. Self-referrals
10. Published books, articles, etc.

Many things help build a referral image, and every therapist strives very hard to have a good one. Without it, his practice of therapy soon comes to a halt, or can never really be a fully satisfying one. As in other professions, there is a pecking order in psychotherapy. Those with perhaps the highest image are the psychoanalysts who are members of institutes. The relatively untrained marital counselor, without a master's degree, represents the other end of the spectrum. A large publications bibliography, frequent papers and symposia at national meetings, a charismatic mysterium of personality, university appointments, affiliation with certain select psychiatric facilities, significant community mental hygiene recognition, reputation as a "good guy," all add their weight to the public and professional image of the healer. Even institutionally, those therapists with the brightest images are to be found in the select therapeutic service centers, the university medical clinics, the psychoanalytic institute treatment clinics, or the Menninger Clinic-type of center. But the best image-maker of all is consistent, satisfactory work with clients, which then seeps into the bedrock of the community, even into the United States as a whole, and is the foundation of the professional's reputation. Referrals, in a sense, become the therapist's Self-definition and his accepted competence.

The client and therapist generally make first contact by telephone. The video telephone, when it is nationally available, should help the prospecting interview a great deal. Reaching for the telephone, dialing the number, then hearing the "voice" is a long and incubated process, one full of planning, inhibition, and trepidation. Sometimes just hearing the "voice," without even appearing, is curative in a paradoxical way.

The telephone is an assessment instrument as well as a communicative one. The client-applicant listens for intonation, timbre, warmth, alertness, honesty, and the other virtues he seeks, and these are probably more important to him than what he hears said. Clients say later, "I liked his voice. It made me feel secure." Or, on the obverse side, "He was direct and curt, didn't seem interested, definitely not the man for me."

I do not recommend (although I understand that this may be impractical) that secretaries handle initial calls from client-applicants. Even the best of them—and they are certainly a well-intentioned lot—have too little knowledge of neurotic suffering to empathize properly with the applicant-caller. They do not, by and large, improve our public relations or satisfy the prospective client, and they have other equally important duties.

When the client finally arrives at the office, do you shake hands with him and provide similar courtesies? This seems a trivial question, but industrial psychologists stress the overriding importance of first impressions in sales work. The client-applicant is almost always afraid, full of despair and depression, and doesn't really know what is going to be done to him. He has heard stories about therapists, not all of them good, and somewhere within he fears a seduction of some kind. It is therefore important to offer immediate assurance of (1) humanity, (2) interest, and (3) gentility. Therapists who come on strong and overwhelm the client-applicant almost always have cause to regret it later. I do shake hands with the client, if I feel like it, and if I am convinced that the client wants it, and that body touching at this stage would not be premature in the relationship. At any rate, I escort the client into my office in the same way I would a guest in my home; I smile, do not make small talk, recognize his pain, the difficulty in coming, and voice the hope that a solution can be found. I am optimistic.

It is always necessary to open the prospecting interview by listening. The client is pent-up with a story he has to tell—and he has been waiting a long time to tell it to you. He has difficulty knowing where to start, but once begun he does not take kindly to comments or interpretations at this point. It is best to let the client first "spill his material," but no prospecting interview can suffice with just this. Indeed, if information-gathering is anywhere involved in therapy, the prospecting hour is the place for it. In addition to the client's complaint-structure, you must learn certain historical facts in order to determine client-status. But remember, the client's style as well as the substance of his presentation is important here.

The following factors may go into the decision to accept a client for therapy. Their import is discussed below.

1. Age, marital status, education
2. Physical condition
3. Chronicity
4. Logical integration of complaints
5. Anxiety level
6. Somatization history

7. Motivation for change
8. Prevailing mood and mood history
9. Earlier treatment history
10. Anti-social history
11. Attainments and dis-attainments
12. Family and social resources
13. Paralogical thinking
14. Paranoid trends
15. Meaning of parapraxes

AGE, MARITAL STATUS, EDUCATION

In a certain sense, therapists specialize in treating people of a certain age range. That is, we prefer, or are more efficient, in treating either infants, children, adolescents, adults, or the aged. It is rare for any one therapist to cover this entire spectrum with equal interest or ability. In addition, office design, equipment, and structures vary distinctly with the age of persons treated. The clients most desired, and those with the best immediate prognosis, are people in their late 20's, 30's, and early 40's, presumably when the solution of id problems are paramount. Any client of any age can of course be helped; but he can be helped more—or more quickly—if the therapist wants to help him, and if he is not too dissimilar in age from the therapist so that introjection and identification are facilitated.[2]

Married people make better clients than unmarried ones if for no other reason than that they are more stable. Even a bad marriage reveals a certain capacity for intimacy, object-libido, the need for social acceptance, and family living. These are all factors which improve the therapeutic chances. It often appears that marriage, and its total ambience, make therapy possible. The fundamental urges and problems involved in marriage are also those with which therapy concerns itself.

Education has already been mentioned elsewhere in this book. Except at the highest and lowest levels, the correlation of intelligence with therapeutic outcome is positive. Therapy is above all a cognitive process in the service of the emotions; without sufficient cognitive ability there is little hope of a corrective emotional experience, with current therapeutic methods. Education indicates as well that the client has values similar to the therapist, who is always an educated man; that he prizes the symbol for its own worth; and that he was at one time open to being a therapist himself, or could become one if he wanted to.

PHYSICAL CONDITION

Surprisingly, the client has to be in good health to undergo longer-term therapy and, indeed, the average client is in good health. Physical ailments

[2]In the case of infants and children, I would say the therapist is capable of temporarily "placing" himself on the child's age level for therapeutic purposes.

drain off necessary energy and, at any rate, divert the client to and enmesh him in physical medicine. Also somatization produced by therapy can be expected with a good percentage of clients. If this is regularly added to existing ailments, the therapy may bog down in first-aid to merely keep the client functioning physically.

It is advisable to check the client's health in the prospecting interview, not only by his statement and his appearance but by the corroboration of his physician. At times it may even be necessary to ask for a new physical examination before proceeding, or at any time during the therapy itself. It works best for any therapist, medical and non-medical, to have a working relationship with a standby physician. This is better than telling the client to go to someone!

CHRONICITY

Chronicity is not necessarily a factor in client selection, at least not in the sense which general medicine uses chronicity. Many clients with long-existing phobias, obsessions, and anxieties, and similar problems, respond more quickly to therapy than those with conditions of acute onset. Their symptoms' resistance to change is often based on their social circumstances rather than on their psyche. Sometimes, therapy and other modes of healing haven't been available to them, or their symptoms are simple confirmed habit, or merely come and go over long periods of time. All people have lifelong crutches and fears they perpetually live with and accept as a part of their existence. What chronicity involves for therapy is the question of whether or not the basic character structure of the person has been diverted by the defensive personality. Are the secondary gains important, and the practical possibilities for a new life after therapy so meager that therapy faces hopeless odds? In another sense, the longer one has suffered, the more ready he is to do something about it. Chronicity can be a motive.

LOGICAL INTEGRATION OF COMPLAINTS

This aspect is best illustrated by people who present a schizoid or schizophrenic complaint picture. Thus the statement, "I slept with him because he explained Kierkegaard so beautifully," demonstrates a porosity and intrusion in the stream and organization of thought which can be an indication of therapeutic prognosis. Psychic symptoms have their own structure, purpose, and organization. In schizophrenia, this organization has long gone by the board, and no one—the client least of all—knows why he is disabled. In the prospecting interview, with or without the aid of a Rorschach, we test this symptom structure and organization. If it is logically functional, the client's chances are better. Paranoia is no exception. Only on superficial levels, or at special times, is the paranoid capable of such logical integration. The history and phenomenology of the complaint structure must reveal a normative and predictable development to make the client amenable to psychotherapy. Lack of logical integration does not rule him out but changes the order of things.

ANXIETY LEVEL

The anxiety level of the client-applicant differs from the complaint pattern but may be a part of it. Some clients seem to have no manifest anxiety at all and others offer a severe panic reaction during the prospecting interview. One client cried for almost six straight therapeutic hours. Anxiety has a devious character and the extreme form of anxiety in the guise of panic reaction may offer better possibilities for therapy than the person completely without anxiety. Most clients who reveal what Viktor Frankl[3] calls a nöogenic neurosis, an existential neurosis, seem well integrated, successful, and without apparent anxiety. But below the surface, the nihilistic character of their Self and their alienation from people make them exceedingly difficult to treat. Free floating anxiety is a tougher therapeutic job than specific anxiety. There are people who also have pan-anxiety and are never free of some manifestation of it.

What is more important for client selection than the absolute level of anxiety is its vagaries and its appropriateness or inappropriateness. The prospecting interview is, of course, an anxiety-producing situation, but the manifest anxiety in situations like this is remarkably stable and appropriate. Where it waxes and wanes peculiarly in the hour, or attaches itself to neutral objects, or shows unique or bizarre manifestations, you should proceed with caution in considering the client-applicant. Large residues of hostility and depression often show up as highly variable anxiety pools. In the final analysis, however, there is less danger in selecting clients with too much anxiety rather than too little.

SOMATIZATION HISTORY

Client-applicants with a history of psychosomatic defenses such as asthma, ulcer, low-back pain, migraine, and hypertension are special therapeutic problems. They usually meet all the stipulated requirements for becoming a client—their psychosomatic status often guarantees this—with the exception of the extraordinary use of their bodies to solve conflicts which may have become a style of life as well.

It was once believed that a single major defense of this sort left the remainder of the personality uninvolved neurotically. I do not find this to be the case. Asthmatics, hypertensives, ulceritics can all have other forms of neurotic problems as well as their psychosomatic ones. There is, as yet, no clear or accepted personality structure associated with each of these diseases. Current psychological hypotheses leave something to be desired. It is possible to treat such clients for the secondary neuroticism surrounding the disease without touching the disease itself significantly, but the client feels and does better. He may also handle his somatic episodes in a more efficient or less painful way. This does not mean the basic psychosomatic problem cannot be reached by therapy but that it is extremely difficult to do so.

[3] V. F. Frankl, *Man's Search for Meaning* (Boston: Beacon Press, 1962).

The therapeutic problem is that the client can never make up his mind whether he has a physical problem or a psychic problem and he tends to have one foot in each camp. He invariably uses one set of defenses to deny the other. Thus asthmatics may get severe bronchial spasms instead of the usual psychological resistances to the transference. Migraine attacks may result from interpretations which should be resisted in other ways and put the client in cold storage for a week. Psychosomatic disorders also confound the therapy by a variety of medications and medical personnel who jump to the rescue in traditional ways which run counter to the psychotherapeutic process.

If the therapist is himself comfortable with somatizers, if he has some knowledge and background of the specific disease involved, if he works well with medical personnel or is himself a doctor of medicine, if he can accept the fact that the treatment will be long and arduous and the outcome problematic, then he should by all means work with the psychosomatic problem presented. In any event, the decision should be based upon the individual and his potentialities and not on the disease.

MOTIVATION FOR CHANGE

The "desire to be cured" as a basis for accepting or rejecting a client-applicant is an overdone thing. No client actually wants to change his unconscious person. What will the client now give up to be relieved of his distress, or to grow in a new direction, is a more useful question. Many therapies fail because the client comes at someone else's request, under duress. This may be so even when he appears to come voluntarily. A client really volunteers for therapy only when he is more or less at the end of the line and the only possible alternative is retreat into insanity, depression or death. There is always some precipitating stimulus-event which frightens the client-applicant and impels him to seek treatment.

At times becoming ready for therapy is a slow, grinding-down process, a wearing away of the vitality, combined with the example of a friend who is doing better. But most people never make it to a therapist, prefering other modes of adaptation. Many come for a single interview and then find the proof that therapy will not work.

If the client-applicant actually appears at the office, he is motivated for treatment. But whether he can tolerate all the vicissitudes ahead, or whether he will stay until the arrived-at therapeutic goals are attained, is another matter. Most clients leave therapy when they get some relief and feel a little better. Sometimes they return for a second or third go-around. The suggestion is offered that no client can be motivated. He must find his own motivation and give up something for it. Give the client every chance to decide and be motivated by honestly offering what you can give him and nothing more.

PREVAILING MOOD AND MOOD HISTORY

Clients with a history of manic and depressive mood fluctuations, even if these have never approached psychotic proportions, must be carefully evaluated for therapy. Therapy can be expected to accentuate their mood swings before it finally reduces them. Also, manics and depressives exhaust their life energy through their episodes so that they have little energy to bring to therapy. They are steeped in, and overwhelmed by, their guilt or ecstasy, as the case may be, and cannot maintain the intense interpersonal communication required for therapy. They are also potential suicide risks. They sometimes need temporary sheltering in residential hospitals, and are often benefitted by medication which has to be prescribed and controlled by authorized personnel.

All clients are, of course, potentially capable of depression in therapy, but fortunately few ever reach that depth of depression or mania which makes it unwise to treat them as outpatients. The swings in mood which regularly occur in therapy are among the phenomena which the "third ear" carefully gauges and evaluates. It is the therapist's job to keep the prevailing mood within defined limits. He does this through control of the transference and by offering his own faith and hope as a model for the client. But occasionally mania or depression comes on with a rush, gets beyond the therapist, and leaves everybody helpless. It is then necessary to protect the client at any cost, and one must not hesitate at this point.

The best approach would be to inquire about mania and depression and ask the client about the frequency and depth of such episodes, if any. You must also find out how the client was treated. The client-applicant is not automatically ruled out if he has had a psychosis. What counts are the resources he now has for coping with any such future defensive measures and the therapist's capability and willingness to carry through with them should they recur with intensity. It is easy to be fooled by depressives.

EARLIER PSYCHOTHERAPY HISTORY

Many client-applicants have made earlier attempts to receive therapy, or have actually been in therapy before. Their earlier therapeutic experiences bear some relationship to, even have some influence on, the current work to be done. Psychotherapy is an evolving process, and the personality grows or declines under the aegis of many social influences. This may have occurred since the client's last therapeutic experience. And therapists are to some extent interchangeable. A therapist usually begins where the other therapist has left off, or if the earlier experience was considered an incomplete or an unprofitable one, the therapist has to understand in what way it was incomplete or unprofitable. Therapy can fail again for identical reasons because the client may set it up this way. Often the client-applicant needs an opportunity to vent his hostile feelings about his earlier therapeutic work, and reconcile himself to it. The prospecting interview is a good place to do it.

But no earlier failure is necessarily a prediction of current failure. Too little is known about psychotherapy for there to be any such unvarying rule. Also, so much depends on the personality and integrity of the therapist. Where one fails another may easily succeed. The client may now be different as well and may have learned a great deal from his former experience, even if he doesn't think he has. Therapy, even the most unpromising, leaves no one untouched in any sense.

The client's comments about his previous therapeutic work are illuminative and give us some insight into what we are up against. Such clients are critical and stress the inadequacies of their former therapist. Passivity, indifference, fees, and personal distaste are frequently mentioned. On the positive side, they mention warmth, humanity, devotion, culture, and education. The basic resentment of earlier clients, however, is that the therapist did not allow himself to encounter the client on a level of depth and meaning. One client transferred to me because her primary therapist had told her she was a psychopath, which she was not. I interpreted this as his warning to her that he was incapable of any form of intimacy with her.

It is wise, where possible, to contact earlier therapists, with permission of the client-applicant, and discuss taking on the client-applicant. This is not only potentially helpful to the client, but furthers inter- and intraprofessional relationships. It leaves good feelings.

ANTI-SOCIAL HISTORY

Some client-applicants have been in penitentiaries for a variety of crimes. Those therapists who work closely with probation and parole departments have many such clients. They differ from the usual client in private practice in that they often must have therapy under an order of the court, by request of a defense attorney, as a condition of probation, or to favorably impress probation or parole officers or boards. Crime and imprisonment as a selective social process reduces the verbal, intellectual, socio-economic and educational possibilities of becoming a client. Also anti-social personalities often scoff at psychiatry as a medium of self-realization and make use of it only when it is distinctly to their practical advantage.

Some therapists find great comfort and efficiency in treating such clients, or in working within institutional confines with detained people. Others cannot handle this at all. It can be a matter of preference and the therapist's unconscious needs. Correctional counseling is quite different from psychotherapy, and may even be opposed to it. I consider it rehabilitative rather than therapeutic, but no client-applicant should be rejected for this reason alone. If he meets the other requisites, is motivated, and comes voluntarily, he should be given primary consideration on his own merits.

ATTAINMENTS AND DISATTAINMENTS

So much of therapy is creativity put back to use that it is small wonder that we look for the most creative people to become clients. The most enjoyable clients, and those helped the most, have been people who have written books, founded economic or social enterprises, were industrial managers or executives, or had personal responsibility for large numbers of people. On the other hand, there are client-applicants who do not have a single, solid creative achievement to show for their lifetime. These are not value judgments, but people who are creatively enterprising also bring this form of enterprise to therapy. Therapy moves faster, is more dynamic, and is more personally satisfying to the therapist with achievers. Psychotherapy can be done with morons and borderline intellectual people, but not many of us do it. Why not? The reason perhaps is that such people have no base-line of achievement, and promise never to have any. We are all imbued with the idea of making a contribution to our fellow men. Again, non-achievement is not a reason for not considering a client-applicant, but it is certainly to his credit if he has been an achiever, or has potentialities for it.

FAMILY AND SOCIAL RESOURCES

I have already discussed this factor to some extent in an earlier chapter. It remains only to say that the truly solitary client-applicant who has no place to go and no one to care for him after therapy is in a difficult social state. Not only that, therapy is designed to give him a family and people to love and if there is someone in the wings it is easier. It is not easy to start making friends from scratch, and this can be a cruel world in that sense.

Despite the obstacles families often put in the way of therapists, their presence is a favorable prognostic sign. As an isolate, a client-applicant has a much better chance of getting into the toils of the formal social institution, the law, mental hospital, and be dehumanized. Someone has to care for him besides the therapist. In doing psychotherapy with three men who had killed their mothers, their fathers, or both, I was always obsessed by the feeling that they could never have anyone to go home to and they were, for this reason, doomed in a certain way.

PARALOGICAL THINKING

Where the client-applicant presents a well-developed thinking disorder, an obvious primitive thinking state, or actual departures from reality testing, one must proceed with caution. The therapist must ask himself: (1) am I competent to treat such an involved problem; (2) do I want to treat it and do I have the time (which may be years) to devote to it; and (3) am I sufficiently unafraid of the primary process and comfortable with it.

My experience has been that only especially knowledgeable people can treat schizophrenic clients and other psychotics, or potential psychotics, successfully. But one does have to try one's wings sometime. If such a client is taken on, proper supervision should be available. Even an in-patient facility should be at hand if it becomes necessary.

The psychotherapy of the psychosis[4] has many unique facets which have to be learned specifically. Learning them is a special order of business, and is probably a post-graduate course beyond the scope of this book.

[4]A. Burton (ed.), *Psychotherapy of the Psychoses* (New York: Basic Books, 1961).

PARANOID TRENDS

Paranoid thinking often reveals itself in longer-term therapy and has to be worked through. It is a regular part of therapy because every personality has a basic distrust and suspiciousness. But a client-applicant with a well-designed paranoid system is something else. In the present state of psycho-therapeutic knowledge, psychotherapy is not effective with paranoid personalities and can even be dangerous. This is true because the client can never detach sufficient libido from his system to apply it to therapy; and because the transference itself becomes part of the paranoid system. Such clients are best treated eclectically, with a variety of medication and psychic approaches, and may at times need the shelter of a residential setting. Some paranoid clients conceal their projective mentation until well along in therapy. It is then necessary to refer the client to someone who specializes in working with psychotics, telling the client honestly that he is beyond the therapist's capabilities.

PARAPRAXES

I watch carefully in the client-applicant for slips of the tongue, confusion, and repetitions. They reveal a great deal which the client doesn't want revealed. They also indicate the presence of complexes and impulses disguised by the censor. All of this bodes well for the therapy. I discourage discussion of dreams in the prospecting hour but welcome parapraxes, for they often say more than the client.

It is of course not intended that the prospecting interview will be a summation of these factors. A therapeutic-diagnosis is more an intuitive event, a structural formulation, which is not the same as its constituent parts. One ultra-important counter-indication to therapy may override all positive factors because it may be precisely that single fact which will play into the therapist's countertransference weakness or a revulsion he feels on a deeper level. Some therapists, for example, cannot treat homosexuals regardless of the other qualities they have. Others feel the same way about chronic alcoholics or exhibitionists. I also have to like the client, be moved in some fashion by his plight, and see that my own growth will to some extent be promoted. Of course, client selection is not a rigid or precise thing. Therapists have to make a living, and society has to help people in psychic distress, so we most often depart from ideal criteria. But selection goes to the heart of the motivation for being a therapist and gives us satisfaction in our work and the strength to go on.

What is perhaps more important than what the client says in the prospecting interview is what he doesn't say. It is now generally accepted that the first hour contains the "kernel" of the client's entire therapeutic problem. I would amend this truism by saying that it is what the client doesn't say in the first hour which holds this kernel. Thus the therapist's "third ear" is busy in the prospecting interview translating what is said into what is not-said, or what is perhaps unsayable, and he makes extrapolations in this way. The basic questions to be asked are: (1) can I help this client;

(2) do I want to help; (3) how dangerous psychologically is it for both of us; (4) how long will it take; and (5) what will be the probable outcome (under the governing conditions).

The client in turn comes with his own questions, some of which he asks, and others he holds for an answer in more appropriate later hours. For example:

1. Do you have therapy time available for me?
2. How sick am I?
3. Can you cure me?
4. What are your fees?
5. How long will it take?
6. How often will I have to come?
7. What specific day and time do I come?
8. What is your theoretical orientation?
9. What methods are you going to use? Will I be hypnotized?
10. Will I be bringing my relatives?
11. Do I need to tell my present therapist about you?
12. Can I call you on the telephone if I need you?
13. Do you want to talk to my physician?
14. Will you be giving me tranquilizers?
15. Am I going to be tested with the ink blots?
16. How do we begin?
17. Are you married?
18. Are you from this part of the country?
19. Do you do this all day?

Some therapists find that their selection of clients improves with a battery of psychological tests, with an anamnesis, and with information derived from earlier client contacts. This is particularly true in institutional therapy, where paperwork seems to be part of the great bureaucratic enterprise. I have always believed, having worked both intramurally and in private practice, that the information factor can be overdone and that too much information is often a hindrance. The client's file becomes the client. Collateral data is sometimes made a substitute for empathic understanding, and such data at any rate requires the final logical act of unifying it into a meaningful dynamic. Psychological tests, for example, are only as valid as the person who interprets them, and the interpretation of a Rorschach has its analogy to integration of the raw data of the prospecting interview. I occasionally give a quick Rorschach to a client during the prospecting hour; but only when I am unsure of myself, or when the client is unsure of himself. Tests convince the client, it should be noted, even when they do not convince us. I do not mean to denigrate the highest levels of psychological testing, but to point out that the highest level of testing is rarely available, and economy is a factor. Many clients will not, or cannot, pay $150 for a battery of tests to be told they cannot be accepted in therapy. Tests have other limitations as well. They deflect energy to assessment which should go to the evolving relationship; and the client also regressively refers back to them again and again when difficulty arises in therapy.

People who do not appear for the prospecting interview, the "no-shows," are a universal part of every single practice. Physicians hedge against "no-shows" by overscheduling. Therapists have some comparable devices, since a single hour out of the working day is one-sixth, one-seventh, or one-eighth of the total therapeutic time available, and can represent a serious loss in time and income. If a therapist has too many "no-shows," his telephonic and prospecting interview procedures should be revaluated for effectiveness. Beyond this, I find satisfaction in the "no-shows," in the possibility that my phone contact, or my prospecting interview, has done some good, the client feels somewhat better, and he will return to me when he is ready. And clients certainly do. Freud writes wistfully of "losing" Emmy von N., against his considered advice, but she did return years later for more treatment.

The prospecting interview goes best when the strain of prospecting is reduced, when the participants can be themselves and drop as much artifice and hedging as possible, and when the data come spontaneously and naturally. It is a principle of therapy that information should be sacrificed for phenomenological quality of relationship, for after all this is what therapy is all about. The possibility that the client can be taken on for a longer trial, say a month, if this is to be long-term therapy, is also open. This, however, is not recommended as a routine procedure. The decision after a month is often no better than that which can be made in the prospecting interview.

BEGINNING THERAPY

IV

The prospecting interview sets the tone but does not begin psychotherapy. Beginning therapy is a formal event and sometimes a difficult one. Each commencement of therapy is a new situation and each client approaches the event in a special way. Both client and therapist will feel they have made an important decision—to start therapy, and that this decision must now be implemented at whatever cost. The consulting room, the client is aware, is off limits to society, and even a court of law cannot intrude. Here, he can drop his defenses more easily than anywhere else in the world.

THE THERAPEUTIC HELIX

It is not precisely known how therapy does its work. Various theoretical formulations which have been offered leave something to be desired. Once therapy proceeds, the individual hours go according to the schema given in Chapter VI, that is, the client opens the hour with a platform statement, incubates it, clarifies it, reorganizes it cognitively and affectively into insight, and then acts upon it. In any single hour of treatment there is a complex matrix of these therapeutic units which operate simultaneously and successively, facilitate and abrade each other, in a dynamic flux only a part of which surfaces in the hour. The therapist presses this associational work forward, supports it, retards it when and where necessary, and provides the necessary and sufficient conditions for it. The client goes at his own speed, but the therapist represents the security backing which makes it possible to begin with.

It is therefore most important, in beginning therapy, to be neutral and just listen. The client must set his own growth structure, but three things have to happen if the therapy is to work. First, the client must begin to experience the therapist in a transferential way, that is, as a significant nurturing or hostile figure of the past. Second, he must begin to bring his specifically neurotic situation into the treatment. And, finally, he must accept the therapeutic situation as a life situation in which he problem-solves previously untouched problems. All of these factors become part of a single approach and cannot be easily distinguished from one another. The client, in a sense, becomes more neurotic to become less so, and psychoanalysts have called this the transference neurosis.

A number of paradoxical phrases have been suggested to describe the growing therapeutic relationship and they perhaps give its flavor best.[1] "Involved detachment" suggests that the therapeutic relationship is affectionate and loving without ever losing its scientific poise. Love, in the marital sense, calls for loss of Self, merging of identities into a new unity, for which passion is the vehicle. In psychotherapy, there is also merger and passion but no loss of Self. If this were regularly to happen in therapy, the growing edge would stop for the experience of being in love itself. This is extremely difficult for people to grasp. Care, interest, love, and devotion are devouring things and in therapy they must always be kept at bay. In this sense, the first hour of therapy is the beginning of its end. Therapy is above all finite and limited whereas the poets describe love as perpetual, transcending, and immortal. The problem in therapy therefore is to be simultaneously involved and detached. And, it is the detachment which does the analysing.

Therapy is a lonely business. Not only are the two participants more or less isolated people but they live in a world of their own making. They counteract their essential loneliness by pooling their resources so that therapy may be called a "related or mutual loneliness." Every neurotic or troubled person has a nagging feeling that he has something of the greatest importance to say, but that no one will listen to him, or that he cannot say it right. Schizophrenics, in their unconscious, believe that their "message" is the secret of life and may save society. The therapist, in turn, is the guardian of individual creativity and he has long reflected on human emotions and the values of life. He, too, is a basically lonely person seeking the answer to the riddle of life. When two such people regularly get together, there is a primary identification and introjection of each other backed by an ontic urge. The human condition the philosophers write about becomes the therapeutic condition. Loneliness loves company and despair is its cement! This situation, even more than the regressive father or mother imposed on the therapy, carries the growing edge forward. Highly accomplished athletes, as an example, lack this being-with-oneself and do not, therefore, usually make good therapists. All the great therapists of the past have been inward-looking people not given to group membership and public affiliation.

Therapy has also been called "a systematic going around in circles." By this is meant the tracing and retracing of the therapeutic dialogue, the waxing and waning, and the reciprocation and facilitation of it. I see psychotherapy as a helix, and the dyadic therapeutic relationship as a double helix. Psychology seems inherently to reflect biology. The chemical arrangement of DNA, as a necessary and sufficient condition of procreation, is bound to the helix form. Variations produce stillbirths or monsters.[2]

A helix is an ever-evolving, multidimensional spiral, reaching ever

---

[1] Helm Stierlin discusses some of these in his admirable little book, *Conflict and Reconciliation* (New York: Doubleday, 1969).
[2] J. D. Watson, *The Double Helix* (New York: Atheneum, 1968).

higher plateaus. The final plateau might be called homeostasis or fulfillment. Each spiral platform is the starting point for the next, and the helix is always in flux and movement, both upwards and downwards, is built into its structure. Hidden within each helix are all the necessary elements basic to interpersonal growth. In the double helix, the therapeutic participants, thus mirror one another in a way that makes them uniquely compatible. If we think of two dynamic helices, flowing and ebbing, overlapping and differentiating, until some final and common resolution comes about, we have a proper model of psychotherapy. Of course the elements of the psychological helix are not atoms or molecules but cognitions, emotions, and drive—parts of the whole we call therapeutic behavior.

Continuing our paradoxical descriptions, "free-floating attentiveness," or rather, "sensitive, receptive relaxation of sharpest concentration" is the way in which the therapist always involves himself with the client. "Do nothing" rather than "take over" and "intervene" is the rule. The therapist's internal perceiving processes, his "third ear," are deeply attuned to the encounter and to what is being said. The conscious, pre-conscious and un-conscious analytic and synthetic creative processes are at work making order out of apparent chaos. The irrational, infantile, paleologic, diffused, frag-mented impulses, wishes, ideas, concepts, feelings, and behavior of the client are patterned into working hypotheses, subject to empirical and symbolic testing. Much of this is tentative and has to be discarded or done over. Hypotheses are creatively formed, entertained and discarded. But when a "hit" appears, it connects with a startling emotional feedback. It belongs! This process is the highest form of concentration and creation. The therapist must learn to let it flow naturally and to follow its course. The apogee of creation, the great discoveries of man, have always seemed absurdly simple. One day, they are suddenly just there. But they also have urgency and a spark of divinity. They have to be solved or created. They sometimes go beyond free will and leave the creator helpless. Therapy is a creative jug-gling act and the more "balls" in the air at one time the better.

A "loving struggle" develops because the client resists what he wants most while the therapist cannot refuse his commitment to his client's freedom and growth. The manifestations of this struggle, things Freud called resistance, are better described in the next chapter under countertransference. They have to appear in therapy sooner or later, and they have to be surmounted or the client will never leave his neurotic perch. A show of strength, tactics, and even manipulation may be part of the therapy—anything to overcome the resistance. The child must not only defeat his mother but himself as well.

Resistances vary in strength from person to person. They may come to light as arriving late for appointments or not arriving at all; a quick cure or flight into health before the treatment has even started; paranoid hostility towards the therapist; even total surrender of the personality. Both over- and under-receptivity and over- and under-participation in therapy are sus-pect and should be subjected to analytic study. Each client has his own growth schedule which must be matched by the therapist. Sudden departures by the client from this base line have to be viewed as resistance and inquired into. Resistance is the personality's last-ditch defense against change, growth, and fulfillment. If resistance is firmly based in the character structure it may be very hard to overcome. Pre-genital personalities, those who never got beyond the anal or oral levels, always show resistance of the highest order. They always fear losing what security and pleasure they have while getting nothing in return,—descending into the oblivion of possible implosion. Clients well know that the alternative to a long entrenched neurosis may be psychic or actual death. Any form or degree of anxiety, or incomplete nurturance, is preferable to the basic confrontation of Self in therapy. A client whose mother used to warm her toilet seat by sitting on it so that the child would be spared that particular form of cold to its "behind," can be expected to show extraordinary resistance to therapy because basically she is still looking for warm toilet seats.

It is technically incorrect, even dangerous, to urge these resistances forward too early, or to insist on resolving them before the client is ready. Sometimes, with some clients, it never can be done. The course of the therapy is actually the course of the resistances and each one must systematically be worked through as it appears. None can or should be ignored.

As I have said, therapy begins by listening. The therapist slides into the zenith of his sharpened relaxation. He may, infrequently, ask for a restatement or clarification, but he never projects himself into the client. Some clients say, "Aren't you going to ask me some questions?" or, "Where do I begin?" or, "Aren't you going to say something?" and always the reply must be, "One can start anywhere," "I don't have anything to say now, but I may later." "Just tell me what you have in your mind." This leaves few clients satisfied. Their helplessness is painful and they may become angry. The client is thus placed in the paradoxical situation Haley[3] describes so well. To survive and grow it seems he must go against his best interests and his survival. A therapist must have the skill to help the client walk such a tightrope without abandoning therapy or sinking even deeper into the morass of his neurotic situation. At this point, clients often set out to prove they cannot be helped. They will sometimes go to almost any lengths in self-punishment to do so. The therapist should recognize and ignore this unconscious perversity while exhibiting perseverance, faith, and humanity in the therapy. His deep understanding of life makes him aware of, and sympathetic to, the client's plight and his resistances. But he must also be capable of getting tough when necessary.

The currency of the unconscious is love and hate. In the deeper forms of therapy one descends into the primary process where the rules of logic and structural language do not apply. The client who said, "Irving Roy told me he loved me when I was seven and it so frightened me that I wouldn't go down Irving Avenue for three years after that," was showing her primary

---

[3]J. Haley, *Strategies of Psychotherapy* (New York: Grune & Stratton, 1963).

process and involving the therapist immediately in the heart of her pathology. Such schizophrenic clients quickly show their pan-sexual and paleological side in a most maladroit way and the therapist begins to feel uneasy with them. Not only that, clients similar to this make their own interpretations, tend to invade the Self of the therapist—"You are kicking your foot because you don't want to be with me today"—and are very good at discovering the therapist's weaknesses and countertransferences before their time. The therapist cannot match this behavior. At any rate, he should not and must not tackle the primary process in the beginning hours. The opening of therapy is not the time to be metaphorical. Reality should be the order of things.

What I call the "therapeutic attitude" allows more and more of the client's neurosis to come into the hour. This always involves significant nurturing figures of the past and the relevant cultural content of money, children, and so on to clothe the transactions. Does one then have to duplicate the entire early neurotic psychogenesis? Or can it be abridged, encapsulated, and symbolized? The answer seems to be that the infantile neurotic situation does not have to be completely replayed on the infant level. The adult client cannot really be an infant again. Even in hypnotic regression the adult is not displaced. In interpersonal psychotherapy, extra-transference, or reality factors, have as much to do with the client's improvement as do the transferential ones. Relationships are invariably straightforward as well as symbolic. Each mental conflict is both a current event and a historical one. To disregard one for the other is sometimes a mistake. The client brings to therapy feelings and conflicts most central to his life at the moment, but the order in which they appear is important. The sequence of mental events is never haphazard or chance. The order in which mental events are brought to consciousness indicates their unconscious priority. The therapist does an involved thematic analysis of what the client brings, and the sequence in which it is brought, and determines the necessary harmonics and reflections of these events up and down the helix. They are then reconciled, ordered, and given a creative formative structure. The discovered themes fall into patterns which are most urgent for the client. Uncovering and synthesizing these themes frees the energy tied up in the conflict-structure. This is a process difficult to describe, but it resolves like a symphony coming to a final crescendo. It is a process which resists analysis into component parts.

RELEASE OF ENERGY

Biological and psychological systems are energy models. Such constructs leave something to be desired on the molar level but they have allowed the best understanding of how the organism works. In one sense, therapy is a redistribution of life energy, an unblocking here and a placement there, making energy available for new purposes. Clients generally have too little life energy and what they have is maldistributed and collected in unusable pools or reservoirs which have to be freed. The symptom is an expression of misused energy and an imbalance in a fluid system. The content of the therapeutic work must thus always be related to the force with which that content is evoked. By this I mean that energy has its own justification in human events.

In the beginning of therapy, ineffective force is the rule. The client applies too much or too little energy in an incorrect and sometimes harmful way. He expends it inchoately, massively, and without regard for his central Self. As therapy proceeds, he does less and less of this. The energy flow starts to approach a proper rhythm. The client seems to become more whole and purposive. This must be what the concept of integration represents: proper and suitable force exerted as a gestalt to complete a need. This is particularly true of clients who turn their conflicts into bodily ills. Energy, in the form of pain, flows to the head as headache, to the heart as a flutter, to the back as low-back pain, and to the stomach, genitals, and anus as well. Conflict energy can attach itself to an already sick or malfunctioning organ, or can invest itself in one which has been previously untouched. As therapy proceeds, such energetic flows and attachments occur less and less because the free-floating energy is first channeled into the transference, and later to more appropriate objects. Intraversive energy becomes extrovertive locomotion. Freeing the repression frees the energy behind it, making it dynamic.

BODY PROBLEMS

Clients starting therapy are more or less disembodied creatures. Their bodies are too much or too little present. Body tonus, posture, face, and appendages are unrelated to feeling and purpose. Body pain is overexaggerated or underexaggerated, very much feared, and must often be dissociated from the body. In the opening hours of therapy, the bodily behavior of the client along with his psyche should be part of the therapist's focus. But I do not believe bodily exercises, as prescribed by Lowen and others, are called for. As therapy evolves, body and mind grow more coordinated. The body is rediscovered and put to more efficient and pleasurable use. The therapist must, however, be alert to any physical pathology of the body which may involve physical disease as well as psychic investment and which may require the services of an internist. Doctors of medicine tend to overexaggerate the body; but doctors of philosophy certainly underexaggerate it.

INTELLIGENCE

By conscious and unconscious selection clients are above average in intelligence. But their intelligence is put to the use of illness. The problem is to return it to the healthy Self. I do not believe, as Albert Ellis does, that intelligence can be harnessed directly to problem-solving or that the client can be forced to use it by special therapeutic techniques. The fact that intelligence is blocked and no longer useful for adaptation has a meaning, that of reducing the danger which purposive intelligence would offer socially.

In the beginning, it is easy to overestimate the client's effective intelligence, ability to be insightful, and intelligent motivation. The therapist must always assume he is dealing with only average utilitarian intelligence, perhaps less, and rigid intelligence at that. While the client may be superb in picking up intellectual nuances, in the use of language, symbols and images, he cannot "educe relationships" from all this intellectual work and apply them to his life. Therapy helps him do this in a number of ways. It reduces the "dangers" of being intelligent, it leads the client creatively, symbol by symbol, to the logical conclusion of thought, and it helps apply intelligence to practical problems.

The proof that this happens is not only that the measured IQ of clients goes up, but that the freeing of intelligence is recognized in job promotions, new creative productions, and a more intelligent circle of friends.

INSTINCTUAL PROBLEMS

Clients are, by definition, people who are not getting enough pleasure. The fact that they alone do not allow themselves to have pleasure does not change the picture. Even euphoriants and releasing drugs begin not to be helpful to our clients. The mechanism of the repression of instinctual needs is now well known, but I believe clients have greater than average sensual needs. Furthermore they need to express them in wider and more perverse ways than others. An instinct, for a client, is not merely an instinct but the sensory basis of existence itself. Life is not very worthwhile to clients without instinct, and ontic thrust calls for a regular quantum of sensation and stimulation. They are like the stammerer who cannot stop talking even though it is his greatest pain and disability.

This sensual background must be recognized at the beginning of therapy and in the developing later hours as well. The client wilfully expects the therapist to somehow meet these pleasure needs of his, or at least to show him how to get them satisfied. Therapy may be described as a process of offering satisfaction and of taking it away. It is the essence of therapy that so much instinctual need can be symbolically satisfied for its direct satisfaction would most certainly destroy it. Therapy, paradoxically, becomes itself the pleasure and primary source of satisfaction. The instincts are displaced to the therapy for the time being. This is perhaps the single most important aspect of therapy. As it proceeds, the therapeutic situation supplies less and less and the outside world supplies more and more gratification. This sometimes begins when the client starts picking up options on old relationships and putting them in new frameworks, as well as finding new objects of instinctual interaction.

SUPER-EGO PROBLEMS

All clients are unhappy participants in a superordinate but concealed morality play. They all have more guilt than other people, and they quickly turn any extraordinary pleasure into more guilt. It is not intended, and can never at any rate happen, that a totally uninhibited or guilt-free person will result from therapy. What does happen is that the client is better able to express his needs without at the same time flagellating himself for his gratification, or developing compensatory symptoms. He will always have the tone of an inhibited person of some kind, but therapy permits the client to go ahead with his pleasures despite guilt, and to live with it, somehow, when it arises.

In the beginning of therapy, the client regularly probes the moral and superego structure of the therapist. He needs to know how far he can go, and the nature of the punishments his wishes and fantasies will call forth. He is also testing the infantile father. It is beyond dispute that psychotherapy is a moral business. We are willy-nilly involved with the "good" and the "bad;" and we grant indulgences in modern forms. But I believe that as therapists, we differ from other community practitioners of ethics in that we bring the "good" and "bad" together in a more unified molar way without formal value or religious judgments, the bribery of an afterlife in heaven, or even of a more paradisaical life right here. The pre-genital, denied by most religionists, receive from us an understanding and acceptance offered by no one else. We are less judgmental than others because of our own personal humility. The moral structure of psychotherapy is designed to humanize morality, and make its social demands more reasonable, meaningful, and profitable. The client perpetually asks the question of Job and receives from the therapist the answer of Man.

Moral neutrality is impossible in man so it is helpful for the therapist to have his own well-defined position on moral questions. Then the client can know where the therapist stands. But these are never offered directly to the client. They insinuate themselves, somehow, into all the interactions between client and therapist. In the initial hours, discussion of them should be led back to the client's beliefs. At any rate, the client should be left free to be moral, amoral, or immoral as he needs and pleases. The therapist should see the best side of his client at all times. As therapy evolves, however, the clarifications and interpretations he offers reveal a covert moral direction which the therapist prefers. Since the therapist believes them, he cannot hide them and he should honestly acknowledge his attitudes without judging. Regardless of their content, these attitudes are on the side of life, not against it, and acknowledgement of them strengthens the relationship. If the therapist consistently denies a certain morality, or hides behind it, his client will find him out and think less of him for it. But therapists are very sensitive to accusations of moralizing and sometimes offer what must appear to the client as insincere denials.

GROWTH OF MEANING

More often than we know, boredom is the basis of neurotic illness. Aloneness, alienation, and the anxiety of not fulfilling oneself are also a part of the neurotic situation. Each person makes some kind of meaning for himself out of life—his project. Without that meaning, he has no overriding sense of purpose or value as a person. All men who seriously create have this sense of mission. While it doesn't confer immunity from neurosis, it adds a dimension to existence which does reduce symptom and conflict. A "meaning in life" reduces the expenditure of energy in useless neurotic defenses or at least makes them less disabling.

By definition, every neurotic client is confused about the meaning of his life. Sometimes his illness is just his questioning. Healthy people do not ask why they are here all of the time. But therapy must produce a better reason for existing than what the client brings to the first hour. It is not so much the ancient infantile attention and love he seeks, as the opportunity to contribute something adult which justifies his identity and the pain he suffers as a man.

Therapy helps clear up the identity confusion, reduces the eternal questioning about meaning, and makes possible life projects not even envisaged before. But these are the products of therapy rather than the techniques. A therapist cannot "intend" giving meaning to a client's life. Meaning grows out of the therapeutic dialogue as a by-product of a successful treatment.

In the first hours, it may be necessary to reinforce the idea that no life is without value and purpose; all that one needs to do is to find them. Clients lack faith in this possibility. They look eagerly for reassurance and, while they don't necessarily buy the therapist's declaration, they are sufficiently encouraged by it to go on. And is it not true! Having a meaning in life—big or little—is part of being human. These are, at any rate, the basic goals of therapy.

The sign that therapy has had its proper beginning is that a certain spontaneity begins to enter the picture. The client's stream of thought accelerates to deliver material for analysis, and the therapist's attention in response to this stream becomes free-floating and sharpened. The partners begin to feel comfortable with each other, even fond of each other, and there is a silent contract that they are together in quest of the great experience of human growth.

THE CLIENT AND
THE PSYCHOTHERAPIST

V

Who is the client and what has led him to us? The simplest answer is that a client is a client. He identifies himself by undergoing a certain set of cultural experiences and by making application through official channels by which our culture labels him a patient. Haley says:

> It is becoming more clear that Sigmund Freud developed psychoanalysis as a method of dealing with a specific class of people. He was faced with the general inability of the medicine man of his day to relieve that type of person who went from doctor to doctor and consistently failed to undergo a change.[1]

He qualifies as sick and receives exemption for it by analogy to physical illness under the prevailing ethic of our culture. But his illness is a very strange one. It has no organic site and cannot be seen by the X-ray or the electronic microscope. In Henry's[2] study, more than half the clients treated by psychotherapists in his sample were diagnosed as having a character disorder. If we add to this those problems called existential disorders, the vast majority of clients who come to therapy are people who have problems with the psyche (soul) or Self. They have a persistent sense of dissatisfaction and are uncomfortable with their being. A vast hiatus exists between their perceived Self and desired Self. They are persistently anxious and afraid. Interpersonal relationships, instead of liberating them, are a source of suffering. Quite often the significant people in their lives complain of being emotionally shortchanged by them, so they feel unloved as well as unable to love. Their bodies under- or over-participate in pleasure-pain mechanisms and fail in their sensual purpose.

Becoming a formal client correlates with the opportunity to do so—with sufficient leisure time to introspect, with a certain level of affluence, with the need to be creative, and with the availability of healers. Of course, a certain world-view which sees psychotherapy as helpful is also needed.

---

[1]Haley, *Strategies of Psychotherapy.*
[2]W. E. Henry, et. al. *The Fifth Profession. Becoming a Psychotherapist.* (San Francisco: Jossey-Bass Publ. Co., 1971).

The mind is now the last frontier and people look to it for salvation. If we add to this the mystical, gnostic, and alchemical tradition of man, then the psychotherapist is the residual of all of those historical forces which drive man to ameliorate his lot by spell, knowledge, incantation, totem, and the like. The great mysterium of life, the awe and wonder of instinct, is still centered on the more or less unknown brain, and we are its approved mediators. Logical positivism, and its primary manifestation, Western Science, stops abruptly when the limits of its knowledge are reached. It refuses to speculate about any mysterium it cannot explain. It either turns its back on needy people or, by indirection, suggests those borderland resources which hover between science and metascience—not totally recognized, but still not rejected as the preconscious resources of man. Psychotherapy belongs in the latter category.

In my opinion, Western society can no longer do without psychiatry and would indeed founder without it. The alternative is revolution—something the young prefer to psychotherapy. There is a reciprocal relationship between a society and its healers. Both feed on each other, but discreetly deny each other. Western civilization, without its healers, would be no civilization at all. Its dissidents are now systematically forced to submit to its healing powers, either as a requisite for support (welfare), for freedom, or as amelioration of the punishment its stringent codes call for. Society's leaders are more and more tempted by the benefits of therapy and as a vocation it ranks at the top in student choice. Psychology even decides who is fit for college, for promotion, and for duty as a soldier. Psychiatry, rather than internal medicine, now presides over the psychological facts of life and death. Certainly the quality of that life or death is ruled by depression or elation.

Of course, symptoms, and bodily and psychic disablement, are the chief reasons for coming to therapy. But rarely is the client as handicapped as he thinks he is. Too infrequently does he realistically total up his personal and social assets. But nobody listens to him any more, to his inner cry, and nobody takes his deepest possibilities seriously. The psychotherapist does both—and he is one of the few in society who will. Rejection is not being left out of a cocktail party, but rather peoples' indifference to one's fantasies. Marriages generally fail, not for the reason given, but because one spouse refuses to take his partner's fantasies seriously. The fantasies have to live together.

Lopez-Ibor[3] believes fear of death is the basis of neurosis and that neurotics have a special relationship to death built into them. Freud came pretty close to such a definitive formulation with his Eros and Thanatos instincts, but he pulled back when they were so poorly received. Neurotics have always seemed to me to put special emphasis on their personal lives. They consider themselves special people exempt from the rigors of ordinary life. Nowhere in their unconscious can they conceive of death, of nothing-

[3]Personal communication.

ness, but neither can they move ahead without fear. For them, immunity and immortality consist of words and complexes.

The structure and mechanism of transference, as a psychological concept, have never been satisfactorily explained. Just as the infant is preserved by his mother, so does the therapist shelter his client. But we call this preservation transference. The need to be "saved" physically and psychologically is still fundamental to human behavior. But today it is mostly the psyche which has to be saved from despair. This becomes painfully clear to us when a client deeply involved in his therapy suicides suddenly and without preparation.

Psychotherapy can be interpreted as a match between two persons who find each other in some way and stay together for a certain period of time for certain purposes. How this happens is not precisely known. But it is recognized that client and therapist have certain attitudes, values, abilities, personality traits, and social background in common. Not only that, the outcome of the therapy seems to be correlated with the degree of this correspondence (or lack of it). It often appears, because of this similarity, that clients could become their own therapists by a simple twist of fate. Some do indeed go on to become qualified healers.

Psychotherapy has arisen as a largely urban, middle-class, Judeo-Christian phenomenon. Its principal practitioners come from this social area as well, or at least adhere closely to it. It is also a product of Western messianic stress. The founding fathers, and those who continue to maintain therapy, feel some urgency to project upon others the solutions they have found to their own personal dilemmas. Freud, Jung, Rank, Ferenczi, Adler, Sullivan, and others, were men in identity crises—crises which they not only had to solve personally, but the solutions to which they were impelled to share with the world. Therapists are missionaries in disguise. They bring the "word" to the uninitiated. In this sense, therapy is like any earlier doctrine of salvation offered man. Each age creates and maintains constructs central to its survival.

It always comes as a shock to therapists that some people in our society reject this form of amelioration no matter how great their misery. It is difficult to understand how they can turn down the healing benefits of catharsis, creative insight, and the pleasure principle. It is difficult for therapists to understand that people live by different premises, and that these premises absolutely govern their choices of means for ameliorating misery. Many die because of their premises but this does not change anything. Tiger Balm and acupuncture are effective healing techniques in Asia. The premise that they work helps them work.

It is a large but select class of society which takes this position towards psychotherapy. I use "class" in the broad sense of Banfield[4] as constituting those members of society—white, yellow, or black—whose life style consists of lack of capacity for self-discipline, need for immediate gratification, lack

---

[4]E. C. Banfield, *The Unheavenly City* (Boston: Little, Brown, 1970).

of planning, social indifference, and a way of life divorced from the Protestant ethic and its values. But it is not only this group in society which spurns psychotherapy. A certain segment of the upper-middle and upper classes do so as well—but for vastly different reasons. Most of society's "successful" men have avoided the psychoanalytic couch. They see psychoanalysis as anti-"self-made", as abject dependency, as effete or feminine weakness. Its lack of personal directivity often appalls them, and they refuse the idea of a life governed by an unconscious, one over which they have no control. The number of great men who have had a single therapeutic interview, and no more, is legion.

Much of the new therapeutic work in the community psychiatry format is, in my opinion, doomed to failure. It involves precisely those segments of society who lack the preconditions for therapeutic healing. Until the healer can offer a closer social identification with those he intends to heal, it will not work. This is why avant-garde community healing programs now involve practitioners who are themselves members of the "sick" order, and who arise from among them.

The vast majority of clients are female and the overwhelming majority of psychotherapists are male. There is a sort of sexual meeting of the needs in this healing ratio. Most devout churchgoers, particularly in Hispanic countries, are women, and priests are always males. Women seek from men a deep spiritual meaning which Christ, Buddha, Lao Tse, and others offered them. But women also seek sexual force and impregnation from still other men and the two have a common symbolic meeting place in psychotherapy. Religion has somehow failed to provide this.

The epicene quality of the new generation, and the sexual difficulties of the old, testify that the biological division into male and female has now become a confused cultural thing. All efforts to bi-sexualize the psyche have come to naught. Jung long ago anticipated that animus could not do without anima and that the universal problem of therapy is to help reconcile the two.

Our clients seem to need more intimacy or ecstasy than others. At times they need an almost constant infusion of it. They have obviously never attained independence from their infantile circumstances and the ever-present possibilities of happy regression to an earlier day. To be exclusively loved, to squeeze the last erg of passion from the body, to have infinite security, to be free of pain, to ride high on the tides of mood, to be protected from the death instinct, these are some of the overriding needs of our clients. Regardless of phenomenology, behind every phobia, the obsession, the fugue, the compulsion, or other neurotic forms lies the supra-human irrational need. It is almost a miracle, and one I have seen, how quickly a phobia or confirmed psychosomatic disability loses its force once intimacy and security and ecstasy are guaranteed the client. Clients respond with bewilderment when asked "by what order of events do they feel they are entitled to paradise." Wheelis[5] says for example:

[5]A. Wheelis, The Illusionless Man (New York: W. W. Norton & Co., 1966).

They are so fortunate, these patients of analysts—money, intelligence, good health, and good looks many of them—and so enslaved! A phobia holds them to one town, even one room. They're afraid of planes and don't travel, have social anxieties and avoid strangers. Always some kind of fear—of incest, guilt feelings, of the strength of impulse, of experience . . . of life itself.

The point is that the clients of psychotherapy are already the blessed of mankind, but they want more. Is this an illness? Yes. For the suffering and social disablement which follow this need is the same as if the body itself were torn. People vary widely in ontic thrust, that is, in the intensity with which they are driven to use their lives. The behavior of inmates of concentration camps illustrates this most aptly.[6] Most people settle for a suitable sublimation but others cannot. They will not give up their Odyssey regardless of how irrational or impossible it becomes. They keep "beating their head against the wall" in the attempt to finally attain it. Sometimes the "search" is converted into the goal itself. Life seems to burn brighter and brighter with such possibilities for some people, but with lesser incandescence for still others. It is the former and not the latter who become the clients of psychotherapy and who seek it with quiet desperation. Distraction and displacement come too easy today for anyone to persist in therapy without an overriding motive such as this.

Are our clients incapable of emotional satisfaction? Maslow[7] writes about the woman of today who replaces one goal, or husband, with another and never really finds what she is looking for. The search again replaces the fulfillment. The endlessness of therapy often results from incapacity to be satisfied; from the impossibility of finding basic fulfillment. This may be why there is no exact and universal stopping point in therapy—satiation thresholds vary so widely from person to person. Of course, each client decides for himself what his life-style will be. But to be useful, therapy must show linear, or at least curvilinear growth, toward some practical life-goal. Boredom, frustration, loneliness, and emptiness are certainly psychic states, but psychotherapy is not yet their specific antidote.

All our clients have had special historical relationships with a mothering-person. They have, in a sense, been vicariously and viciously imprinted in the Bowlby[8] sense. It is as though an unwritten contract in blood had been made between mother and child which has not yet been fulfilled. The client everlastingly presents the contract for payment. To feel unconsciously cheated as an adult in this significant way is one of the most painful of human experiences. Every therapeutic client seeks in therapy to have the contract (or its equivalent) paid up, or to have it finally abridged or cancelled. Many of my clients actually recall promises of this sort made by their parents which were never fulfilled. "If you lose weight, I will take you—and you alone—with me to New York on my next trip." "I love only you and no one else matters. Be mine." "We'll be together the rest of our lives." "I'll never let

[6]V. E. Frankl, *From Death Camp to Existentialism* (Boston: Beacon Press, 1958).
[7]Maslow, *Motivation and Personality*. (2nd ed.).
[8]J. Bowlby, *Attachment and Loss* (New York: Basic Books, 1969).

anybody hurt you." But most contracts are more subtle than this, and the contract lies unfulfilled and often unfulfillable because the clauses contain double-binds. Fortunately, for most children the contractual disillusionment is tragic but not irreparable. But for some, our clients, the contract stands everlastingly.

Are our clients narcissistic? Of course they are! But narcissism need not be looked down upon. Some of the most revered and saintly people in our society are heavily narcissistic. The greatest forms of creativity are narcissistic. The problem is that clients cannot relinquish their narcissism even temporarily when relinquishment is required for the good of the Other. They are perpetually caught in it like a dinosaur in a tar pit. Therapy, hopefully, helps them to shelve narcissism, here and there, by revealing that it has no proper payoff. But no client ever really completely relinquishes his narcissism. He learns to do with less of it.

The problem of neurosis is in a sense the failure of aggression. Aggression, according to Spitz, is the carrier wave of humanity. But what happens if one does not know when aggression is appropriate, how aggressive to be, and how to stop being aggressive? The client who said to me that love and sex were two entirely separate things meant of course that one was aggression and the other love. He could never put them together and thereby demonstrated a basic split in his personality. Love as aggression is the order of the integrated person. One client said that marrying a man meant, at the same time, marrying her (1) beloved father, (2) her therapist, and (3) Jesus Christ. No aggressive human relationship can successfully contain this trinity. Aggression, instinct, and power are the stuff of living. Anyone deficient in them, or sadly overburdened by them, is at a disadvantage with his fellow-man.

Is therapy a disillusioning process? Do our clients have too many illusions about Self and Other? Yes. What we substitute for this in psychotherapy is a more realistic, a more satisfying, set of illusions. Therapy is, therefore, a metapsychology put to the service of the Self, and we offer hope in the sense of more useful illusions, which make the paradoxes and absurdities of life more bearable.

There is no need for pessimism about our clients. In terms of intelligence, literacy, sensitivity, physical health, and economic circumstances, they have the basis for a fulfilled life. They have to seek it and find it in their own way. The therapist doesn't provide the answer; he helps clear away the undergrowth to reveal the question.

THE PSYCHOTHERAPIST

The most recent, and possibly the most definitive study of psychotherapists, (clinical psychologists, psychiatric social workers, psychiatrists, and psychoanalysts) is that of Henry.[9] He interviewed and psychologically tested a carefully selected sample of 300 of them in Chicago, Los Angeles, and New York using a variety of data-designs. His work represents an ethno-

[9] W. E. Henry, *Careers in Mental Health* (1970 Mimeo).

logical base line for our discussion of the nature of the psychotherapist. I have abstracted a small amount of his data for illustration here.

If psychiatric social workers are excluded (60% of all female practitioners in this study were social workers), then most psychotherapists are men. Interestingly enough, 39% of the entire sample claimed Jewish affinity; but Jewish ethnic background must be even more common. As might be expected, continental influences and values rank high. While only 14% were foreign-born, 51% of the psychotherapists had fathers who were foreign born.

The sample was skewed toward the youthful side; but the modal points of this distribution were as follows: 36% were between 31 to 40 years of age, and another 34% were between 41 and 50.

About one-third of practitioners in the sample said they were either atheistic, agnostic, or had no religion at all. But a larger proportion of young psychoanalysts (under 40) were atheists. There was no indication as to how seriously the majority take their religious identifications.

The majority of psychoanalysts and psychiatrists work in private practice settings. This is less true of clinical psychologists and psychiatric social workers who are predominantly institutionally oriented. Very few psychotherapists now work in traditional mental hospitals.

What is the workload of our therapists? Henry found that if we take the total number of patients being treated by each profession and divide by the total number of corresponding professionals, we find that the mean patient load for psychoanalysts is 22.4; for psychiatrists, 32.7; for clinical psychologists, 14.6; and 10.8 for psychiatric social workers. For all professions taken together, the average number of patients being treated per week per respondent is 18.

More than three out of four psychotherapists have themselves received psychotherapy. Those who were found to be in the high or moderate success category are much more likely to have received psychotherapy than the low success group.

An earlier study on the same topic, that of Schofield,[10] is less revealing. He identified 140 psychiatrists, 149 psychiatric social workers, and 88 clinical psychologists who were psychotherapists through their respective parent professional organizations, such as the American Psychiatric Association. Psychotherapist was defined as "a worker in the broad area of mental illness who specialized in 'intrusive personal endeavors of a corrective or therapeutic nature, utilizing the interview as his primary tool.' " Schofield was more interested in the differences between the professions whereas our interest is in the aggregate. I have therefore extrapolated some general conclusions from his data.

He found that psychotherapists show pressure toward upward social mobility but that professional training homogenizes social values and thus restricts the basis for empathy.

The typical case carried was male (female for psychiatrists), 20 to 40 years of age, married (single for psychologists), with high school or higher

[10]W. Schofield, Psychotherapy. The Purchase of Friendship (Englewood Cliffs, N.J.: Prentice-Hall, Inc., 1964).

education, and professional/managerial in job identification (unskilled or semi-skilled for social workers). The average client who was seeing a psychiatrist had an income of over $8,000, and less for the other professions.

When asked what the ideal clients would be like, the psychotherapists preferred married females, 20 to 40 years old, with some college education, having professional/managerial status. "Unattractive" clients in this study are under the age of 15 or over 50, widowed or divorced, with limited education (or too much education), employed in services, fisheries, forestry, semi- or skilled labor, etc.

The psychologists and psychiatrists were mostly males; the social workers female. Their average age was 44 years; but the social workers tended to be younger. Divorce was more common than among the general population.

The psychotherapists of schizophrenia have always impressed me as a more intense and more dedicated group than other therapists because their clients are so difficult to approach and work with.[11] As a part of a study, I asked a number of outstanding therapists of schizophrenia to describe themselves using only adjectives. Here are five examples from that study:

> *Therapist 1.* "Sympathetic, conscientious, sensitive, ambitious, energetic, tenacious, and grateful."
>
> *Therapist 2.* "Sincere, honest, brusque, libidinous, tough, erotic, and tender."
>
> *Therapist 3.* "An extroverted introvert, thoughtful, homeloving, curious, critical, perfectionistic, and tolerant."
>
> *Therapist 4.* "Aggressive, ambitious, impatient with personal limitation, vacillating in mood when reacting to the latter, generally content, zest for life, periodically self-critical."
>
> *Therapist 5.* "Friendly, reserved, optimistic, hardworking, tolerant, 'giving', mildly nihilistic, and self-indulgent."

From these studies, it must be clear that psychotherapy is not a profession like other professions. It is rather a "calling." Rieff,[12] that philosopher of culture, calls psychotherapists the new priesthood of Western culture. He makes a case for the possibility that we are now somehow chosen or designated for that role. Of course, priestly functions call for moral suasions of one kind or another, and a sense of overriding social mission. Whether we like to see ourselves this way or not, we are the guardians of the sacred in culture; But of course, when we hold individual values in our clients to be superogatory to cultural ones, we are subverting culture. But our function is to bring order out of chaos, and society is above all the ordering of persons into working units.

Many recent studies indicate that we are an elite, and that we prefer to work with elite clients.[13] By elite I mean certain qualities of intelligence,

---

[11]A. Burton, "The adoration of the patient and its disillusionment," *Am. J. Psychoan.*, 1970, *29*, 194–204.

[12]D. Rieff, The impossible culture. *Encounter*, 1970, *35*, 33–34.

[13]A. B. Hollingshead, and F. C. Redlich, *Social Class and Mental Illness* (New York: John Wiley, 1958); Gurin, G. et al., *Americans View Their Mental Health* (New York: Basic Books, 1960).

verbal ability, socio-economic membership, race, creativity, and sex. And we do our best work with precisely those clients we like to work with. Carl Rogers was puzzled and chagrined that the farmers of Wisconsin, the control group in his study of schizophrenia, did not share his enthusiasm for plumbing their personality depths or for this particular form of humane intervention. They saw no purpose in it.

Psychotherapy is "clean," white-collar work, unlike what most of our fathers did, and it offers status, income, and a desirable style of life. Its setting is indoors—not the landscape—and it is civil, humane, and stylistic. Aggression and force are talked about but rarely exerted. It is a life style preferred by many people, shunned by just as many, but is in the established European talmudic and scholarly tradition. Rabbis were in the field before Freud and they did not do such a bad job! We talk a lot about sex but are not very lustful. While some therapists have certainly slept with their clients, in the face of the opportunities available, it is an extremely rare event. This is evidence either of considerable control or sublimation on the part of therapists. It takes sensuality to become a therapist—sensuality not acted-out but displaced into "care."

One would, therefore, expect that therapists have happy and ideal family backgrounds and lives, and that in this setting they find their sensuality and happiness. But the statistics for highly gifted scientists, as well as for therapists, do not confirm this. Bush,[14] after systematically reviewing 73 articles on scientific creativity, comes to the following conclusions about the gifted creators:

1. There seems to be an unusually high incidence of absence of a parent from the home in childhood, either due to death, divorce or other causes. The lack of fathering seems more prevalent than the lack of adequate mothering (in later childhood remoteness is reported in both parents).

2. Family relations were notably lacking in warmth, closeness, and intimacy, and remained tenuous throughout life. Mothers have often been reported to have been insecure, inconsistent, frustrating, preoccupied, and not too warm, giving, or protective. While there was usually even more distance between father and son, the father seems to be less disparaged than the mother and viewed with more respect.

3. The break from home toward independence occurs relatively early and without much apparent conflict or guilt.

4. Periods of extended childhood isolation are commonly reported due variously to physical factors (illness or physical deficiencies and/or voluntary or imposed social isolation).

5. Both psychological and psychosexual development are retarded. Peer relations are slow to develop and dating relationships usually begin quite late.

6. Intellectual interests and achievements appear very early and their significance is

[14]M. Bush, "Psychoanalysis and scientific creativity," *J. Am. Psychoan. Assoc.*, 1969, *17*, 136–190.

highly overdetermined. They provide the child with important sources of self-amusement and solace, and in many instances are one of the few gratifying ties to his parents, teachers, and other people.

While therapists are also scientists, they do not perfectly conform to the personality picture of the physical or biological scientists. But it is true that in the case of psychogenetic development Henry[15] and Burton[16] find distress in the early lives of therapists similar to that noted among other scientists. The residue of the family romance must act as the charge or motor through which the therapist finds the incentive to give himself to his clients in his characteristic way. There is no drudgery and boredom like therapy when one is not "involved" in it. The statement of a clinical psychologist, "What, me work with the nuts!" describes it very well. It is an attribute of psychogenesis that unmastered and unintegrated impulses in childhood have to be mastered, and apparently even training analysis doesn't completely do the job.

Therapists are thus left with an affective sensitivity in their personal lives. They put this quest to use in their work and even find major gratification in it. It is their particular form of poetry, and they become highly attuned to it. A perceptual mechanism selects the necessary clients for them. They respond positively to despair while others flee from it. They become guardians of it and their clients park a part of their "badness" with them. Of course, this brings with it an overinvolvement and narcissism which people have called arrogance. While this is not necessarily commendable it seems to me to be necessary. Therapists are ambivalent about their clients just as clients are ambivalent about their therapists. Too much narcissism, at any rate, is damaging and clients have magnificent ways of reducing it. The arrogant therapist is apt to be a professional failure.

Historically, psychotherapy is the residue of 2,000 or more years of applied humanism. The therapist is today the symbol of the Judeo-Christian individual life, and the central issues which surround that life. He fights vigorously against anybody and anything which limits the fulfillment and completion of that life. Neurotic suffering, for him, is wasteful because it is life not put to use. If psychotherapy should ever become political, it would be the first true Western liberalism with values centering around the person and his inner life—something current politics gives only lip service to.

One would expect people devoted to such a task would be highly religious. All the inner structures and purposes common to the psychotherapist go well with people who have "soul." But the evidence consistently shows that therapists are rarely formally religious. How can this be? There are many ways of having "soul," and I believe therapists are religious but not as defined by institutional religions.

We need to be close to the birth of creativity. This calls for a sensitized

---

[15]W. E. Henry, "Some observations on the lives and training of healers," 1965 (Mimeo).

[16]A. Burton, "The adoration of the patient and its disillusionment."

person to help mold the creativity. Perhaps, on the simplest level, the therapist demands the *epistemic* life. By this I mean, he is dedicated to "knowing," and to helping other people "know." Knowledge is for him not only power but life. His chief tools are the cognitive mechanisms: the intellect and language, but he is by no means limited to these media.

By definition, every therapist is a defender of linguistics and he sees reason and reality as the sole way to salvation in the world. He may be a phenomenologist, an existentialist, or an artist/scientist. But he basically subscribes to logical positivism as the philosophical way out of the human maze. Cognitive and affective closure are his peak experiences, and the unity of the fragmented his watchword. He makes wholes out of parts, after first making parts out of wholes.

Some people apparently need to be close to the unconscious, to the demons. Leopold Szondi would say that it wouldn't matter much whether the form this took was theology, psychiatry or madness. Therapists are more comfortable with the Furies than other people are. The mystical, the arcane, the bizarre and the marginal are the stuff of their work. Possibly we need to show that we can best Beelzebub, that right does win out, and that persistent neurotic suffering has some kind of reward. What the man on the street fears is the therapist's forte. We flourish in the presence of anxiety instead of being reduced by it.

According to Jung's typology, most therapists would be feeling, thinking, introverts. They would also be close to the animus-anima archetype, to their feminine impulses—and they would acknowledge and put them to work. Their inner life, their dreams and fantasies, would be at least as important as their outward behavior. Loneliness is a condition in which the Self cannot commune with it-Self.

Let me close this chapter by saying what therapists are not.

They are not athletes, although they may be athletic; they are not hunters or fishermen, even though they may like the field, stream and sea; they are not marksmen or gun collectors, even though they may own a gun; they are not bankers or real estate developers, even though they invest their money; and they do not usually run for political office even though they are intensely interested in politics.

On the positive side, they are people who have strong creative drives, and who feel a certain incompleteness of Self. Each client permits them to complete themselves, and in this way resolve some of the unfinished business of the family romance. But above all, they are dedicated to the idea of the Self, its fulfillment, and the reduction of despair.

MAINTAINING
THERAPEUTIC FLOW

VI

The heart of psychotherapy is the process of working-through. This is a procedure by which a wish, idea, or concept of the client is followed through to its cognitive and emotional conclusions.

The following statements, made by clients, about their specific life dilemmas, suggest the flavor of the problem:

1. "I can't put love and sex together."
2. "I don't have any valid life. What I have is punished."
3. "I want a story to tell which will make sense."
4. "I am followed by an aura and it may be death."
5. "I have a failure of nerve."
6. "I always feel that I am behind in the game of life."

The problems are not so much specific disabling symptoms such as phobias or compulsions. More basic is the concept of self which falters in critical human situations. These statements illustrate a basic and central hunger for wider parameters. This is, of course, related to the specific symptoms which set the limits to the client's life. The technical problems during the middle course of therapy are not only to fully relieve manifest symptoms such as anxiety, guilt, and motor dysfunctions, but to help reconstitute the inadequate and failing conception of self. How is this to be done?

THE THERAPIST AS MEDIUM

Therapy works with the psychotherapist as intermediary or midwife. He has a number of functions, some of them real and some projected upon him. He fulfills these functions successively and simultaneously. They are the vehicle by which psychic growth occurs. The concept of transference helps account for some of the functions described below, but too much value has been placed on transference at the expense of conscious functions which occur at the same time and produce change.

Wise Old Man

One consults another person because he possesses something such as information, power, technique, or prescience, which the supplicant does not have. Man has always tried to look behind the veil. In ancient Thebes, Sparta, the Delian Confederation, and Athens, no significant step was ever taken without consulting an oracle. Even Western science makes a fetish of prediction—its own particular form of wisdom and soothsaying. The wise man in every culture gains an aura of mystery because of his wisdom. This is true both in primitive and civilized cultures.

Certain areas of knowledge about life are delegated to wise men. They are rewarded well for their knowledge, and they are both feared and respected for it. In years just past the physician, who presides over birth and death, has carried the mantle of the wise old man. Earlier the priest, who was the guardian of the soul and after-life, the warrior or samurai who guarded land and person, were the wise men. Today the psychotherapist has inherited this position. No really significant moves are made today in our society without directly or indirectly consulting a psychologist, a psychiatrist, or his equivalent. Wisdom, while often derided, is the basic commodity and research, its source, is supremely extolled and rewarded.

Clients come to "wise old men" in the same way the Athenians went to the Delphian oracle. They ask Nemesis or the Furies to foretell, intercede, ameliorate, or palliate their specific human condition. In modern times knowledge has been institutionalized and formalized so that only those who are licensed may be "wise old men" for a fee. But, as far as we know, all psychological approaches, the licensed as well as the unlicensed, confer equal benefits upon the client. (I would hastily add, however, that the formally approved probably do less harm.)

The therapist offers not only this form of metapsychology but solid scientific substance as well. The wisdom of the therapist encapsulates at least a hundred years of knowledge about how the psyche operates, and what to do when it falls into disrepair. Of course, therapeutic knowledge is rudimentary compared to a field like genetics, but it is the best available. It cannot be matched by astrology, meditation, religion, or faith healing. The client seeks the latest informed word on his malady and the latest technique for correcting it. Heart transplants created the stir they did because "wise old men" had made it possible not only to extend life but to have a new heart, meaning psyche. To patients like these it made a difference whose heart they were getting in the transplant.

All therapists accept this function of therapy. Some load it more heavily than others. Communication from wise men is always unidirectional. Truly "wise old men" do not promiscuously offer their counsel. The fact that they are bearers of the wisdom and are most sparing of it is sufficient to have effects on the client. These effects are a motivation to learn from the wise one, to be like him, and to be similarly wise and compassionate with others.

Fount of Affection

All forms of psychotherapy offer the client similar emotional regard. His illness, helplessness, hopelessness, pain, lack of pleasure, absence of love and relatedness, isolation, and fears of all kinds are recognized. The therapist's stance must counter all of these negations. But, most of all, he has to have an affectionate regard, even "love," for his client. This cannot be faked. It must involve the therapist's own deep need for affection and existence. It may be a happenstance that the couch became the symbol and method of psychoanalysis, but I do not believe so. Most erotic acts are done lying down. Why should this also be the classical analytic posture? Of course, the clients are mostly women and the therapists mostly men.

In order to grow and become authentic the client must re-experience the earliest love, particularly where he failed to master it in certain particulars. The proper aim of love is a most fragile thing and it is almost a miracle that so many of us succeed. Our clients have failed in it, have struggled unsuccessfully with it for years. They not only need affection but they need also to learn how to gain it and reciprocate it. Obviously, the therapist is immediately in the center of such needs.

There is something Dionysian about therapy in the sense that it celebrates the triumph of love in human events. Even though little is acted out in the therapeutic hour itself, the fantasies of therapy are quite affectional and erotic. The dyadic community gets its share of deferred impulses. It is fortunate that images and symbols work so well; otherwise there might be no psychotherapy at all. The most authentic therapist is the one who accepts therapy as a labor of love, is comfortable with that love, and uses it for the good of his clients.

In the middle course of therapy, positive feelings (and their negative counterparts) build to a crescendo. They are often outrageously fictional, or full of illusions, but therapeutic love was never meant to be rational. The important thing is that the client has such feelings, feels safe with them, and later transfers them to more appropriate objects, as he probably failed to do in the Oedipal period. Affection invariably works wonders in mobilizing passion and unlocking inhibition. It reveals what is possible in life, the beauty of life, and confirms that the effort to obtain it is worthwhile. It transcends and transforms the client's reality, and the neurotic is above all hooked on the "facts" of his condition.

No one knows how love and affection operate, but we are personally and professionally aware that they have effects. Often, merely the fact that the therapist cares about the client is sufficient for him to go forward. It is a somewhat amusing commentary that the wives of therapists never exactly know what goes on in therapy, and they make no great attempts to find out. But they do know they have to share something with their spouses' clients. Apparently, by selection, they are glad to do so. Comparisons of wives and clients are taboo at therapeutic sessions themselves and at cocktail parties the therapist and his wife attend.

The Devil or Shadow

Repression of wish, impulse, and image is still a perfectly valid sign of neurosis. The unconscious becomes stuffed with unusable monads which drain energy. Most of this blockage is amoral or immoral in content and it defends against guilt, anxiety, and dissociation. The fantasies and dreams of clients, when analyzed, reveal that they are more pursued by the Furies than non-clients. The therapist, whatever else he is, is also symbolically the devil in disguise. In Jung's sense, he is the shadow side of the client. The two shadows must meet and compromise if the outcome is to be beneficial.

I have said elsewhere that clients deposit their "badness" or demon temporarily with the therapist, who is professionally glad to assume it, and who is furthermore capable of accepting it. We still exorcise and purify. Catharsis is the purging, not of digestive contents, but of devilish inchoate forces which raise hob with self order and integration. Demonic matters are full or partial impulses towards incest, cannibalism, murder, torture, and rape. All men have these impulses and all must deny them. Goya and Hieronymus Bosch have perhaps best presented the demon in their lithographs and paintings.

Dialogue with the therapist is also a dialogue with the devil or unconscious. This is the only time and place in which society permits and even approves of discussing such arcane matters. The fact that clients uniformly become hostile and aggressive toward the therapist, and see him as satanish at this time, indicates the universal projection of their own shadow side on him. This is different from the father-transference discussed below. It represents rather an anthropological and sociological residual to which all civilized men fall heir.

The Rival

Therapists become siblings as well as fathers and mothers. The family position of a sibling is always competitive. In this sense, the therapist becomes an older brother or sister. But therapeutic rivalry goes beyond this. Just as the client needs to become more powerful, the therapist needs to avoid giving him too much power, or power too quickly. Interpersonal psychotherapy reveals that when clients do get power this way they may use it against the therapist. Much of the negative force in therapy is rivalrous. The client often resents and envies the status of the therapist, his happiness, and even his material things. Thus the therapist represents the anal retentive as well as the oral nurturance. Some clients even come to feel that the therapist has usurped what is rightfully theirs.

If the therapist is aware that a rivalry will occur, he is in a better position to cope with it. Presumably, he will have worked through his own competitive family feelings in his training or personal therapy and will not be challenged by the rare client who has a better station in life, or more achievements, or who has more promise for the future. It is better to let the client have his feelings, to acknowledge and clarify them, but not to compete with him. In any event this would be no competition at all. Sometimes we envy the client his unbridled libido, his good looks, and his fecundity, but the authentic therapist doesn't need these things from the client. He probably matches them in the community, in his family, and in his own sublimations and adjustments.

Masculinity-Femininity

The original state of man was unisexed. With the coming of Eve, Jung's animus-anima problems came on the scene. Man has apparently never given up the quest for unification, for total self-sufficiency. This is most apparent in the hip generation. It also reflects the oneness and interdependence of nature. Men have problems with women; women have problems with men. And men have problems with the feminine side of themselves; and women, with their masculine side. This is by no means new, but what bears discussion is its function in therapy.

Freud found the ground of the neurosis in sexuality and pleasure. This is still basically true of modern man. In therapy, the problems of repression and of getting pleasure are no longer so simple. For Freud it was a more quantitative thing whereas today it has unique qualitative aspects. Our clients demand an ecstasy in their sexuality which even a fin-de-siecle Viennese would have thought uncalled for.

For our purposes, the therapist is the masculine model and animus-anima problems are worked out through him. This of course involves the pull toward homosexuality, unresolved Oedipal remnants in the personality, penis envy, castration feelings, and the like. The therapist uses his masculine and feminine side to do this in subtle ways.

Father Surrogate

Inevitably, through transference, the therapist will become the client's father. Fathers have been derogated in dynamic psychiatry but they have a greater importance than we have heretofore realized. In my experience when a father is fully masculine and sexual with his spouse and family, double binds and similar covert pathological mechanisms are either rare or non-symptom formative. Fathers are Mosaic, Don Juanish, Promethean, Apolonian, and Aesculapian all rolled into one. It is no accident that Christianity preaches about God the Father, that youth rebels against the Father, and that Father is still the source of all pro-creation.

The client has somehow missed the growth influence of the father. The explicit reasons for this we need not explore here. Female clients particularly have Father deficits and a certain desperation about them. Society, furthermore, while it pays public homage to Mother, extolls Father in ways that count. Clients also want to be their own fathers.

In therapy, transference supplies them with one. Reaction to the therapist, who is a stranger after all, in this way is often uncanny. The same feelings and modes of transaction toward Father reappear despite anything the client can do. Of course, there is both affection and anger—affection for the felt tenderness, and anger because it never came to full fruition. It is not the child who pulls back in the Oedipal situation but the Father. They are, in a developmental sense, notorious cowards.

Those therapists who have children of their own see a very close analogue in them to their clients. They symbolically adopt the client, and proceed to be fatherly to him. Problems of course arise. How fatherly should one be, and when? How and when to set limits and to punish? Clients are, in a sense, "bad" children who want and need to be better. Most often the therapist simply needs to let the transference develop, but he hangs up when he stops short of becoming the ideal father, with all the extraordinary demands this implies. Only by being a perfect father can he demonstrate there is no such thing. Fathers are merely men. Clients seduce, threaten, fall into depression, somatize, anything and everything not to permit father to be father, and to prove his culpability and cupidity. The therapist must demonstrate his sincerity, and then lead the client to be a more appropriate man or woman.

Mother Surrogate

So much has been written on this topic that I fear being redundant. The mother, or mothering person, is crucial because she has the survival of the infant in her hands. More than we care to recognize, mothers are selfish, ignorant, manipulating people. Why not: the infant and child is at her disposal and if she has self-hatred she will certainly hate her child. But her hatred is, of course, disguised as benevolence—for the good of the child. The maternal instinct is more than a biological need. Psychologically, motherhood justifies being women. A child is proof positive of womanliness.

Mothers promote mastery and autonomy through the various developmental ages and phases. They should do this in a way which does not encourage fixation at any one stage or regression to earlier ones. When the child fixates or regresses, the mother is herself anxious or neurotic. Or she is serving her own needs through the rape of the child. This is, of course, involuntary but the mother's own existence provides the backing and force for it. This is not the battered-child syndrome. These children are usually better off. Rape comes in the life promises which are never fulfilled, in the life which is not allowed to be, and in the gradual subversion of reality.

Obviously, the therapist has to help undo and re-do this. He becomes Mother—with a difference. He has no hidden agenda. His life does not depend on the child, and he has a mature vantage point from which reality can be returned to the child. This dispassion within passion does the work since the actual mother cannot step out of herself. Some therapists may not make good parents, but they are invariably good parent-therapists.

If therapists allowed it, clients would suckle at their breasts. When some clients actually are offered milk in a bottle, they take it greedily. Thus therapy is symbolically and transferentially offering a new nurturance—in carefully measured doses. This helps change the significance of the original mother and of the feelings toward her. These feelings become more positive and unencumbering—they can be set aside. Making this possible is the therapist's prime goal.

SILENCE AND OVERTALKING

Among the barriers to maintaining therapeutic flow are silence—and overtalking. People who come to therapy have individual styles of communication. Some talk from the first moment of the interview and do not stop until they leave. Others say very little, say nothing at all, or speak only in bursts or ejaculations. The therapist must make allowances for variances in style. Beyond this, some stages of therapy normatively call for more verbal communication than others.

Blocking can come at any time and it has to be taken seriously. It not only has dynamic significance for the therapy—estranged married couples do not talk to each other either—but it may lead to premature termination. Persistent silence, without dropping out of therapy, is the most aggressive thing the client can do. When this happens three or four sessions in a row, it becomes urgent to resolve the situation. Most often the therapist waits the client out, giving only sufficient reinforcement—generally nonverbal—to provide headway to the encounter. In most cases, the client will then pick up the thread and go on. But once in a while the client will not continue. Why not?

Invariably, these clients have a history of being punished for talking, for giving information. Or they use silence as a means of attaining secondary gains. Most therapists would prefer to be screamed at, to have four-letter words thrown at them, than to have the client maintain continuous silence. Of course, silence is speech, and non-talkers do use body language in their silent periods. Silence makes everyone uncomfortable and guilty if for no other reason than that clients come to talk and pay heavily for the opportunity. If the therapist gets no talk from the client, he may have to talk. This may knock him off his more or less prepared "presentation of self." No therapist likes to lose his aplomb, his studied professional poise, or his deep interest in the moment. Continued silence aggravates all of these pressures.

There is no universal rule about silences in therapy. Each therapeutic hour, and each client, has to be taken on its own merits. The client's silence has to be respected, and this is often the only way he can fight back. Respect calls for understanding, so that no long silence should be merely passed over. There are as well many kinds of silence: the *in memoriam* type; the helpless silence; the murderous silence; the orgasmic silence; the silence of death; the fulfilled silence; the silence of awe; and so on.

Pre-silent clients will say, "You are not talking today. Please say something." It may be that on this particular day the therapist is a little more withdrawn than usual, or he is still working on the problem of the previous hour, or he really has nothing to say, or "it isn't his turn." The therapist may then just smile, or say, "I have nothing to say at this moment. But I'm with you; I'm here; I'm listening." But no more!

The client feels safer when the therapist talks. The client then gets to the therapist's problems and not his own, and he can resent this deeply. When I have talked out of turn in therapy, I have been taken to task and paid for it later.

How long, then, should a silence go on? Only as long as the silence is communicating something, serving some function, and is not too frightening a thing for the client. If silence is a regular recurring event, the therapist had better reconsider what he is doing. The therapeutic process is a flowing stream and if dirt and debris dam it up, it must be opened. If recognizing and respecting the silence doesn't terminate it, other approaches are necessary. Some of them are:

1. Begin a soliloquy talking mostly of yourself and not dealing as such with the silence.
2. Provide a stimulus for the client's anger or mourning in a gross provoking way.
3. Interpret the silence on a deep understanding level.
4. Give the client body support while talking affectionately to him.
5. Restate the goals of the therapy in a loud voice relating the silence to them.

There are other approaches as well, but these work. Furthermore they give the client an opportunity to meet the needs the silence is the cover for.

Some therapists have their own problems of silence as well. That is, they are silent when they should be saying something. Classical psychoanalysis did not allow too much dialogue, but today such passivity is rare. Why, then, is the therapist silent when he should be talking? For the same reasons the client is silent. But silence is not expected of him. He has gotten the silence out of his system in his therapeutic training, and his obligation is to keep the dialogue going. Not saying something at the right time is as much a technical error as saying it at the wrong time, but its effects are less immediately discernible.

If the therapist himself falls passively into lengthy and total silence while the client is verbally communicating and he is challenged, he should quickly say to the client, "I don't know why I have so little to say today. Maybe I've dried up. I'm very much here with you but feel a sense of quietness." If the therapist is silent because he is hostile to the client, he should reveal this if it will not be destructive to the therapy. Clients can accept anything if it is honestly offered, and given with proper humility. Of course, there is the therapeutic silence which serves as the backdrop for fulfillment. All important things happen in silence. This form of silence must not be confused with silence that destroys.

Some clients begin verbalizing and free associating the moment they enter the consulting room and never stop until the hour is up. They keep this up hour after therapeutic hour *ad nauseum*. Overtalking can be as much a resistance as silence and it can be as hampering to the evolution of interpersonal psychotherapy. The client saturates the field with images, icons, and symbols, repeats himself, and is finally caught in a verbal maze from which he cannot extricate himself. Obviously, most of this material does not come from the unconscious. When this happens, the therapist must correct the situation. Usually he does this naturally after first allowing the client to "talk himself out" for awhile. Then clarification and interpretation should lead him to deeper issues and a more reflective silence. If this fails, if the therapist is hampered in his own participation by overtalking, the matter should be brought up for deeper analysis. If this does not clarify it and provide the necessary security the client requires, the therapist just asks the client to stop and maintain silence for a few moments. The client and the therapist then face each other and communicate nonverbally for the period. Or the client can be asked to paint or sculpt outside of the hour to achieve fuller expression of self.

It has also happened that therapists overtalk. Clients complain that their therapists are always telling them about themselves and that they "do not get their turn." More than we know, therapists love an audience, and the client is such a captive audience. They also give us concentrated attention which others may not do. And clients are rarely in a position to interfere. Most clients don't know how to turn their therapists' verbalizations off. As a result, they fail to come back. The therapeutic task is to learn just how much to say—and when to say it. This may be the most difficult interpersonal task of all.

AMBIVALENCE AND FIXATION

Ambivalence and fixation are hallmarks of the neurotic person. Most people in the world manage in some way to come to decisions. Even if their decisions are incorrect, they live with them. The client, however, acts as though the world turns on his decision, and he gets caught up in a tremendous inner trial and error from which he cannot free himself. He wants both sides of his decision, and therefore comes to have neither. Ambivalence shows up most strongly in schizophrenic clients. In its most extreme form it is recognized as catatonia, or its equivalent.

Much has been written about fixation and its causes. The principle cause seems to be the client going back to or getting caught on the point of greatest success or comfort and not being able to move. Also, habit plays a great part in fixation. It seems most family environments help maintain fixations in order to preserve their own homeostasis. The client gets little help in moving or growing even though this is everyone's hope. When the fixation is oral, anal, or even Oedipal, considerable effort is required to alter it.

Ambivalence and fixation cannot be attacked directly and rationally. They are the products of a long history of personality failure. They can only be changed by a total process which offers new hope, a demonstration of greater effectiveness, and which shows that authenticity is a more rewarding state. The ambivalent alternatives are each analytically considered for their meaning, choices of any kind are encouraged, and the decision made by the client is fully supported and incorporated into the personality. The therapist must not be hasty and make decisions for the client. He must be able to withstand countless failures of decision. Of course, with this comes a new sense of self-responsibility. Once ambivalence is resolved, fixations change of their own accord because their principal motive force has been undercut.

LOVE OF SELF

Progress in interpersonal therapy is often held up because of the client's inordinate narcissism. This means the client's love of self cannot be transformed to love of another. Such clients are often deceptive for they pay attention and seem eager to do what has to be done in therapy. But nothing ever happens! They go on in their blithe way undoing what is done in therapy, sometimes making slight gains, but clutching desperately to their situation and to their narcissism.

Possibly clients like this are unable to detach energy from self and place it on objects outside of themselves. This may in some way be a developmental anomaly, a failure of early mastery. I find that such narcissism in the client is always the counterpart of the mother's narcissism—an identification with it as well as a supreme resistance to it. The child is, so to speak, stigmatized by his election as a special person, by his being placed in the center of things, by his value. Eventually he incorporates this into his personality. Freud himself, called "Das Goldener Zigie"—The Golden One—by his mother, was narcissistic. This accounts, to some extent, for his systematic alienation and continuous estrangement from people.

Highly narcissistic clients are exceedingly difficult in this phase of treatment. They need to have their narcissism fed, but interpersonal psychotherapy calls for a reduced schedule of feeding. When it is considerably reduced, the client balks, and he very reluctantly accepts the therapist as transferential lover. A battle or impasse is apt to occur at this point which may well determine the outcome of therapy.

Firmness, positive regard, and restatement of goals work best. The therapist must not be shaken from his stance by any crises the client may bring, and he must always be as empathic and understanding as possible. It may take months, even years, to work through this phase. If it is successful, the therapy will be fruitful. Such clients are very good at trapping the therapist in his *own* narcissism, so that both feeding and non-feeding of the client as an authentic mother is the only thing that will work. I have many times become angry at the arrogance of such clients, only to find that I had been trapped into doing precisely what they wanted me to do.

SUICIDAL IMPULSES

Interpersonal psychotherapy recognizes the importance of the Eros-Thanatos equation and the fact that therapy works within these polarities. Every client is fundamentally depressed, and every client is potentially a suicide risk. The difference between a trained and untrained therapist is precisely that he understands this statement and can use it. If the client is approached this way, the danger in clients being suicidal is somewhat reduced.

Long-term psychotherapy, if it is to be effective, must bring the client to question his life and its values. Since these are so often found wanting, suicidal impulses come as no great surprise. They have constructive as well as destructive aspects. A person who contemplates dying really wants to live —but in a different way. Most such people are sensitive, feeling, thinking persons who reflect deeply upon themselves. They are, therefore, precisely the kind of people who also find their way to a therapist. The significant factor is that the therapist must not be frightened by the possibility of the client's death, which by introjection may also be his own death.

When suicidal impulses arise in therapy, they are indications that (1) the client is being reached, and (2) he needs to be reached even more deeply. This is not the time to pull back unless a major error has been made. Many times more frequent hours, contact by telephone, and person to person rather than transferential relationship is indicated. Most important the therapist must stand for Eros rather than Thanatos, and he must make this evident in a number of ways. The client has to do what he has to do if he is not psychotic. In any event, he cannot be watched perpetually. The goal is to give the client sufficient protection, support, and motive to continue living. Most often, situations like this are handled nominally. Sometimes the intervention of the family or a residential psychiatric setting is necessary. But it is a mistake frequently made to call for hospitalization too quickly.

DELUSIONS

Some non-psychotic clients develop delusions during therapy. These may involve the body, as in the case of the lady who said her head was filled with dry ice, or misinterpretations of a paranoid kind, or a mild hallucinatory-type phenomenon. This is not surprising since therapy is itself lusional. Perception and thought are in constant challenge and turmoil within this process.

When reality is distorted to this degree, the therapist must ask himself why it has now become evident. He should not be concerned with whether or not his diagnosis was correct but rather with the dynamic events which make the delusion necessary. Often these are the last major defenses to change, or necessary preludes to change, or an attempt to ameliorate the life or therapeutic circumstances which have become too hard. Delusions require the sympathetic understanding of the therapist. He should not attack them directly or take part in them. Instead, their substrate, and the general state of the therapy, should be reviewed by the "third ear" and increased effort given in the deficiency direction indicated. Such delusions are mostly transitory and even self-limiting. If, however, they indicate a coming psychotic episode, the procedure for working with the client must be changed.

If the client becomes overtly psychotic, a determination is required as to whether or not treatment can continue. This may require the use of a consultant experienced with psychoses. Medication may also be indicated as well as brief residential sheltering. At any rate, therapeutic procedures have to be altered. Clarification and interpretation have to stop. The intensity of transference must be reduced, and the client must be given more obvious security. Covering rather than uncovering is required for a time. But even psychosis is no counterindication to interpersonal therapy as psychotherapy with schizophrenics proves. It simply makes therapy more difficult and requires more skill on the part of the therapist.

ACTING-OUT

Acting-out is considered deleterious to therapy because the client does what he should merely symbolize. That is, he takes ill-advised action impulsively before proper insight and judgment are available as controls. Not only that, the client's outward behavior directly challenges his character history, as well as his experiences in therapy. The timing and quantity of these actions are out of phase. For these reasons, every therapist attempts to reduce the amount of acting-out which arises in interpersonal psychotherapy.

I have contended that acting-out isn't the bugbear earlier textbooks had described. Some amount of living-out is necessary. The client after all needs to attempt things in his world during therapy, and who is to say when is the best time to do so? The therapist works with what the client brings to the session instead of trying to shape what might be brought there. But acting-out can also be a defense against the therapy itself and can place serious complications in its way. The acting-out client may make new contracts of a more or less permanent sort—such as a new marriage, or a business venture, from which he can extricate himself only with difficulty. To protect him, Freud asked the client to agree to take no new major step in his life without joint concurrence. Acting-out usually brings the community into the therapy, and often it impairs the transferential relationship.

As a practical thing, it is impossible to regulate the life of the client outside of the hour, even if this were desirable. The therapeutic situation cannot be kept this pure and, at any rate, the client needs material to feed the therapeutic session. When the primary focus was on the history of the client, contemporaneous events were considered interferences of a sort. But today, when the here and now takes equal place with influences of the past, acting-out behavior is not so much an inhibition as a source of analytic material. It must be dynamically interpreted rather than severely proscribed.

However, too much acting-out or too much ill-advised acting-out can destroy the therapy. The best corrective is prevention. The proper prosecution of the treatment precludes most acting-out. At any rate, the acting-out can be anticipated when it does come, and abridged or ameliorated. For example, some acting-out takes place as a displacement from therapy. If the client is given an opportunity to be hostile, impulsive, and molar in the hour, he may not have to do it outside. Often it can be symbolized if expression of the impulse is not tabooed by the therapist. At least its implications and meaning can be discussed. The client can then do what he has to do.

It remains only to go on after the acting-out has occurred. No special issue is made of it and the client will himself incorporate it into the body of his therapeutic work. Eventually, he comes to see the meaning and purpose of his acting-out and has a better basis for reflection if and when it occurs again.

THE BODY

As therapy progresses, the body resists treatment as does the psyche. Whatever somatizing or physical impairment the client originally brings can be expected to get worse before it gets better. Not only that, clients make poor use and poor social presentations of their bodies. Their bodies are certainly out of phase with their intellects. Many of them still have polymorphous perverse needs and reify or become phobic about one or another erogenous zone. The body image of our clients reveals not only poor differentiation but inchoate organization, ranging from mild disturbance in the neurotic to total disorganization of the schizophrenic. Therapy must help change the body image. The Draw-a-Person test, given before and after therapy, does show this happens.

Most therapists ignore the body in treatment and consider it a passive encumbrance. They prefer to deal directly with the psyche. This becomes even more paradoxical if the therapist is a doctor of medicine and has a social mandate to "touch" the body. Interpersonal psychotherapy gives equal weight to body and mind, observing and participating in body communications, and giving full status to bodily fulfillment. I clarify and interpret the client's face, body tonus, appendages, and adornment, in the same way I do his verbal associations. They are all of a piece, and sometimes even more revealing.

Body resistance manifests itself in overfunction or underfunction as, for example, in suddenly becoming highly active sexually or becoming temporarily impotent instead. The body may develop sensory deficiencies or become remarkably acute. It may shrink-up or dilate, and endocrine, metabolic, and neural processes either pace or follow the change as the alarm or ecstasy reaction prevails. The body becomes depressed as well.

Clients carefully observe the body of the therapist. If it is vital, physical, sensual, and purposive, they incorporate it. (It has always seemed to me in this regard that a therapist I know who was enduringly confined to a mobile bed and could only move his head and speech organs suffered in his therapeutic work because of this body deficiency.) Clients comment on the therapist's person and it is not so much the clothes they perceive as the body beneath. The fantasies of the client are always more bodily than he tells us. It is, therefore, very important that the therapist know his body, love it, and be able to use it for therapeutic purposes.

THE PLATEAU

If a stalemate occurs in interpersonal therapy it will come in the middle of therapy. I call this a plateau since the client rests on a part of the learning curve and cannot proceed further. He cannot actualize the potentialities of his helix. The next question is whether this is the maximum possible attainment for him, and whether or not he can be aided to go on. These clients do not drop out of therapy, but neither does their growing edge go forward. They just keep coming and nothing much happens after the plateau is reached. It also becomes the most problematic situation of all for the therapist who cannot long tolerate such emptiness. Often the client preserves the appearance of movement but not the actuality.

There is not too much the therapist can do about the plateau. In the first place they have to be waited out for they require time to mature. Perhaps the client himself must recognize it for what it is and become bored with it. During this period the therapist regularly affirms the goals of treatment, the beauty of life, and the possibilities of finding fulfillment. He does not participate in the plateau negation, and he does not assume responsibility for it.

At this point the adjunctive techniques described in Chapter IX come into play. The client may not be able to move from the plateau as therapy is presently experienced, but he may be able to do so if he can do it outside the therapeutic situation. I therefore ask him to paint, sculpt, write poetry, or whatever seems indicated. I offer this in the concentration needed and I suggest more frequent interviews. I also depart somewhat from my conventional passive stance and become more active and perhaps personally intervening.

It sometimes becomes necessary to force the situation by facing up with the client to the plateau's desperate qualities. I tell the client of my pessimism about his therapy, that it has occurred to me that termination may be necessary, and how unhappy I am with it all. Also, that I feel helpless and useless. But I do not role play. This is genuinely frightening to the client because he knows the therapist cares for him and now he too is on a plateau. This mobilizes the client to use his greatest potentialities to get off the plateau. If he has within him the motivation and strength to reach for higher authentication levels, a break-through will occur and therapeutic movement will come to the fore in the following hours. This is always accompanied by outbursts of energy, impulsivity, affect, tears, and anger, and it requires the utmost in support, tolerance, and understanding of the therapist. Sometimes, it should be noted, nothing works!

DREAMS

A dream may sometimes point the way out of the impasse and interpersonal psychotherapy makes use of dream analysis where indicated. Dreams are mental activity which take place when the client and his defenses are in a greater state of participation. They signify the deeper repressed wishes of the person as well as his intercurrent conflicts. Dreams are part of the client which let him soar above his mundane life, and be himself, but the soaring is of a metaphoric kind. Dreams can be helpful even if they are not interpreted, for the client knows that they are his and that they represent in some way his fulfilled life. He feels pursued by his dreams but also actualized by them.

Interpersonal psychotherapy does not follow any single system of dream interpretation but draws eclectically on all of them. It sees the dream as a coded wish of the client, with a symbolism peculiar to the individual himself while having archetypal significance. Dreams occur and are recalled most often when there is an immediate problem to solve in the life of the client. The dream points the way to a solution. But clients resist dreams in the same way they resist therapy. They bring only those dreams they feel safe in bringing. Of course, they are unaware of the dream currency, and the dreams which are brought are precisely those needed to get on with the business of therapy. But the overdreaming client may be destroying his therapy.

The following two dreams are not intended to be definitive. They merely illustrate certain procedures for the use of dreams in interpersonal psychotherapy.

DREAM I
Sara and Franklyn were just leaving for somewhere. Frank asked to borrow my sweater. He put his hand in the pocket and pulled out a dead and withered insect. I took it back and it withered a little more. I put it on a piece of green canvas, sprinkled with water on it, and it turned into a flower —a red flower, with a chalice, and tinted with yellow. I couldn't get it to stand up. It all happened on the second story of the building, facing south towards the garden, and with lots of glass around.

Associations to the dream were:

Franklyn—Dark; Jewish; speed-freak; stutters; really like him a lot; likes Sara, my girl friend. Both making a pass at each other. Disciplined; highly moral; good artist. They go well together.
Bug—Smoothest I ever saw; incredibly beautiful; big wings; could glide or soar; about size of small plate (could fit in pocket of your sport coat). Found it dead and put it in my pocket.
Green—Trees; flowers; soft green; most of the world this beautiful.
General Comments—Dreamer (Darian) revitalized the bug he had found dead and which he put in his pocket. Wings withered like on a peach. Became a spring flower, with a cup, red and yellow, cut off. Beautiful, lying there.

Darian, the dreamer, is 23 years of age, a university student, majoring in psychology, and hoping someday to be a therapist himself. He had been in therapy with me for 125 hours and never before brought a complete dream for analysis, or even one so vivid. This one was so manifestly numinous that he pressed for an interpretation even though he had resisted others in the past.

After a borderline psychotic episode and hospitalization induced by marijuana and methadrine, he had come to therapy. He was severely coarcted, with highly repressed hositilities bordering on paranoia; violently loved and hated women (but he could not do without them); was somewhat dilapidated in his emotions; had a lively intelligence; showed schizophrenic ambivalence and similar schizophrenic manifestations; had tremendous sexual confusion; and reacted with panic when he had to confront authority figures. Darian was a rich and complicated boy with an involved family history.

Each dream has its own inherent fantasy and reality properties. The question was why this particular dream had appeared at this time? It presaged something to come, some thought or action, incubated but not yet conscious. It was a testing of a wish, a fitting of reality to a fantasy, and tremendously important as an indicator. Despite Darian's knowledge of psychology, and deep intuition, he had no insight into the meaning of this dream. He also missed the next session after reporting the dream. Then he came and said he was going to marry Sara, which he subsequently did, when the therapist was out of the country. She was the feminine principle he had long struggled with, as the Laocoon struggled with his self-evolution.

The interpretation of a dream can be elemental or sophisticated depending on the style of the therapist and the needs of the client. Every therapeutic hour can be given over to dream analysis in the middle of therapy, if one wants to, but little else would be accomplished. I use dream interpretation selectively when the client feels this is his way of bringing his unconscious to therapy, when he cannot voluntarily produce associations in the hour, at crucial periods of working-through resistances, and when breakthroughs in therapy are imminent. The dream is the property of the client, and after introducing dream analysis as a technique, I let him bring them as he is impelled to.

The client should be allowed to tell the dream as he recalls it (or has written it) without interference, give his own interpretation of it, and then free associate to each concept and item of it. The way he goes about doing this, the affect connected with it, and the acceptance or rejection of its meanings are carefully noted. The therapist does not interpret the dream as such. He helps the client find its meaning, that is, he brings the client to it. The therapist must never fully reveal the total meaning of a dream, for it can damage the client, unless sufficient preparation has been made for it. Certain constructions of the dream are used for analyzing the client's thematic personality structure which is in turn to be used later as the basis for interpretations.

Each symbol, image, metaphor, icon, and action in the dream must be studied for its denotation, but the sum of this dream analysis is not necessarily the meaning of the dream. The therapist develops propositions by this procedure, and these tie in with data gathered during the sessions. He puts these propositions to the internal test of existential "fit" and then offers them tentatively to the dreamer for his reaction. Obviously, Darian's statement of "incredibly beautiful" for a bug which is usually the obverse of beauty, and in a therapeutic history in which beauty never came up and was not lived as well, indicates a new vision and transformation to come. The colors in the dream—green, yellow, red—are the growing affect in a surprisingly affectless person and, manifestly, the conversion of bug to flower, the chalice cup indicate sexual definition, certainty of potency, desirability of femininity, and its equation with beauty in life. He commented at the time, "The bug adds sensuality to the house"; and "I didn't believe I could ever be a beautiful person"; and "I have 'revitalized' the bug."

In hours following the dream, Darian felt he could now compete with Franklyn, could be a man, could marry Sara, could declare on the side of life, give up his ambivalence, and go on to become a therapist. These goals were his never really acknowledged wishes, which he has implemented.

DREAM II

I am asleep but my boyfriend awakens me and says that he must tell me a big secret. For some reason I have a child in the dream, and I begin to feel afraid. He tells me that he knows who the Zodiac Killer[1] is. The latter showed him five telegrams he was getting ready to send to his next victims. "My boyfriend said that if I revealed the secret to anyone, even my child, the Zodiac Killer would kill me, too." I know I have to eventually tell my child the secret and he therefore will kill her.

This 27-year-old divorced woman of exceptional musical talent has neither found a place for herself nor for her person. She has wandered from high-level job to high-level job, and from man to man, seeking only not to be rejected, and she has revealed some lesbian latencies as well. But she has never been able to act consistently and find peace and authenticity. Her narcissism is tremendous but is coupled with an extraordinary will to live and to be authenticated. She is both attracted to and repelled by her family, who are at once her greatest enemy and her greatest source of affection. She seeks a form of nirvana given perhaps only to gods, deems it her right, and is oblivious to her privileged status consisting of youth, health, talent, intelligence, and money. She wants primarily to "care" for people; and to have a child would be an act of caring.

Her therapy cannot yet be called brilliantly successful. She has made considerable gains in insight, in elevated affect, and in family relationships, but has not been able to give up much of her infantile narcissism. She has unconsciously played the divorced man she is living with against her father—she recently moved only five miles from the family home with her boyfriend—and her father spent a few days in the hospital for a heart attack which turned out to be an incident of hyperventilation after the boyfriend said certain things to him at a family party. She has not yet made systematic gains socially, occupationally, or artistically, as befits her abilities. Also, she has not convinced the man she has been living with that marriage would be a desirable state, even though it frequently comes up in therapy. She is obviously holding back. Before the dream I discussed possible future termination with her on a failure of therapy basis, and she violently resisted the idea. I have had the impression that perhaps her boyfriend wants out of the relationship as well.

Her free associations to the dream were:

Kill—Frightening; obscene; unhappy.
Child—Mother; nursery; babies; motherhood.
Secret—Not telling; hidden; private; dishonest.
Boyfriend—Lover; sweetheart; partner; father.
Zodiac Killer—Mentally ill; terrible; frightening.
Five—Five men I have been deeply involved with.

There are four figures in the dream: the Zodiac Killer, the boyfriend, the child, and the dreamer. All seem passively related to the dreamer except

---

[1]The Zodiac Killer is a notorious murderer in the San Francisco area who as of January 1, 1971, was as yet uncaught. His crimes were notable for the warning he sent his victims, for the publicity about his crimes he sent to the press at the same time, and for the seeming indifference with which he selected his victims.

the Zodiac Killer. She in fact has no child, so that the child represents her key wish for the future. The fact that the child seems doomed to be killed reflects the possibility that she may never find fulfillment, that she will kill her own unborn child, destroy her hope for the future. And she herself must be the Zodiac Killer. His irrational vagaries and murderous interests are indeed similar to her own.

She is obviously reacting catastrophically to my suggestion of termination, as well as to her boyfriend's current, conflict-ridden involvement with her. In her own narcissistic way she feels she has been a Zodiac Killer. She has idiosyncratically destroyed everyone of greatest importance to her, and particularly those she has loved most. She is a Medusa in San Francisco form.

In interpersonal psychotherapy dreams are not, as they are in psychoanalysis, the high road to treatment. They are only one of several ways of tapping the unconscious. There are clients who cannot, or will not, ever bring a dream to therapy, and some of the newer evidence on sleep and dreams[2] works against rigid dream analysis as Freud propounded it. In interpersonal psychotherapy, dreams have the following functions:

1. The dream actualizes the material of the therapeutic hour.
2. It brings the client's major symbols and archetypes to therapy.
3. It gives the client a feeling of being deeply involved in his problem and in his therapy.
4. It reveals the basic life wish, the various sub-wishes, in the client's personality.
5. It provides a fantasy release for something which cannot yet be released because of repression.
6. It quiets moods and anxiety by draining off the horrific and devilish.
7. It copes, at the moment, with life and death wishes in a way superior to waking life.
8. It reveals how the therapy is going.

PARAPRAXES

The interpersonal psychotherapist listens carefully for the expression of conflict as it is revealed in language. A study should some day be made in depth of the linguistics of therapy, but at any rate slips of the tongue reveal the unconscious at work. Such slips of the tongue are passed over by the client as nonsense, but the logic and sense in them has to be revealed to him. I analyze any and all parapraxes by asking the client to give associations to them, by comparing them in their context to correct mental formulations, and by attempting to determine the wishes behind the slips. The problem most often involves the transformation of persons, places, or actions which have to be reinterpreted.

---

[2]W. C. Dement, "An Essay on Dreams: The Role of Physiology in Understanding Their Nature," *New Directions in Psychology II* (New York: Holt, Rinehart, Winston, 1965).

The analysis of parapraxes is valuable. The sequence and way ideas appear may be as important as the ideas themselves. The way a concept is delivered, when and where it is delivered, its linguistic structure, are significant for the study of personality. Slips of the tongue, language fixations, perseverations, redundancies, bizarrities, subject-predicate distortions, are all grist for the analytic mill. Linguistic structure which is the vehicle of the neurosis becomes a part of the treatment of that neurosis.

CATHARSIS

The basic therapeutic principle which backs up all the others operating in the main part of therapy is catharsis. Catharsis became the therapeutic keystone of Freud's system. Having placed repression squarely at its center, he had to find a way to reduce repressions. Cathartics have been known for a long time and the fact that they relieve is elemental.

It is well known that the memory of the client is cluttered with useless impulses, images, signs, symbols, icons, and metaphors. All of these require energy to be kept stored. When they return to the system, they produce distortions in it. In industry, clearing out old files and useless information is one of management's most important and expensive problems. People have similar problems keeping data and information currently relevant. The client's data is what we call emotional. It appears to have no survival value, and yet the client clings to it at all costs. And no human system can function with such an overload!

In therapy the client must come to abreact, to give forth most of this data. But it can be dangerous to have it disgorged violently and all of a piece. Most people cannot confront the hidden realities of life head on. Encounter groups have exaggerated the remedial value of their spontaneously-induced confrontations. It works, after all, not like Pandora's Box, but rather through slow and certain materialization of the shadow part of the person. The guilt and anxiety which accompany such "secrets" have to have their own indigenous devestment procedures. Otherwise the pathology remains even though the content is divulged. The client's need to retain illusion, myth, and metaconstruct must be understood and a more realistic substitute offered. Freud over and over again stressed the point that psychoanalysis had to give something in return for what it took away. Interpersonal psychotherapy understands that often therapy may be nothing more than a better set of illusions, problems, or sublimations than the client had originally.

Each cathartic monad is matched by a structural equivalent which arises from the phoenix of the therapeutic encounter. The client, so to speak, gives up a "secret" in return for an insight. Often therapy seems to amount to nothing more than the exchange of such currency. Whether or not the client will therapeutically cathart, depends not only on his opportunity to do so but on the rewards involved. I have over the years participated in the revelation of countless such secrets, most of them of an asocial or antisocial nature. What the client was usually guarding was not homosexual, incestuous, or murderous items, but the fact that he was a special person of a kind he could not reveal to anyone. The person who represses, who has such secrets, is a distinctive person because he represses, and not because of what he has repressed. Catharsis is always a matter of awe, a mysterium, a special state of being, and we must never forget that Martin Luther fought the demons of Catholicism best while sitting on the toilet, while catharting.

Does the client have one trauma, one secret, or a series of small ones in his psyche? Are they real or fantastic? Do all of them have to be catharted before the client can be authenticated? The answer, from the point of view of interpersonal psychotherapy, seems to be that there is no single central trauma. Furthermore some traumas are fabrications built upon facts of some sort. Therapists start their work in the quest of truth; later it appears to them that not the trauma but the revelation or telling of a trauma is what counts. This is not to mean that clients do not have traumatic experiences, but only that they assign different meanings to them and, more important, their traumas serve as vehicles.

The therapeutic hours justify themselves on the basis of catharsis. The client unloads something, feels better, and replaces it with something else. But the process is basically an energetic one. The important thing is that there is now communication between the various parts of the personality. The taking-in is as important as the giving-out.

INSIGHT

During the middle course of therapy the materials necessary for insight-formation are developed. Through catharsis, and through the clarifications and interpretations of the therapist, the conditions are laid for new emotional and cognitive organizations. Clients are generally puzzled by their new insights, or by their previous inability to perceive these insights. At first glance, these insights do not seem earth-shaking. Sophocles has Oedipus blinding himself and wandering forever on the face of the earth for unknowingly marrying Jacosta, his mother. This is his penalty for having opened his eyes to the truth—for having discovered his true identity. Insight can be blinding but it is rarely as dramatic as Sophocles presents it. Therapeutic insight consists mostly of small insights, viable insights, credible insights, and humanistic insights. These insights, all coming together, produce the sudden flash of cognition. From this flash the motivation to change something basic in one's life can develop. But insight as therapy is not enough. There is the danger that the client will feel satisfied with just insight into his life. Freud was wrong in believing that knowing about something inevitably leads to a change in behavior. Knowledge does not necessarily set one free.

The step correlated with insight, but going beyond it, I call post-insight. Not only does the therapist help facilitate the cognitive and emotive parts of the motivation to form a gestalt, but he sees the process through to some kind of resolution in action. He presses for use of the insight in some areas of the client's life. Insights of this level and quality pervade the warp and woof of existence and affect the entire personality. The therapeutic task is to help the client understand this. How is this done? By not letting the insight drop from sight, become inactivated or re-repressed. By constantly confronting the client with it and silently expecting or having faith in results. Infrequently the therapist may even come right out and ask the client to review what has happened with the insight.

Clients do not take kindly to this persistence, but the possibility of insight stopping at that point is a greater danger than the client's momentary displeasure. Sometimes the insight is "unfortunately" acted upon, but its application is a learning process. Trial and error techniques are appropriate. Of course, both the derivation of the insight and its application must have a certain timeliness. They cannot be rushed. An insight may not come to full fruition until very much later, but allowing it to develop is certainly different from permanently shelving it.

Here are some insights that have come out of interpersonal therapy:

1. I am unable to love.
2. I am a latent homosexual.
3. I wanted to kill my mother.
4. The best pleasure comes from the anus.
5. The best pleasure comes from the mouth.
6. I loved my father (mother).
7. I am impotent (frigid).
8. People are really kind.
9. My fantasies are truly self-defeating.
10. I hate all men (women).
11. I want a penis (vagina).
12. The world is green.
13. Life is fun.
14. My boss is really my father.
15. I don't need to play games anymore.
16. That turns my migraine on.
17. I've been beating myself over the head.
18. I guess money has been the wrong goal.
19. There is power in powerlessness.
20. I'm getting back at him by being fat.

The number of insights is not a measure of recovery, but no interpersonal psychotherapy can be considered successful without at least one. Some clients, unfortunately, have too many insights. They turn therapy into a game of insight-discovery. If this does happen, the therapy has become intellectualized and one must look to the transference which may be defective.

INTERPRETATION

The real vehicle of therapeutic growth is the interpretation. An interpretation is a peak moment which encapsulates past, present, and future events into a single concept—and its possibilities. Interpretations are preceded by preparation, incubation, formulation, announcement, and incorporation. They are the revealed truths of psychotherapy. The experience of interpretation is always euphoric or depressing. At any rate it releases repressed energy. Interpretations also have great intellectual beauty analogous to a mathematical equation. To be authentic, a therapist must be able to make proper interpretations. The over-interpretive or under-interpretive therapist is handicapped. He always just misses the boat. Knowledge of how to make interpretations grows with experience but it also requires a great deal of intuitive and introjective capacity.

An interpretation is not an explanation, a new fact, or even a rearrangement of existing facts. It is a way by which the deepest truths about human beings are communicated from one person to another. Therapists are coders and decoders of sorts. Their messages involve the highest metapsychology of experience and existence. An interpretation is an existential truth, hidden from the client, which he needs to know to get on with solving his problem with life. This truth springs from the central creativity of the therapist and it must be backed by relevant intellectual constructs. Schizophrenics interpret a great deal, but they make poor therapists because their senses of timing and relatedness are poor. The statement, "My mother is holding my emotions in trust for me" is both an interpretation and a statement requiring interpretation. On one level it says, "I am not allowed to have any emotions because my mother is the Great Mother," and on another, "My mother has left me an underprivileged person." One doesn't interpret a great deal with schizophrenic clients because they know their unconscious pretty well. With a neurotic, the statement, "My mother was a perfect woman" can be interpreted as (1) she was a perfect woman; (2) she was an imperfect woman; or (3) she wasn't a woman at all. Each of these interpretations opens the door to further development of a historical and contemporary process aimed at a certain life validation. By making the interpretation, we accept a line of development and urge it forward, submitting it to the client to have him see if it "fits." It is comparable to the field forces in which a percept operates. The perception becomes whole, unified, and meaningful when it completes an historical process and neutralizes a field charge. The historical and personal growth process produces a psychic field with a certain readiness for a metaphoric or symbolic key, which is the interpretation. Interpretations in general are neither ultra-sagacious, ultra-sophisticated, or ultra-complex. They are simple formula keys to locked doors. All passwords are elemental, but they are not to be cheaply bought. They grow out of the special experiences of mankind such as suffering, joy, care and disease. A technical process sets the stage for the interpretation, but whether it is realized or not depends on the creative formative structure of the therapist's own personality being in tune with the client's.His interpretations reveal the depth and breadth of his own being.

WORKING THROUGH

The process by which repressions are released and reintegrated into the personality is called working-through. Working-through means seeing a symptom through its final meaning and worth, as well as the solution of the client's neurotic state of being itself. The term implies effort applied systematically to a barrier—the client himself. The force of therapy, its logic, has to be so persuasive that the client cannot avoid change. To continue to cling to his neuroses would embarrass him. Working-through, in a sense, presents the client with the ultimate dilemma: "accept yourself as an ill person and give up your hunger for more in life, or take the possibilities therapy affords."

The therapist offers this dilemma again and again in manifold ways to the client insisting on its reality and possibility. But nothing can be forced on the client except an opportunity to choose. But the neurotic does not have such choices when he comes to therapy. The fact that they are available comes as something akin to shock. The world has been closed for so long that to find it open gives rise to incredulity, disbelief, and downright denial.

What counts most in the choices the client makes is the dignity, sincerity, and integrity of the therapist. The client is aware that the therapist has, so to speak, placed his own existence on the line to help him, and that this is an extremely rare thing in our society. His life counts for something, when all of his life he has believed and had proof it did not count. Faith is very much a part of the helping process and therapy works best with those who have faith in it. Hope, a special kind of faith, which offers the promise of a changed future, is also necessary.

Working-through involves tracking down every significant image, icon, metaphor, and symbol relating to the core existence and core conflict. This process has to continue until the client has sufficient energy for change, makes a choice to do so, and follows through. The amount of tracking down required differs with each client. Only enough of the unconscious needs integration to accomplish the client's ends. Otherwise, therapy may become an intellectual exercise or a detective story. And the analytic process has coterminous with it synthesizing properties as well as encountering ones. The meeting of the therapist and the client in the middle course of therapy is one of those significant encounters which occur rarely in each lifetime. It ranks equally with any encounter which alters the stream of life. How could it not have growth effects?

As the main part of therapy proceeds, the client takes more and more responsibility for the hours. He structures them and relates them to what has already taken place. He begins to see the end of therapy and he drives toward that kind of closure. He also begins to tackle more and more things in his world. This, of course, is accompanied by its own special form of anxiety. When termination begins to appear possible, the final phase of treatment is attained.

RELATIONAL DYNAMICS

VII

This chapter deals with the intradynamics of the single interview rather than with therapy as a total process. What takes place in any therapeutic interview? What is the structure of that interview? How is any single interview integrated into the total therapy as a whole?

I have elaborated Benjamin's[1] suggestion as to the structure of the therapeutic interview in the following way:

OPENING OR PLATFORM STATEMENT

Every therapeutic interview has an opening statement or platform. This is the jumping-off place for the rest of the hour. It can contain either progress or regress. I listen carefully to what the client says or does not say with his opening words. I look at body posture and the other nonverbal cues he is offering, as well as the prevailing mood of the platform statement. The previous hour has left him uncompleted. He needs to maintain continuity of purpose and identity from hour to hour. Not only that, the stream of thought makes the flow and resolution of unsolved ideas mandatory. Therapy goes on between therapeutic hours as well as during them. The platform reveals to the therapist what has happened in this intervening period. The "third-ear" assessment of the client's growth or regression, hour by hour, is most often based on the way the client begins and carries the hour forward. This is particularly true if an intervening crisis or success has occurred since his last session.

The following are examples of platform statements:

1. I didn't feel like coming today.
2. My mother and I had a big fight yesterday.
3. I had a date this week.
4. I couldn't go to work Tuesday because my migraine bothered me so.
5. I got a good erection Wednesday.
6. I've decided that you were wrong in what you said in our hour on Monday.
7. This was a good week.
8. My boss is absolutely impossible. I hate him.
9. I don't know whether or not I should accept that promotion.
10. I had a dream last night.

[1] A. Benjamin, The Helping Interview (Boston: Houghton Mifflin Co., 1969).

Platforms invariably involve broad themes of life such as love, hate, money, sex, relatives, or children. They usually focus, however, on specific persons or events as jumping-off points. No platform statement is irrelevant and every one must be analyzed in its own right. Sometimes clients "prepare" the platform statement before they come, but what counts is whether the therapist is prepared to hear it. Many clients carefully appraise the therapist first to see that the climate is right for their opening. One client, a remarkably perceptive one, knows my moods almost as well as I do. She will often refuse a specific platform when she feels I am not ready to receive it. Clients feel they need to give us what we want, but that may not be what is actually most important to their personality growth.

INCUBATION

After the platform there follows an incubation period which can be as short as one second or as long as the hour, or even several hours. Nothing in therapy is ever lost or misplaced. Feelings and concepts require creative sharpening and delivery. Depending on the barriers involved, they find the proper time to come forth. A client should seldom be urged to complete his conceptual idea for there may have been insufficient incubation time for him to do so. Clarification, reflection, and restatement are fine interviewing devices, but they must not force the idea or concept. This plays into resistance. These techniques should only be used to show that the therapist is in rapport and prepared to wait. One must develop sufficient intuition to know when incubation is incomplete, or when blocking is taking place. Even ideas and concepts need to mature. There are a number of ways of breaking the block but nothing compensates for incomplete incubation. Insight is the product of incubation. Perhaps the longer the incubation, the greater the insight. While the client drops his platform and moves on to a new idea, he may be incubating the platform. Clients sometimes start the hour with a statement such as, "I feel I may be a homosexual," and then say no more about it for some time. Another opens with, "You were wrong in the idea that I really hated my brother whom I loved dearly," and then goes on to another topic or falls into a lengthy silence. But these are statements which, after incubation, will be placed on the agenda once more for development. Incubation is the preconscious and unconscious at work at the creative reorganization of unstructured and unaffiliated data necessary to the production of a mental form or ideation. It is the shaping and forming part of every creative act.

An example of *incubation* might be a dialogue like this:

Client	Sometimes I feel like murdering him.
Therapist	You felt like killing him.
Client	I saw a fine motion picture this week. Do you like the cinema?
Therapist	You want to know whether I appreciate Bunuel and Bergman.
Client	Yes. They portray life in its most dramatic form and in visual symbols.
Therapist	Hmm.

Client	I get all wrapped up with the lead or hero. I don't care for Antonioni. He seems contrived.
Therapist	Yes.
Client	I know now why I felt so murderous. He missed my signals last night that I wanted to make love.
Therapist	A man in love ought to be attuned to signals.

DEVELOPMENT

Development carries the idea and concept to verbal maturity. It is cognitive organization based on a new or reorganized feeling. It carries the concept to a more rational or logical conclusion. As part of this process, the primitiveness of the emotion connected with the regressive aspect of the concept reaches higher level response in the sense of orderliness and humaneness, which makes something new of it. The cognitive and the affective become more appropriately joined, so that behavior is more unified and the feelings of distress less raw. This is the stage where trial and error, gestalt learning, symbolic realization, and higher order conditioning, as well as other processes come into play. A product of some kind results at this point of development in the form of a new insight, attitude, feeling, or bit of behavior. The client has a coordinated positive feeling about himself.

Development is difficult to illustrate. It takes place over longer periods of time. The following may, however, give an idea of the concept as I am using it:

Client	I had one of those raw feelings of panic yesterday. I really thought I was going to flip. Almost called you from a pay booth.
Therapist	You had that feeling of blowing up again.
Client	Yes, they frighten me and I can't tell why they come and when they are likely to come.
Therapist	Could there be some constant related to their appearance?
Client	I don't know what it could be. We've discussed this before many times. They seem to be getting worse.
Therapist	(Silence)
Client	You're not saying anything?
Therapist	I'm hoping you can find the key.
Client	The key!
Therapist	(Silence)
Client	You know, every time it happens Jack sort of seems to be in the background. Could he be related to the extreme anxiety I feel?
Therapist	You like him a lot.

Client	I love Janice but Jack is a good friend. He makes me comfortable. I don't have to be on guard with him.
Therapist	He's different from Janice but you need them both.
Client	Janice says I should drop him, but I can't do that. She thinks we're too close. She feels competitive.
Therapist	Janice resents him.
Client	No, not resents him. Doesn't want me spending so much time with him.
Therapist	What could be wrong with that?
Client	(Silence—three minutes)
Therapist	(Silence)
Client	Could I be in love with Jack too? . . . What a horrible thought. Ugh. But I did have a dream about him. It made me uncomfortable.
Therapist	You felt uneasy.
Client	Yes, as though it were wrong.
Therapist	(Silence)
Client	He has a nice body and is an athlete. I envy him.
Therapist	You admire him.
Client	He has asked me to share an apartment. I wonder if I should?
Therapist	You would be together more.
Client	(Thoughtfully) Do you suppose he and I have something going? That I panic because underneath I might have some latent homosexual tendencies?

CLOSING

Closing is that part of the therapeutic interview in which the idea or concept stated and developed is substantively adopted and the energy it contains reduced to a basal point. Often, each interview, or segment of interview, closes appropriately when the time period allotted for it has run out. But this is not always so. With skilled therapists this happens routinely, but learners never seem to have enough time to close. Closing completes the dynamic interview unit and supplies the building block which is the particular unit of therapeutic growth. There may be one or fifty closings in any single hour. Each closing adds its part to the matrix of closing which, hopefully, is the total fulfillment or growth of the client, the total therapy.

The following is an example of closing:

Client	I fall deeply in love with a man and marry him but the day after the wedding he becomes repugnant to me.
Therapist	You say this has happened four times.
Client	Yes. I know there's a reason, and we have discussed this.

Therapist There is something about the man the morning after which changes him?

Client It must have something to do with sex. With his penis.

Therapist It's a possibility. Want to develop it?

Client It's ugly. Men become Christ, Father, and lover for me. I can't handle that trinity. And yet, I want a man with a penis. I'll work at it but for now I'll just go on living. It doesn't bother me in the old way. Maybe I'll try a man with a small penis for a change!

Therapist (Laughter)

ACTING-UPON

The culmination of the platform, incubation, development, and closing is the acting-upon stage. This is the natural outcome of a change in mental status. Without this final step, therapy often becomes a mere intellectual exercise with the client going on and on in his confirmed pathways. Acting-upon can be as simple as an elemental reorganization of thoughts or feelings, an internal event, or it can be a visible change in behavior. In either case something changes. Neither form of growth is unimportant. Therapy is, in a sense, a series of acting-upons, leading to behavior which the client believes offers the fulfillment he seeks, or at least release from his demons. He becomes content.

The acting-upon phase may take place within the therapeutic situation or outside of it. It is psychologically compelling because new understanding demands appropriate action. A client in therapy who found his life restricted by chiefly passive pursuits took up skindiving as the outcome of an interview. A highly schizoid woman began organizing—successfully I might say —weekly bicycle expeditions for the people in her office. But acting-upon need not be as blatant as this. It can consist of saying "no" or "yes" to something one could not take a stand on previously. Evaluation of the effectiveness of therapy is limited by the impossibility of seeing the client in this phase of the interview or of total therapy, but I suspect we do better than we know. Acting-upon is a part of every interview.

INTERVIEW DYNAMICS

The following processes occur during every therapeutic interview. Some are more apparent than others during any single interview. The interview structure is constant. If any of the stages fail to appear, it may be that no therapy is taking place at that particular interview. It is a wise idea to occasionally break an interview down into parts to see whether or not the interview develops in this way. The therapist has a large repertory of responses available to him in therapeutic interviews. These responses serve as the vehicles for the client's movement. They usually pass unnoticed or are eclipsed in the professional's work because they become ingrained in the woof and warp of his technical experience. The learner has not yet come to be able to document them and it is helpful to understand them. They are the means by which all schools of therapy do their healing through interview.

AFFIRMATION

The entire therapy represents an affirmation of the client. But affirmation can also be used within any single interview for dynamic effect. Clients have varying needs for affirmation and varying needs for it from moment to moment. The schizophrenic needs affirmation constantly. The neurotic is suspicious of it. The psychopath denies it to begin with. Clients, by definition, lack confirmation. They must have affirmation on the way towards finding a new identity. Clients want more than recognition. Any hint that they are being rewarded for reward's sake is considered patronizing. Affirmation is instead a deep inner feeling of the therapist that the client has attained mastery. It has nothing to do with whether or not the therapist is pleased. A schizophrenic client slapped me once. While I brooded over it, it was the greatest act of affirmation possible for her. I could not prevent it, and I would have if I could, but I affirmed her need to touch me, and it opened a whole new area of investigation in our work.

An example of fairly blatant affirmation is the following:

Client   I thought I did real well on my GRE exam. I'm really not that bright.

Therapist You feared that scholastic aptitude test.

Client   All graduate students are scared silly by it and they count it so heavily.

Therapist (Silence)

Client   I'm pleased. Now I'll probably make a Class A graduate school.

Therapist Until now you doubted you could do it.

Client   Yes.

Therapist I never had any doubt about you.

Client   Really? And you have such high academic standards.

Therapist Yes.

Affirmation may be a nod, or an "uh-huh," or a "hmm," or a posture, look, or statement, or a silence, but it always communicates "we are together," and "we are finding our authentication." It is a special feeling, a communion, and much of it may be nonverbal. What affirmation does, essentially, is to confirm the being of the client and the courageous thrust to fulfillment which his statement represents. It is perhaps the most subtle of the interview dynamics.

CLARIFICATION

By their very nature, statements about emotions and behavior are rarely straightforward. The symbolization of events which the process of imagination makes possible alters direct communication and makes man vastly different from other primates. Also, the neurotic complicates his feelings and emotions, and the language involved in their expression. For him, clarity with Self and with others comes with extreme difficulty. One of the important functions of therapy is to help clarify feelings, ideas, concepts, and images, and to provide an explicit correlation between them and behavior. Most of us believe that once such matters are clarified the decision to be made will seem obvious and a choice between them will be made by the client. The "noise" in the system is reduced and the carrier wave opened. Possibly too much is expected of clarification in therapy today but it is certainly a necessary prelude to interpretation and acting-upon. However, therapy may merely stop with clarity without really new options in life. It is distressing to see a clear and vivid intellect which cannot change a thing.

Clients cannot usually clarify their feelings and concepts because (1) significant persons in their lives do not permit it; (2) they have a major investment in not doing so; and (3) the truthful nakedness of a tabooed idea or feeling is perhaps the most frightening thing of all. To say that "I love you," or "I hate you," straight out, and mean it, is a rare thing in our society, particularly if it has no hidden pay-off. But perhaps it was never intended that culture would be as direct as this or that symbolization or social ambivalence would never be required. That everything in life is to be clear is a sad delusion. In therapy the major myths and metaphors require clarification. The corrupted metapsychology of life may be integrally dishonest and hamper fulfillment. Too much clarity, however, makes for a pedantic and moralizing therapy without taste and effervescence.

One must always insist that the client "say" what he is "saying." The therapist cannot allow anything to go by which he does not hear or does not understand. It is always permissible to say, "But I don't understand what you are saying," or, "Let me get this straight. By this you mean . . . ," or any of ten other ways by which the client is asked to make clear what he is saying. Sometimes I get restive and move about more in my chair than is customary, and the client may then, without prompting, clarify what he has said. But clarification requires timing as proper as interpretation.

The client needs to face his suffering in his own way. Clarifying certain pleasurable actions too soon may destroy them. In the early stages of therapy, comments by the therapist are taken as strictures. What has to be clarified are the major avenues to fulfillment open to the person, the channels which lead to a different outlook and behavior, rather than the irrelevant minutiae of life. What these avenues are, for any client, is for the therapeutic partnership to decide in its work together.

Critical conflicts invariably invest themselves in a few people, a few processes, and a few events. These come to stand for the total neurotic dilemma. They focus themselves in therapy and come up again and again. Clarification works best with these focal conflicts. If they can be clarified, the rest of problematic existence may fall into place. Masculinity-femininity, sex, mother love, money, pleasure-pain, vocation, marriage, children, life-meaning, death, matters of the spirit, and similar things are the stuff of clarification. These are all areas which lend themselves, not only to mental conflict, but to the indirect or concealed statement. This is the basic arena of our work.

In the following example the client clarifies her feelings about her father which are related to her recent marriage:

Client   I am a victim so to speak of my famous father. He made me what I am.

Therapist   Your father has a special relationship to you. His beautiful and talented daughter.

Client   Yes. He is revered by everyone but I know what a narcissistic and perfectionistic person he is.

Therapist   But he had a special place for you.

Client   He wanted to make me his equal in the arts and he tried hard enough.

Therapist   Umh-hmm.

Client   That last concert did it. I couldn't meet his standards and I literally begged for approval . . . but it wasn't forthcoming. Damn him.

Therapist   You wanted him to say you were great . . . at least good.

Client   I needed it. But I understand him better now and I don't have that old rage any more.

Therapist   But are other males exempt?

Client   My husband is getting the brunt of it now, and unfortunately the love and the hate. . . . I understand it now, I think.

REFLECTING BACK

Reflection or reflecting back was developed to a high art by the classical Rogerians. With this school, the therapist's participation was so minimal as to be on a par with the psychoanalyst who sat behind the couch where the patient could not see him. Of course, the um-hmms were more frequent and the Rogerian counselor did face his client. Even Carl Rogers agrees today that this was sadly overdone.

In handball, tennis, or ping-pong, hitting the ball back in any way is often good enough to win. If you can continue to get the ball back, you can defeat opponents quite superior to you who will fall into their own errors. Reflection in therapy is somewhat similar. The lead is passed to the other party who must make something of the situation and fall into his own mistakes. This "leading" becomes grist for study in the therapeutic situation. If, on the other hand, the client is forced to always counter the therapist's lead, he may never get around to stating or solving his own problems.

It is, therefore, very important to allow the client sufficient opportunity to bring his neurosis to the therapeutic situation. Reflection is more than just bouncing the ball back. Done properly, it adds its own dimension to treatment. Reflection signifies understanding and empathy and interest and respect for the client. No one bothers to reflect something back if he is un-interested in the person or the transaction. Termination can easily be made by direct comment. Proper reflection opens the way for further contact and permits the platform to become development, closing, and acting-upon. On the other hand, if reflection becomes repetitive and automated, and is really a mask for lack of technical ability, it breaks down as an interview technique.

Reflection implies, "I know what you are saying and I am confident you can solve it, but let's see if I have it right." Often the reflection is necessary because there has not been enough time for incubation and development to bring the concept to the point of reorganized insight or action. There is a dilemma, not yet resolved, but on the way to solution. Reflecting it back to the client encourages that solution. Reflection takes a high degree of skill because the therapist must first understand what the client is saying and then merely rephrase without endorsement or embellishment. Reflection must not hinder or force any direction. It should increase the level of involvement.

The following example illustrates reflecting the client's material back with clarification:

Client   My boss objects to my being persistently late. He says he is going to demote me since docking my vacation time hasn't worked. I can't under-stand why he takes this attitude. I simply can't get up that early. I stay up very late and sometimes even take a sleeping pill.

Therapist   He's a stickler for office routine.

Client   They watch me. I can't get by with anything the others get away with. It isn't fair . . .

Therapist   You're singled out as an example.

Client   Yes. No one says anything when I am on time. They don't know the hell I go through to be there at 8 o'clock.

Therapist   Hmm.

Client   Of course, I've had the same problem before. Got fired over it, I think.

Therapist   It has happened to you before.

Client   Yes. But what does it matter? I get my work done.

REPEATING THE CLIENT'S STATEMENT

Repeating the client's words exactly is a common interview technique. It signifies that the therapist has heard what has been said but he neither re-flects it back nor interprets it. But he doesn't remain silent either. Sometimes I repeat only a part of the client's statement—the most significant part. Of course, repetition serves as a reinforcer and brings attention to something important which might otherwise be passed over but does not deserve higher elaboration. Sometimes, the therapist is simply waiting for the follow-up to come.

Repeating the statement is not always a voluntary act with me, just as "um-hmm" is not always deliberate, but the genuine expostulation of an involved person. A number of what I call "flow mechanisms" to keep the interview moving are integral to the interview itself. Repetition is among the more important of these mechanisms.

The following is an example of this interview technique:

Client   If only my husband would stop drinking we would have a really fine marriage. That's the problem.

Therapist   If only he would stop drinking.

Client   He gets mean when he drinks and then he is sorry; but the damage has been done.

Therapist   He's mean when he drinks.

Client   He stops for awhile and then bang! he's back at the bar—and we repeat the cycle.

Therapist   He stops for awhile.

Client   His father drinks, too. It runs in the family.

Therapist   It's in the family.

INTERPRETATION

A great deal has been written about interpretation, possibly because it is the cornerstone of psychoanalytic practice. It has been a vastly overabused and unabused thing. Interpretation is the cognitive vehicle by which one person communicates to another a self-truth which, up to that moment, could not be a truth. Interpretation requires the most careful preparation and incubation. No self-truth can be accepted or incorporated unless an adequate basis has been laid for it. Not only that, interpretations are expected to change life-long attitudes, and even life-styles. Even though they carry tremendous reorganizational force, they can be expected to meet an equal counter force in resistance. No one gives up even inadequate behavior for an unrealized promise. At least, no client does so until that promise has sufficient scope to invite him to take a risk.

Interpretations have a dynamic of their own. It is as though certain neuron potentials finally find their proper switching mechanism. The result of a proper interpretation is a peak response of awe, glow, surprise, and contentment. If there is any shrine in which the intellect reigns as the god supreme, its manifestation would most certainly be in the psychotherapeutic interpretation. But one must not underestimate the emotional bedrock of the interpretation. Thought can only occur when feelings give the green light. In therapy, interpretation is merely a sign that an emotional restructuring has taken place and that the client is ready for a new vista.

The following excerpt portrays how an interpretation might work:

Client	I felt absolutely up-tight yesterday. I had that old paranoid feeling for which they hospitalized me before I came to you.
Therapist	You found it necessary to distort reality again.
Client	I really wanted to hurt you . . . I felt you were manipulating me again and you have to cut it out!
Therapist	I seemed to be your enemy?
Client	I can't live up to your standards for me. I could never be a Jungian analyst. You're like my mother in some ways.
Therapist	Paranoia is a good cop out.
Client	I can't believe in myself. It just won't work. I'm condemned to be nothing.
Therapist	Somebody always sold you short.
Client	Yes. She wanted something. I did it. But it was never any good. But my brother couldn't do anything wrong.
Therapist	You wanted her approval so badly.
Client	Yes. But pain always and invariably followed . . . oh, the humiliation and depression!
Therapist	You're afraid I'll do the same to you. Lead you down the wrong path again as she did.
Client	I can't trust anybody. You seem to be OK but how do I know? But I guess I have to trust somebody. I do admire you.

Interpretation should be a rare thing in therapy, but sadly this is not the case. Too many therapists feel that if they are not interpreting they are not earning their bread. Every learner can be expected to err in this area of therapy. Interpretations have little place in the first half of therapy. They are properly the culmination of a discovery relationship and not its vehicle.

The most significant interpretations are those which clarify the client-therapist relationship, insofar as it comes to represent past as well as present interpersonal situations, particularly difficult relationships. Transference is promoted or reduced by interpretations; but, more than that, the interpersonal commerce of the hour brings with it all the neurotic limitations which hamper the client in his social world. They can be observed and worked through in a special setting given over to this process. Interpretations are, in a sense, intelligence put to the use of freedom of personality, and they are an important part of the covenant made when therapy is begun. Growth completes itself in this interpretive dialogue and cannot tolerate pathology of relationship, but interpretations incorrectly used can also be a way of reducing therapy to naught.

When does a therapist make an interpretation, and how does he follow through on it? A proper interpretation arrives naturally and is not programmed or prepared for specifically. The therapist's "third ear" is everlastingly at work synthesizing and making useful and meaningful the data which the client supplies. Interpretations are products of this mental work. Some clients even insist on making their own interpretations, and one client of mine would not allow me to interpret for long stretches in her therapy. "Don't say anything," she would say to me. But it is not unusual to bring the client to the interpretation in this way, particularly with ambulatory schizophrenics.

Interpretations are closures whenever the Self requires thrust in new areas of thought and feeling. They delimit roles, masochistic tendencies, fixations, narcissism, obsessions, and self-pity, by revealing them as inefficient and nonproductive, noncreative and nonrewarding ways of behaving. They point up the absurdity of symptoms in a way which is neither comic nor critical, and certainly not defensive. It is often painful to be stripped in this way. In a proper interpretation, the client sometimes feels like a dupe, or a dunce, a tragically paradoxical victim of himself.

Interpretations point the way to insight and to new ways of existing. A female client, who continually used four-letter words to maintain a painful persona she did not want, gave them up when an interpretation helped her to see how they deprived her of any possible inner sense of her own femininity. Another client took sodium dilantin for years for epilepsy he never had to begin with. An interpretation about orgasm and epileptic equivalents helped him to give up his useless medication—in stages, of course. It seems the more useful the neurotic crutch the greater the importance of the interpretation about it.

Interpretations are often tentative things. An interpretation may be offered and then dropped. Hot irons cannot be immediately grasped! But no interpretation in therapy is ever lost. Mistaken or premature ones come back to hound the therapist again and again. They are also the materials of suicide. An interpretation which fixes a client as homosexual, or one which implies relief or cure is impossible, can have devastating effects on the person. A good rule is that no therapist has a right to make an interpretation he would be unprepared to receive about himself were he the client. Some therapists use the power of interpretation as a platform for their own elevated place in society or for feelings about Self. They feel a certain strength and dignity in interpreting and find it the motivating core of their work. This is an incorrect use of perhaps the greatest technique for change and growth we know.

SILENCE

Roszak[2] describes society's attitude toward silence in the following way:

> Oriental mysticism comprehends argumentation; but it also provides a generous place for silence, out of wise recognition of the fact that it is with silence that men confront the great moments of life. Unhappily, the Western intellect is inclined to treat silence as if it were a mere zero: a loss of words indicating the absence of meaning.

[2]T. Roszak, *The Making of a Counter Culture* (New York: Doubleday and Co., 1969).

Some clients talk from the first moment they enter the consulting room until the time they leave—not necessarily on an anxious basis, but as a life- or therapeutic-style. Others maintain passive silence in quietude and contemplation. The importance of talk as a medium of growth in therapy has been overemphasized. The free-associational process uses words as vehicles but words may not really describe what is happening in the stream of thought. We get uncomfortable without words. Therapists, by some hidden selection factor, are verbal people. The clients who come to us may have this investment in language as well. The surgeon, on the other hand, speaks primarily through organs and the body. Silence can be the most effective way of saying something in therapy. Silence is also the basic form of communion with the inner Self, and beauty is an important aspect of this communion. We are always silent in the face of the truly moving experiences of life, as Roszak states. Silence is also related to hostility. During extremely long silences in therapy, I offer the client my hand without saying a word. I sometimes do this several times until the silence is broken, and it seems to help resolve the impasse. The therapist must learn to be comfortably silent, to pace his words, and to be sparing of them. Popenoe says therapists need to develop large ears and small mouths.[3] Classical psychoanalysis was overly "silent," and erroneously believed that only in this way would the client come forth with the necessary material for analysis. Clients today demand some form of dialogue and will no longer accept a totally "silent" therapist. They withdraw from therapy if they encounter only silence. The younger clients particularly, like college students, who see in "rapping" an answer to social working-through, explicitly refuse the earlier model.

The principal function of silence is incubation of something that cannot yet be hatched in preparation for a creative act. Yet, silence can be a hostile withdrawal, a resistance and it often requires handling as a resistance. But many clients are silent because their therapists make them so in covert ways. By this I mean the client is not involved in his therapy, does not see the necessary lines of therapeutic growth, and is afraid of both the deficiencies and the power of the therapist. No one is silent when he has something to say, and when the circumstances for saying it are right.

I allow clients to be silent as long as they want to if the silence is well based. But if silence prevails over therapeutic hours, I begin to examine myself for deficiencies and I examine the premises of our therapeutic work. Sometimes there really is nothing to say in therapy and it should be terminated. In most instances like this, I have failed the client in some affective way, and this needs to be changed before the client can talk. Sometimes I am continuously silent when the client is not. My silence tells the client his material cannot be commented on, or that it is worthless and I am being cheated, or that I am communing with my "third ear," or that I am distancing myself to protect him. I am silent when angry until I can express it appropriately. At other times my fantasies or my "third ear" are at work syn-

[3]P. Popenoe, Address at Sacramento State College, May 21, 1970.

thesizing the client and testing his various possibilities. Words interfere with this and they should be restrained.

Some of the most salubrious moments in therapy are meaningful silences spent with the client. This is an aesthetic and affective experience. A great deal is said without language. Since I also use adjunctive expressionistic techniques such as painting, sculpture, or writing, the client may have said what he had to say in the hour partly in this way. We sometimes use his artistic production to delimit his silence if we have to, as I describe in a later chapter. Depression uses silence and the client has a right to develop his mourning. It is important that the therapist understand and share the silence. Otherwise, it cannot be considered therapeutic. Biological healing takes place in silence. The same principle applies to therapy.

HUMOR

Most textbooks fail to mention humor as playing any part in therapy. They consider therapy a grim business, which indeed it may be. But I always find that while clients cannot laugh at first, their improvement brings laughter with it. If the client doesn't show a growth in humor, I am probably failing with him. Humor and wit are so definitely connected with the personality that it is surprising so little has been written about it. Humor is invariably used against the Self in the neurosis. It is also a way of displacing and sublimating instinctual impulses. Humor is considered dangerous by most clients because they fear being laughed at—or having their own laughter redirected at themselves. Also, they cannot really distinguish the comic. Laughter is freedom-to-be, and they cannot aspire to this so early in treatment. Much wit and humor is sexual, and involves logic put to the absurd. Clients cannot, in any way, handle the paradoxes of laughter.

One thing every therapist must have is a feeling for the comic. This balances his feeling for the tragic. I am suspicious of any therapist who never laughs. So much of life is absurd, that unless humor can temper the discrepancies in it one may fall into a continuously pessimistic mood. Humor resolves paradoxes, tempers aggression, and is generally acceptable socially as non-aggrandizing and cementing. When, for example, someone can joke with his mother, double-binds can have little place in their relationship.

An employer, the epitome of judgment and authority, responds in a different way to the employee who can laugh with him. He recognizes that he is being accepted as a person as well as an authority. "He is a card," means Bill is a regular guy who puts things in proper perspective. Bosses have a deep fear of losing their humanity.

The therapist should not be afraid to laugh in therapy although most of us are. The client may be puzzled by it, perhaps even offended, but eventually he will see that humor is part of the interpersonal and part of his life. He will at, some point in therapy, try it himself, watching carefully for the reaction, and being terribly frightened. If his humor is well received, if it is actually funny, he will use more and more of it to buttress his personal tragedy.

What does one laugh about in therapy? Some parts of the therapeutic situation have the same tension, irony, and paradoxical nature jokes have. If these cannot be resolved in traditional ways, they can be relieved by appropriate humor. A client who comes at the right time but the wrong day is open to humor. A client who calls his present therapist by the name of his former therapist is also fair game. When, on rare occasions, the therapist wears socks which do not match, laughter is a good way of showing that the therapist is perhaps a bit "crazy" himself. Of course, humor is the most sparing of dynamisms, and is to be used with the greatest caution. It calls for a very secure therapist, a well-based therapeutic relationship, as well as a feeling for humor. In the severest kind of impasses, it is often useful. It can be releasing and helpful.

Here is an example of humor in therapy:

Client   Women are central in my life. They are the source of all nurturance, beauty and pleasure. But I keep violently blowing up at them at unpredictable times. I don't have any control of it and it is not like the rest of me.

Therapist   It's somehow related to your asthma.

Client   Yes. My psychoanalysis revealed that like other asthmatics I could neither love my mother nor break from her. That even now she keeps me symbolically tied to her.

Therapist   But you have moved beyond her in your personal freedom and creativity.

Client   Well, we have a detente and it works. But lately I haven't been doing very well with the ladies.

Therapist   Very well?

Client   My appreciation of them is sometimes more than monogamous. I love my wife but she can't fill all needs—and I no longer expect it.

Therapist   Um-hmm.

Client   There is this other girl, quite nice, with a very lively mind. She has gone to a neighboring university and has called a couple of times suggesting I come down. Maybe I will.

Therapist   She attracts you.

Client   Yes.

Therapist   What would you do with her if she were attracted to you?

Client   That's the problem! I might just get her and then I'd be in real deep trouble!

(Therapist and client break out in grins and then in rollicking laughter for several seconds. A long . . . long pause follows. Both realize that the laughter represented the resolution of the paradox presented by the client which they both deeply understood.)

GIVING ADVICE

Clients come to therapy expecting to receive advice—to be told something. The medical model, the one they are most familiar with, supports this expectation. They are, therefore, most chagrined to find the therapist has no direct advice to give them, nothing to say as such. Some psychiatrists and psychologists do give a great deal of advice in short term therapy. So do some marriage counselors. Advice (information) is a costly and valuable thing and is not to be demeaned. In industry, personnel administration, law, education, and similar fields, information is a key commodity, much sought after and very expensive. Good advice prevents costly mistakes, adds to the efficiency of operations, and even improves the elegance of technical operations.

The following dialogue illustrates some of the problems with giving advice to clients:

Client	Well, I haven't seen you for about six months. Got married and I'm happy now.
Therapist	Sounds good.
Client	I'm out here from the East Coast. Thought I'd call you for an appointment. Sort of renew myself.
Therapist	You wanted a contact at this time.
Client	Yes.
Therapist	(Silence)
Client	(Pause . . .) I wanted to get your opinion about something. . . . My back has been bothering me again and I was thinking of having that spinal disc removed completely.
Therapist	This would make your third major spinal surgery.
Client	The first two helped for a short while. But my neurologist says I need it.
Therapist	Your neurologist is for it.
Client	Well, he hedges and won't promise anything. I haven't told him much of my past psychiatric history.
Therapist	You feel it better not to give him too many details.
Client	Since you know me best of all I want to ask you whether or not I should have the surgery done. There's a chance I'll end up permanently in a wheel chair.
Therapist	(Silence)
Client	Aren't you going to answer?
Therapist	Yes. But the question in my mind is what I can tell you. You've probably

already made up your mind and want confirmation of your decision. Also, I don't feel competent to advise on spinal matters.

Client I know, but you are the only one who knows intrinsically about me and how I operate. Is this another example of my unconscious wanting bodily nurturance and rewards?

Therapist We've worked hard together and I'm confident you can now make your own decisions about yourself and your body. It's true that you have looked to surgeons for the resolution of problems of the psyche in the past but it isn't necessarily still true. I'm confident you will make the correct decision, and will stand by you.

Client (Pause) OK. Thanks.

The situation in therapy is similar to the problems of industry but also very different. A client's proposed business merger or marriage may turn out to be a very costly mistake, and the therapist may have insight into its coming failure and I suppose could sometimes prevent it. Why then does he not? The disruptive effect of analysis was, of course, recognized by Freud. He forbade major changes in the life of the analysand without his concurrence during analysis. But this has not been the generally accepted pattern in psychoanalytic psychotherapy or its derivative forms.

The simple answer is that the client doesn't actually want the therapist's advice, even though he thinks he comes for it. The experience of every therapist is that once you start offering advice, things go badly in therapy. Of course, the client, on one ground or another, rarely follows the direct advice given him. Indeed, he may do just the opposite. The therapist is not, at any rate, gifted with divine knowledge. All of us are well aware of the contingent state of psychology and psychiatry as an area of man's knowledge. This should make the therapist humble about giving advice. Many of us as well may feel our personal lives are not so Apollonian that we can offer our clients heavenly advice.

The therapist's function is to make decisions for his client possible rather than to make decisions on behalf of the client. Therapy improves the precision and success of those decisions, but this results from the new freedom with which they are made, not from a different intellect. Mistakes, while in therapy, often become less damaging and destructive and thus aid learning. Therapy is not all success. It is often preceded by a whole series of failures. Some grand ones even occur while treatment is taking place. To deny these mistakes is to inhibit the learning process which therapy is.

When pushed very hard for advice by a client, I usually say, "But you can make this one as well as I can. Can I possibly help you, though, with the data involved in your decision?" I then carefully refrain from advice-giving, but do help clarify the background of the decision. Once in a while the question may be whether or not the client should continue in therapy. Here, again, I first quickly consider whether the therapy has actually been going well, and what the client is really asking. If the therapy has, in my opinion, been going well the client may feel he hasn't been given enough love, or he cannot recognize the progress made. Then we discuss the last several hours and I offer a great deal of support. In most instances, however, I say that leaving therapy is up to the client . . . that I want to continue our work together, am ready to do so, but the decision is his. I then abide by his decision.

There are certain situations however where intervention, by advice, or even by action, is mandatory. This involves behavior which might lead to the client's suicide, to physical injury to someone else, or serious harm to the client's good reputation. These are situations in which the ethics of humanism and psychotherapy override the technique of psychotherapy. Protection of the client is basic to the therapeutic ethic, and it is also usually a legal duty as well. Do no harm, or, as I paraphrase it, do not allow serious harm to happen, is one of the oldest principles of medicine and it applies equally to psychotherapy.

PERSUASION

Suggestion and persuasion are part of every therapeutic interview although they are somewhat tarnished concepts today. They smack of an unhappy directness or underhandedness which are anti-egalitarian. They are associated with the commercial marketplace which uses them regularly to sell goods. But they should not be sneered at. The therapist is selling a service himself and he competes with other therapists for clients. Also, clients seem to do better, or think they do, with the self-assured, positive therapist who offers charisma along with scholarship and technical ability. He offers them the suggestion of himself as assured, and successful. This suggestion and persuasion form a part of the model and is a powerful ingredient for change. Such suggestions are regularly a part of general medicine which, however, exploits them, sometimes shamefully.

The trouble with suggestion and persuasion is that they tend to be overused. They defy careful analysis since they have global and undefinable aspects. Sometimes they seem to be more geared to human engineering than human therapy. In behavioral and hypnotic therapies they have a most important place. Indeed, many symptoms are mitigated through these techniques. Placebos work through persuasion. They are very commonly used, directly or indirectly, and they do relieve symptoms for some people. But these approaches have only a small place in interpersonal psychotherapy where treatment is based on two equal human participants experiencing and growing together. Despite this, one does *suggest* and *persuade* preconsciously. No interpersonal relationship can dispense with these techniques entirely, nor should it. At times I say to a client, "You can do it," because I am confident he can. This is usually at a critical time, when new insights and feelings are being put to use while they are still hedged with fears and trepidation.

The following is an example of persuasion with a student in therapy:

Client   I have this interview with the psychiatrist in the medical school whom I'm going to work for . . . assist him with his research. But I can't even think of the interview. It blows my mind and I get deathly afraid. I'm going to blow it!

Therapist   Psychiatrists are imposing people.

Client   Yes. I'm sure he'll know what's going on in me . . . how sick I am. I can't cover up with him.

Therapist   They understand about being human.

Client   He's a sharp guy. Walks around in a white coat and always confident.

Therapist   Takes a lot of training and understanding to be a psychiatrist.

Client   I don't want to be judged and maybe ruin my record in the Psych Department.

Therapist   Psychiatrists know no one's perfect.

COUNTERING

There are a number of interview techniques which have been used to shock or confront the client into movement and insight. These are: (1) disbelief; (2) ridicule; (3) telling the client he is wrong and (4) insisting that his problem is not important enough. These are lumped together here because they are generic, and the comments apply equally to all.

Today, confrontation is a much more acceptable technique in the basic encounter group, Synanon type approaches, and in many group therapies. These are all useful devices for promoting confrontation. They also have their place in crisis intervention and community-oriented therapies. I, myself, have led a number of encounter groups in which I have used them. I now accept the obvious fact that confrontation, whether dyadic or polyadic, is much less dangerous than we had formerly believed. It has a place in interpersonal psychotherapy, as in Synanon, but in a somewhat different way.

Interpersonal psychotherapy does not strive for explosive confrontation with the client, with a rapid stripping away of resistances, impulses and values. If this is indicated for the client, he should be referred to an appropriate marathon or Esalen-type group approach. Our way is a more ordered, better paced, less hysterical way of approaching growth through basic confrontation of the Self. I agree with Maslow[4] that the basic encounter group has not demonstrated that it has cured anyone yet. It is merely a provisional set of concepts which are acted upon as though they were true. Little attempt is made to validate encounter therapy's awareness and sensitivity techniques against some broader criterion of validity.

However, countering approaches in interpersonal psychotherapy have an extremely limited, but definite, use. Some clients may maintain such rigid neurotic fixations that they are little moved by affirmation, clarification, interpretation, and the remaining techniques of the interview. These techniques wash off the client like water off a duck's back and nothing works.

The therapist must then set out to prove to the client that his psychological position is untenable. This calls for provoking him within a loving at-

[4]A. Maslow, *Op. cit.*

mosphere. The client is paradoxically put in the position of not wanting to listen to the therapist but of a greater need than ever to stay in therapy. He is, in a sense, caught between two systems and two people—himself, of course.

When this occurs the therapist feels genuine anger and hostility toward the client because he persists in clinging so to his erroneous beliefs and ways. I may then tell him that I believe he is making too much of his symptoms, that he is "stroking" himself in an infantile way, and I indicate disbelief in the credibility of his inner world as he has related it. I may come right out and say he is downright wrong in one or more of his feelings or ideas and that they approach delusion. I may even turn my back on him. Of course, he fights back. It is then necessary, as Searles[5] says, "To give as good as one receives." Such a "pitched battle" often has good results with clients whose therapy is otherwise doomed to fail, but not always. At best, this technique shows the client that the therapist will fight for the client's health, and that he can stand up to the client's symptoms and his unconscious. At worst, the client feels put upon, overwhelmed, beaten, and threatened, and he withdraws from therapy for a while.

This approach is only indicated when it seems obvious that, as things are going, the client will not and cannot find fulfillment and that a referral or a consultant will not help. It also calls for a maximum of genuineness and positive regard. You can become angry and use disbelief only when you really care for the client. The therapist who frequently finds himself using countering techniques is, perhaps, himself a candiate for self-examination. These are emergency techniques only.

The following example illustrates countering by telling the client he is wrong:

Client   I enjoy seeing Dr. X on Thursdays and you on Mondays. It seems to be working real well.

Therapist   I don't share that with you. Dr. X and I never conferred on you being a part of his therapy and you haven't been working here since going there.

Client   I don't see any harm in it. I like him and it's free. I'll also come here.

Therapist   As I see it, you can't have two therapists in this way. At least, I can't work that way.

Client   But I think it's OK.

Therapist   But I don't. I talked to Dr. X and he agreed that you were talking about your own problems and not family ones. He also feels that the maximum has been attained for your family and wants to terminate.

Client   You son of a bitch!

Therapist   It's up to you to choose whom you want to see, but you can't see us both.

Client   Go to hell.

[5]H. Searles, *Collected Papers on Schizophrenia and Related Topics* (New York: International Univ. Press, 1965).

FOUR-LETTER WORDS

Most clients in therapy are forty and under. Youth, in search of identity, is an avid patron of the many varieties of therapy. The intellectual, the creator, the symbolizer, the introspect, primarily find relief this way. The therapist, in his work, must be aware of new customs and folkways and of new attitudes toward traditional morality and authority. This is particularly true when working with young people. This new freedom has invaded language. The question of four-letter words (other than love) in therapy must be dealt with.

I have found myself, almost in spite of myself, saying "shit" and "fuck" with my young clients in response to their use of these words. Such words have pungency, imagery, and color. Use of these words feels good because it seems the generation gap is thus bridged and that rapport is maximized. I do not analyze the concepts themselves, but use them as a way of communicating with a client on a level meaningful to him. Is this a desirable practice? Any way of getting on with a client is a good way. The use of special argot of a subgroup of society tends to confer membership in that group. Even therapists have their own cant, as one can judge from national meetings. I have, however, given up using these four-letter words because it simply isn't *me*. All of my life has been, in a sense, devoted to the use of elegant language applied to science and I cannot change now. My aping of this language is only the manifestation of a poseur and is really never accepted by my clients.

I suggest that if such language is natural for the therapist, if the client uses it, and if tact and dignity can be maintained, then it is recommended. Some women use four-letter words consistently in therapy. I have noted, however, that as their therapy progresses they have less and less need for it. They discover ways of conveying their frustration and demands that are better than this pseudo-masculine way.

THERAPIST DISCLOSURE

Much has been written about the value of self-disclosure, varying from the extreme position of O. Hobart Mowrer on the one hand to Sigmund Freud on the other. In this chapter, I discuss it only as an interview technique. Only the part it plays in furthering the structure of the interview is of interest.

The client attempts consistently to reveal himself in order to be understood and to find new ways of thinking, feeling, and behaving. He continuously monitors the therapist's response to his output, and further revelations depend on that response. Clients believe, indeed have to believe, that their therapists are problem-free people, fulfilled in every sense. When, however, I disclose to a client that I have, in the past, struggled with the same problem he is coping with, such as an over-controlling mother, the barrier to our communication is often quickly lowered. Two people in the therapeutic situation become temporarily bonded by a common and limiting experience.

The following is an example of this interview technique:

Client	My mother is a bitch. Because she couldn't love my old man she put me in his place. And I tried to fill it. Now look at me today: neither man nor woman . . .
Therapist	Your mother needed somebody and found you.
Client	Did you know that I slept in the same bed with her until I was eight years old. Wow!
Therapist	(Silence)
Client	I'm fine, and then she phones and I'm right back where I started. She can undo six months of work in two seconds.
Therapist	My mother was a problem, too.
Client	Your mother!
Therapist	Yep. She didn't find intimacy with my father and looked to me for things he couldn't give her. Oedipus had a rough time in my family.
Client	Then you know what I'm talking about.
Therapist	From personal experience.

Therapist disclosure is a delicate thing. It is not to be done for any hidden rewards. That would be taking advantage of the powerless client. It is occasionally useful when nothing else works and you have to tell the client you are at one with him in a way you cannot do by words alone. You can say "My mother was that way, too," or "I sometimes have the same longings," or you can relate a segment of experience, or a metaphorical "story" about yourself, or go into a soliloquy. Mowrer[6] and Jourard[7] show, in detail, how well self-disclosure works in general.

NONVERBAL RESPONSE

Nonverbal techniques in the therapeutic interview are not so easily described. They usually operate outside the realm of awareness. This does not mean they are not regularly used or that they lack effectiveness. Therapy is a controlled situation and the absence of control or understanding is usually to be avoided.

The client's posture is an important part of his communicative repertoire. Scheflen[8] has shown that the preening behavior by female clients is a seductive mechanism which operates out of awareness and is designed to gain concessions for her. The therapist himself has his favorite nonverbal means of communication. Because of this, too many words are spoken in treatment. I myself tend to slip down in my upholstered chair when I am feeling certain things, or run both my hands through my hair, besides cross-

[6]O. H. Mowrer, *op. cit.*

[7]S. Jourard, *The Transparent Self* (Princeton: D. Van Nostrand & Co., 1964).

[8]A. E. Scheflen, "Quasi-courtship behavior in psychotherapy," *Psychiatry*, 1965, *28*, 245–251.

ing or uncrossing my hands or my feet. I know other therapists who stand up, relight their pipes, or clasp their hands in characteristic ways. Of course, the face is the most expressive of all even in silence. All therapeutic training should now include one or two sessions on video tape so that the therapist may become aware of his nonverbal modes, and be able to use them.

The conscious act of reducing the distance between the two by moving the chairs closer together, or by actually touching the patient, or by closing the distance, or by looking and feeling sad or joyous can also be very significant. Our body has a way of speaking for us when we cannot speak, a primitive but effective form of talking.

Of course no analysis of the dialogue between psychotherapist and client does justice to the interplay of forces to be found there. There is always a *supra* factor which goes over and beyond any of the elements one finds in it.

INSTRUMENTAL PROBLEMS

VIII

The practice of psychotherapy involves certain housekeeping chores which are sometimes burdensome if not handled efficiently. If they are done routinely, they ease the path to the client's fulfillment. Ignored or maladministered, they make therapy a minor nightmare. Most textbooks on therapy tend to ignore them, but I feel that therapy cannot be properly practiced without some knowledge of these aspects of our work. There are probably a number of good ways of using the telephone, writing reports, seeing relatives, setting and collecting fees, accepting or rejecting gifts, but I have found the following ways work best for me. Each therapist needs to adapt his procedures to his own style of practice, but the discussion which follows should prepare him for the problems he will encounter.

THE TELEPHONE

The telephone is an aid and an interruption but no therapist can survive today without it. It is part of the current life-style and it will soon include visual as well as aural. The phone has tremendous implications for the practice of therapy which are invariably overlooked. Mackinnon and Michels[1] summarize their experience with the telephone as follows:

> Patients resort to telephone interviews for various reasons. The problem of physical distance prevents some patients from coming in person. Other frequent motivations for telephone interviews are the fear of inordinate expense associated with psychiatric help or the fear of humiliation as the result of discussing embarrassing material face to face. Some patients experience such intense desires to commit suicide that they fear that they may not live long enough to be interviewed in person and, therefore, are using the telephone contact as a measure of true desperation.

Most clients, if encouraged, would prefer their therapy via telephone. The most powerful reason is that they would not have to face their conflicts or guilt, and they would still get some help. A friend of mine, a blind, nonprofessionally-trained therapist, has a long waiting list of people, many of them physicians, priests, and therapists. I believe this largely true because he cannot see them and their agony. But therapy is the facility to see what

[1]R. A. Mackinnon, and R. Michels, "The telephone in the psychiatric interview," *Psychiatry,* 1970, *33,* 82–93.

one has not seen and does not want to see. The telephone is sometimes an evasion; its use must be based upon a proper rationale. But the phone also appeals to the therapist who can save time with it and also be impersonal. We do many things on the telephone we would not do in the interview. Mainly, we minimize human encounter, and maximize advice and electronic support. Lives are, however, saved by telephone, as in suicide prevention centers. We should not scoff at its value.

The telephone saves money for the client. While some therapists, like some pediatricians, impose a charge for time they use treating on the telephone, most do not. Some clients try to save money, but in doing so they also follow the medical model which discourages patients from asking for house calls, or even coming to an already overcrowded office. The client often feels that all he needs when he phones is some minor guidance or support. He knows that extra therapeutic hours are often out of the question with his therapist. Most therapists are practically incommunicado during the treatment day. Many have unlisted telephone numbers, so that use of the telephone is often an act of desperation as well.

Clients fear initial confrontation with the therapist where they will be deeply evaluated and possibly rejected. They do not want the therapist to see them helpless. The telephone shields them from this, while they can, in turn, evaluate his acceptability. In this way, they can offer only those parts of themselves which they think are agreeable.

The telephone call can, itself, be healing. The initial telephone call to a therapist sometimes takes years of incubation and maturation. Picking up the receiver, dialing, making contact, and "hearing the voice" is enough to quiet anxiety and promote reorganization in some people. These are cures without encounter and are known to all therapists. Beyond this, the telephone has reinforcement properties for clients already in therapy. Mackinnon and Michels say that they hold 45-minute therapeutic interviews by phone, and presumably charge a fee for this. This is not recommended except for rare emergencies as, for example, when the therapist is overseas or otherwise out of touch. Stand-by colleague assistance is frequently demeaned on the specious ground that no one can take the therapist's place, not even briefly.

Since the first contact with the therapist is usually by telephone, I recommend that wherever possible the therapist speak to the applicant himself. Secretaries, no matter how qualified and well meaning, lack sufficient knowledge about neurotic suffering to appreciate the situation of the caller. They create resentments and bad public relations without intending to. Direct contact with the caller improves the probability he will become a client. It helps the cause of mental hygiene whichever way it goes. It is important to "feel" the client's voice, to understand the configuration of his complaint, and to know what he is really saying. This reveals a great deal. Some clients merely ask for an appointment. Others want basic information about fees, theoretical orientation, therapy time available, and so on, before they will make an appointment.

Some of this information should be given, but phone contact must not be made a substitute for the prospecting interview itself. If prospective clients are referred by a colleague, they may already have some of this basic information. More knowledgable clients know enough to consult biographical material available in any library. If the therapist has published, they may read his books. The therapist also needs some basic information before he can offer or refuse an appointment. The call can supply this information, and not everyone who calls should have an appointment.

It is vital to master the telephone so that your personality is, to some extent, communicated through it. Clients listen carefully for manner, intonation, diction, volume, and so forth. They may base a choice on this rather than on what is said to them. Charisma and the telephone go hand in hand! One must also learn how to listen on the telephone. Most of us feel the telephone was made for talking and not listening.

I also believe that all changes in formal appointments as well as new appointments should be made by the therapist. Where the therapist's practice is large, or when several therapists share one appointment secretary, this may be inefficient by business standards. However, I am willing to sacrifice efficiency for the personal touch. This is, after all, what psychotherapy is all about. But there are some restrictions on this principle and these are outlined below.

Clients should have your home telephone number, or that of an answering service which can be in instant contact with you. This is sometimes abused, but it need not be. It will ultimately prevent a suicide or two. I am reminded, at this point, of the client who called me at 1:00 AM and said, "Dr. Burton, I just had a nightmare and wanted to know if you were there." Situations like this call for humor, particularly since she started calling me three times a week, at 1:00 AM, for the same reason until we could analyze the reason for the calls.

Phone calls from clients in therapy are best handled by supportive listening. Often they simply need to know you are still there—still alive. If the calls come frequently, I offer extra hours temporarily. If they are refused, I tend to become impatient. Occasionally, the therapist must call a client. This happens rarely, when the therapist has made a mistake and wants to reassure himself of his client's welfare, or when a special form of support is needed. For example, the client may be physically ill in the hospital, or may have delivered a child.

Should one receive calls during sessions with other clients? Clients tend to resent this intrusion and feel they are paying for the therapist's telephone work. Still, there are emergencies which will not wait. I disagree with Mackinnon and Michels who feel such interruptions have therapeutic value for the client who listens in *ad hoc*. But since every administrative procedure is, more or less, a compromise, I recommend never having more than one interruption per session. These should only be permitted from on-going clients. If possible, they should take place out of hearing of the client you are with. Answering services, recording devices, and similar equipment for making callbacks are now available in such profusion that they can be used in a variety of ingenious ways. Consistent response is probably more important than what is actually responded since the client wants contact more than anything else.

Here are three examples of calls for initial appointments and the way they were handled.

CALL I

Caller: Hello, Dr. Burton?

Dr. Burton: Yes, this is Dr. Burton.

Caller: Do you have any therapy time open? I need to see someone.

Dr. Burton: Well, it varies from time to time. May I ask who referred you?

Caller: Dr. Yule, in New York. I was seeing him, but my husband got a job at the University. He recommended you. He's read your books.

Dr. Burton: That's fine. What seems to be the trouble? How can I help?

Caller: My old phobias have come back and my stomach is acting up again. I'm afraid.

Dr. Burton: Can we schedule an hour and see if we can work it out?

Caller: When?

Dr. Burton: Friday at 1:00 PM, or Monday at 8:00 AM.

Caller: Monday. I'll be there.

CALL II

Caller: Dr. Burton?

Dr. Burton: This is Dr. Burton.

Caller: Can I see you? I'm in trouble.

Dr. Burton: What kind of trouble are you having?

Caller: I'm sorry, I can't talk about it on the telephone but I'm desperate. I may lose my job if I don't do something.

Dr. Burton: How did you locate me?

Caller: One of my coworkers took a class from you. He recommended you. Can you help?

Dr. Burton: I hope so. Will tomorrow at 6:00 PM be all right?

Caller: I'll be there. Thanks.

CALL III

Caller: I'm calling to ask what your fees are.
Is it very expensive?

Dr. Burton: You need some therapy but you want to know what you're getting into economically?

Caller: Yes, that's it.

Dr. Burton: I don't usually discuss fees on the telephone. Could you risk an hour and we can explore this and other matters necessary to treatment? My rates are standard for this community.

Caller: Well, I don't know.

Dr. Burton: What seems to be the trouble?

Caller: It's my husband, he drinks and is cruel to me. I want him to come to you.

Dr. Burton: I see . . .

Caller: Guess I'd better call you back. Is that satisfactory?

Dr. Burton: OK. Good luck.

Caller: Thanks.

THERAPIST ABSENCES

Some therapists cancel appointments at the drop of a hat. Others almost never miss an interview. Some therapists appear at their office with a fever. Others regularly stay away with a pedestrian cold. Some find pressing private business a good reason for cancellation. Others would not think of missing a therapy hour for personal business. What is proper?

Successful treatment does not depend on compulsive therapy, but neither can it be attained by hit-or-miss application. A therapist at either extreme may have unresolved neurotic countertransferences. The therapist is, above all, human. As such, he will need time for vacations, time for himself and his family, time with colleagues, time to be ill, time for community mental hygiene activities, perhaps even time for his training analysis. All these things make him a more individuated and fulfilled therapist and thus more valuable to his clients.

As therapists, we must help the client understand these needs. As a rule, they envision us as some kind of supermen who never need vacations, never become ill, and never need pleasure. Even the loneliest and most desperate client must come to respect this part of the therapist's life. But if the client is given the feeling that the therapist's participation is arbitrary, idiosyncratic, or that he is just another client, resistive problems will come up. It is no accident that many therapists flee into full-time research, administration, or teaching. They can no longer meet the rigors of unconditional positive regard. And it is no service to clients to have this happen frequently. The therapist's respect for himself, his coming to terms with what he can and cannot do, and his furthering of his own authentication are part of being a qualified therapist. Frequent absences from clients are signs of lagging professional commitment.

I usually tell clients where I am going if I will miss more than two interviews with them. To clients who have extraordinary difficulty with separation, the ambulatory schizophrenic clients, for instance, I give an itinerary, or the name of someone who will always know where I am. Or I provide them with the name and phone number of a colleague who can help them, if need be. Sometimes I use a modification of the Harrower letter-writing technique,[2] or the client and I talk over the trans-Atlantic or trans-Pacific telephone at rare intervals.

Clients also take vacations and miss appointments. The problem is to differentiate resistance from the reasonable lapses. No approach is really adequate. The therapist is in business and too many lacunae in his schedule mean he is a bad businessman. One of my former clients cancelled every other appointment presumably for business reasons. I discussed it with her, and then referred her to a colleague. I could neither tolerate nor analyze it satisfactorily. I require clients to give me 48 hours' notice of cancellation. If I fill the hour, I do not make a charge. Even then, I am liberal about it, as far as the dynamics allow. Clients' vacations, professional meetings, and so forth are handled routinely. However, I try to evaluate whether, within these client-absences, the growing edge is steadily going forward as planned. If it is not, I may ask the client for more frequent interviews. If the cancellations become too onerous, I bring the matter up for evaluation.

When therapy is central to the client's being, no problem usually arises in this connection. Problems occur most often when the client has not yet made a transference, or as a manifestation of major resistance, or when the client is approaching termination of his therapy. These things must be appreciated in their proper setting.

FEES

Therapeutic services can only be provided for a fee whether it is paid by the client himself, or by a private or government agency. Whether or not a fee (paid directly by the client) helps the client's recovery is a philosophical question I cannot discuss at this time.

White and partner have this to say about fees:

> The measure of the worth of the private practitioner is not determined by his position in salaried governmental employment, but is assessed by ordinary social values such as his market value, successful treatment of his patients, and his income. These are the normal values of the community at large, which the average citizen can understand and appreciate. The setting of a fee between patient and psychologist is the normal reality aspect of private practice as it is in other areas of daily life. A psychologist in private practice sells his skills and capabilities and the client pays so that both have a vested interest in getting the best result for the money spent. The simple and direct contract of the fee has been found, from experience, to remove two major obstacles to the effective conclusion of the relationship between patient and psychologist. It removes the guilt of taking from the psychologist without direct personal exertion and the implication that the patient has not the resources in money at a practical level, and personal strengths at an emotional level to pay his way as a person and a citizen. It also removes the social service dependency covert in the patient's attitude that he has already paid for this service in his taxes to the State in advance, and that the services of the psychologist are his right.[3]

[2]M. Harrower, "Therapeutic Communications by Letter-Notebooks and Recorded Transcriptions," in L. Pearson (ed.), *The Use of Written Communication in Psychotherapy* (Springfield, Ill.: C. C. Thomas Publ., 1965).

[3]J. R. E. White, and P. M. Sarfaty. "A report on the Division's working party on private practice in clinical psychology," *Australian Psychol.*, 1970, *5*, 184–190. P. 189.

More important is the fact that the therapist in private practice invariably makes his living from his practice. Fees are something he is very much concerned with, even though the politics of fees are such that they are considered vulgar, guilt-ridden, or tactless material for discussion. Right or wrong, the size of our income determines many social facets of our living, and that of our families, and our income needs no apology.

Clients resist paying fees for a number of reasons. They have, to begin with, considerable background resentment toward members of the medical profession who they feel have exploited their misery for economic gain. Often the only recourse they have is not to pay the bill. Apparently they do this with great facility if the number of collection agencies in existence is an indication. The therapist is specifically portrayed in movies, television, and novels as a very highly paid person who does very little to earn his pay. Mothers scratch and scrape to provide orthodontia for borderline dental problems in children at fantastic fees. But they will resist needed child psychotherapy until the "last dog is hung."

Some clients really believe therapy is friendship, not a commercial venture but a humane gesture from one well-meaning person to another. In their unconscious, they fully believe their presence alone is its own reward and they are stunned at the size of the fee asked. Also several outstanding psychotherapists who are paid by universities or from research foundation funds have publicly stated their objections to fees of any sort. In my view, a fee is necessary to successful treatment. Further, it is part of the unconditional positive regard of every therapist. Those who deny it have a hidden agenda as to what they want from the client.

It is important, at any rate, that fees not be allowed to arise again and again as the subject of resistance in therapy. For many therapists it becomes a recurring battleground. The wrong campaign is being fought in this instance. An agreement on fees, their amount, how they are to be paid, must be clearly established during the prospecting interview and firmly held to. This is an enforceable contract, and conforms to all of the statutes and stipulations like any other business contract. The therapist must learn to give up his tender feelings concerning fees and be practical and realistic. This clarifies things in the long run. Money is sometimes as much a problem for the therapist as it is for the client. Some of us want a lot of it, and others look down on it as being just a little dirty. However, therapy has to be done in a businesslike way, like law, banking, and engineering. In the long run this is best for both the client and the therapist.

During the prospecting interview, client and therapist agree to work together for a time. Sometime during the hour, the conditions of treatment are discussed. These include things like frequency of visits, time of visits, how cancellations are made, fees, method of payment, health insurance.

Collecting "bad debts" arising from therapy is not good for the client or the therapist. There is no best way to do it, and it leaves a bad aftertaste in many mouths. Most medical practitioners are reconciled to a certain percentage loss in bad debts as a cost of doing business. They raise their fees proportionately. I believe the effective therapist has fewer bad debts than the ineffective one, but this begs the question. My suggestion is that the client not be placed in the position of owing thousands of dollars he cannot pay, or later doesn't want to pay. If collection does come up, the bill should be turned over to the best commercial collection agency available routinely and dispassionately. Some clients probably do not pay other debts as well, so the therapist needn't feel he is being slighted!

GIFTS

Some clients bring gifts frequently and others never offer one. There is no correlation between the service provided and the frequency and value of the gifts tendered. Should a gift from a client always be uniformly accepted or always rejected? Many wealthy clients, or former clients of therapists, have made vast donations to mental hygiene causes. Medicine systematically promotes such gifts, particularly for hospitals. Should we disdain small gifts from grateful clients while accepting sizable ones for the promotion of the overall well being of man?

A gift has to be considered in the light of when it is offered and the background of both the donor and the recipient. There is no absolute rule. Each gift has to be understood for its specific dynamic meaning. I sometimes accept one from a client and then reject a second one from the same client. One brings fruit from her garden, another antiquarian statuary, still another a book, and still another ballet tickets. What determines the gift giving— and its frequency?

I accept a gift when I feel I want one from that particular client, when there is some rational basis for gift giving, and where the dynamic implication of the gift is not counter to the goals of treatment. I myself, on the other hand, have never given a client a gift in more than two decades of practice. Fritz Perls, humorously but bitterly, remarks at one point that he gave his lovely, Junoesque female analyst a gift during his training analysis, and "all he got back was an interpretation."

Clients should get more than an interpretation for their gifts, or they should not be accepted. The gift is a person to person token, a recognition of a kind of friendship, over and beyond the recognition of the professional involvement itself. It can, of course, be a bribe, a guilt-reducing device, and other things as well. Therapy cannot be a primary occasion for gift giving and receiving. But the impulse does come up, sometimes quite often. Much damage can be done by arbitrarily rejecting or accepting such offerings. It is better, in my opinion, to err on the side of acceptance rather than rejection.

ACTING-OUT

Acting-out, as a technical problem, has been overemphasized. There is really less to fear from it than we had supposed. But it is intrusive and time consuming. Also, if it is not handled properly, you may lose your client to institutional forces of one kind or another. Also, intensive forms of therapy make clients susceptible to acting-out. They simply act on latencies long present which are just activated. Such acting-out is often the first sign of a change in the client's life.

We must protect such clients, but I think psychoanalysis overreaches itself in this regard. Life cannot stop because of therapy. The so-called transference neurosis does not change the fact that the client must also get pleasure outside of the consulting room.

Many clients attempt marriage or divorce during therapy, become pregnant, or undergo equally compelling experiences. Others visit surgeons with more than customary frequency or start new business ventures with poor probabilities. It is often apparent that these are ill-advised maneuvers and that if the client will only wait, the probability of success will be improved. But no therapist is omniscient or omnipotent. I do not believe our clients should be enjoined from such behavior. Of course, these things are all grist for the analytic mill, and should be analyzed before and after they occur. Hopefully the client can learn more from his mistakes while he is in therapy!

Acting-out sometimes brings the wrath of the family or community down on the therapeutic participants. How far does the interpersonal therapist go in extricating his client? Does he represent the client in court, or at least talk with the client's attorneys, phone the judge privately, or even testify about the client's less sane aspects? When a client refuses selective service induction, do you help reduce the prison sentence on psychiatric grounds, or help make available more humanitarian services in lieu of imprisonment, or offer mental hospitalization? Does the interpersonal therapist arrange for abortions or vasectomies, or even give information about them? Psychiatry and psychology are extremely powerful today as forces of manipulation. People in authority do listen to us and read our reports. They are also sometimes afraid not to.

Hard-won experience reveals that the therapist should stay out of most of this even though his heart says rush in. The central purpose of interpersonal therapy is to help fulfill the client. This does not include an old-fashioned rescue service. There is no end to it with some clients, and it is invariably fatal to the therapy. Such intervention is the hallmark of the inexperienced therapist. One puts one's moral and humane feelings aside for the moment in light of the truth and value of the more overriding purpose: the total treatment. Clients, in retrospect, approve of our non-intervention. However, there are exceptions, and each case must be examined on its own merits.

INTRUSION OF RELATIVES

No client is an island. Their relatives are very much involved in their condition and their fate. Indeed, relatives feel they have to protect their vested interests. Sometimes these are economic as well as emotional. Therapy is handicapped not only by the client's inherent resistance to cure but by the resistances of his loved ones. Mothers and spouses refuse to yield any increment of intimacy to the therapist. They are suspicious and internally derisive of such efforts. They see themselves as downgraded by it. And, in a sense, they are correct. The outcome of successful psychotherapy may result in divorce half the time.[4] Family therapy recognizes these limitations explicitly and sets out to alter them by total family participation.

It is easy to see why relatives intrude on the treatment. Often this intrusion involves active attempts, even threats, to get the client to discontinue treatment. They noticeably reduce their love for the client to get him to stop coming. The healthier the client becomes, the greater his family's panic and efforts. Many times the relative honestly believes the therapy is not the proper approach for his spouse, or that a different type of therapy is best, or that simply a rest or vacation will do it. They want to take care of the client themselves. In still other instances, family members do not want their own guilt, complicity, or pathological involvement revealed to anyone else. They also fear becoming clients themselves.

When I first began therapy, I refused to talk to relatives who called me on the telephone, particularly when I did not have the permission of the client. I know therapists who still follow this procedure all the time. Today I not only talk to them on the phone but willingly see any relative for a single interview if the client approves. I sometimes see the relative alone or together with the client, whichever seems most helpful. This helps dissipate much of the hidden family hostility to interpersonal psychotherapy, and reassures the relative of the goals of treatment and the process involved. This doesn't solve the problem, but it helps. In marital counseling I often see the married couple together, and each of them individually if it can be worked out. This complicates the straight-forwardness of the dyad, but it helps the client practically in the world he has to live in. Sooner or later he will have to apply new attitudes and feelings to his significant Others. Anything which makes that application easier is beneficial.

The problem when relatives intrude is that they change the object and goals of treatment, or severely delimit them. They say to the client, in effect, "do not go beyond this or you cannot have me."

SOCIAL RELATIONSHIPS

Is it possible to meet clients socially and still carry interpersonal psychotherapy forward to completion? A client with severe schizoid, depressive, and somatizing symptoms finally reaches the point in therapy where she has the ego-strength to plan and give a beautiful cocktail party for office colleagues and new-found friends. She hesitantly asks her therapist to come. Should he go? Another client fortuitously meets his therapist on the streets of San Francisco and asks him to have a drink in a bar. A client learns from the newspaper that his therapist will deliver a paper at a convention in Washington, D.C., where he lives. He invites the therapist to dinner at a posh and delightful place the therapist has always wanted to see. Should all these invitations be refused?

It is, of course, clear that the traditional psychoanalytic aloofness was

---

[4]This figure has been cited by a world-famous psychoanalytic in- and out-patient treatment center.

overdone. It was motivated more by a lack of interest and time for seeing the client outside of the hour than by the real possibilities of damage to his treatment. It is probably true that we would not voluntarily select many of our clients as personal friends in place of those friends we already have. If the therapist has no friends, or cannot stand his own loneliness, and is dependent on his clients in this way, he is not ready to work intensively in treatment situations. But what guidelines can we set for social interaction?

In general, social relationships with a client are to be avoided during treatment. After therapy the client is usually not much interested in seeing the therapist. The reason for this is that therapy does not leave the participants free to be friends. It biases the relationship in many unique directions and limits its freedom. Posttherapeutic social relationships tend to become tense and semi-exploitative. They often cannot exist in and for themselves. Still, some therapists have successfully married their clients or have made life-long friendships with them.

If a social invitation is extended by a client, if the therapist feels like accepting it, and if its rationale is clear and meaningful, the therapist ought to be human about it. I did go to that cocktail party and found it helpful to the lady's treatment. And I enjoyed myself. If, however, the client repeatedly and irrationally seeks social encounters, the client should be referred to someone else.

KEEPING RECORDS

Records about therapy should be kept to a minimum. Some therapists take notes during the interview, some make notes during the break between clients, others tape interviews, and others make notes at the end of the day. My statement that note-taking should be avoided assumes there is no research activity which would require extensive notation.

I recommend minimal record keeping in therapy because the mind becomes highly acute while listening and concentrating on the substance of the hour. It senses, perceives, and organizes in a supra-memorial way that which it needs, then stores it, and returns it when needed. Very little is ever forgotten. If it is, it becomes an object of countertransference. Obsessive note-taking detracts from attention process and interferes with storing and recall of material.

At any rate, supervision and consultation in therapy are best done, not from notes, but in a dialogue in which the therapist's phenomenological and analytic and synthetic functions can be observed. Video tape and other means are now so extensively and cheaply available that notes seem obsolete.

Also, the facts are often less important than nuances of the interpersonal relationship. To buttress such observation there are sometimes the social work anamnesis, medical findings, social welfare information, and collateral information from other sources. Of course, whatever basic documents are required by insurance companies, by law, or by administrative regulation must be kept, but these require little depth.

Interpersonal psychotherapy is a confidential process. It exists by virtue of the fact that there is, in society, a group of people who are privileged to hear what no one else is allowed to hear. Unfortunately law and psychotherapy often disagree about what coheres to justice and what to the individual himself. The nonmedical practitioner has a more ambiguous and difficult role than the psychiatrist who is a licensed doctor of medicine. I recently received a subpoena to present all of my therapy records on a client to an attorney who represented my client's adversary in a civil suit. The client had fallen and injured herself and the adversary believed her psychological incompetence might have induced the fall. I discovered the attorney had the legal right to my records and failure to comply would subject me to a fine or imprisonment.

In this situation, I called the attorney and explained that I kept only financial records on clients and that he was welcome to them. I told him my records were "in my head," and that he could subpoena me, or we could meet and talk informally if he would reimburse me for my time. He was incredulous, but it was true! Often the law stops right there.

It is helpful, however, to make a notation or two on a 3 × 5 card after each hour or two with the client. Often a single sentence suffices. This serves as a stimulus-cue to bring forth all the material about the client in your memory bank should you otherwise fail. It is also helpful periodically to write a detailed case summary of a client tying disparate things together, for self-organizational reasons and not for record purposes.

REFERRALS

Making and receiving referrals is not customarily considered a technical therapeutic problem but it certainly can be. To whom do you refer a client if it becomes obvious you can no longer be helpful or effective? To whom do you refer the spouse or family member of a client when he requests a referral? How do we select a consultant when we need one? (The selection of a consultant is, of course, never accidental. It has both conscious and unconscious determinants.) Do you really want the client to be successful with Dr. Smith when he has failed with you? Is Dr. Smith, doomed to failure, chosen because he is inadequate, so we can show the client we were clearly right? Do we want a consultant who is sympathetic with the technical difficulties we have run into, and the terrible hardships we have had. Or do we want one who is objectively and critically helpful but who is not careful of our vanity? Of course, the reply is always on the side of the angels, but in practice the demons are often involved!

Each therapist should have a standby consultant available, and several additional people he can refer clients to. This panel should not be determined by friendship, hearsay, economics, or convenience but by tested qualification of the therapist himself. I usually ask such people to have lunch with me, outline my philosophy of therapy, ask them for theirs. I tell them the kinds of clients I have, my training background, publications, and ask the referral-therapist-to-be if he would like to reciprocate by giving me information about himself. I sometimes even swim, play cards, or golf with him. I often present several real or hypothetical cases to him and ask how he would handle them. I also inquire about his reputation in the community. In this way I form an opinion of his competence, motivation, personal traits, and his availability for referrals. More often than we know, therapists are not interested in receiving or making referrals. This is true for a variety of reasons, including the fact that the best therapists do not need more clients.

I feel no obligation to accept a client even if he is referred to me by a therapist whose friendship I value highly. The referring source has, of course, to be considered, but it is better to evaluate the client on his own merits. I have, at times, gotten people off the "hook" by accepting such referrals and struggled and regretted it. I always acknowledge, by letter or telephone, my gratitude for the referral and mention the reasons why I can or cannot be helpful.

There are, of course, many other technical or instrumental problems which come up. Most of them can be handled by common sense, therapeutic apperceptive background, or sound business or management judgment. One should not be fearful of looking for outside help if it is needed.

ADJUNCTIVE
HEALING PROCEDURES

IX

It is easy for a therapist to come to feel that the growth of the client will take place in the consulting room with him and nowhere else. He may make some grudging acknowledgement that life goes on outside of the hour, but since he cannot see, experience, or evaluate it directly, he puts it aside. This may be why, for some clients, therapy temporarily becomes their life. The taboo against meeting clients socially may arise from just that confusion of the clients' "two lives" and the need to keep them sorted out.

I believe that a great deal of therapy goes on in between therapeutic hours—I have called this interval therapy—and that this fact should be recognized and used by the therapist.[1] Clients bring to the hour their memory of major achievements or disaffections that have occurred in the interval since their last appointment. But this is always a partial, biased and distorted recall of what occurred. They strive for relevant continuity in their treatment, usually following the design erected by the therapist as most efficient for achieving a cure. But this design is always somewhat short of completion and perfection. Whether we like it or not, therapy is an artificial construct, and the participants themselves are perpetually on guard against each other. Anais Nin was probably correct when she said "Psychoanalysis makes illusory friendships," by which she meant that psychoanalysis could never really take the place of life itself.[2] Any technique, therefore, which helps bridge the gap between the consulting room and the client's living environment is highly useful.

CLIENTS AS WRITERS

Most longer-term clients want, at some point or other in their therapy, to become writers. By this clients mean they want to express something ineffable or inexpressible and to tell it to a wider audience than they currently have. Very few clients ever actually become professional writers, but the need to write does arise as a part of therapy and is supported by it. Thera-

[1]A. Burton, "The Use of Written Production in Psychotherapy," in L. Pearson (ed.) *The Use of Written Communications in Psychotherapy* (Springfield: Charles C Thomas, 1965).
[2]A. Nin, *The Diary of Anais Nin* (New York: Harcourt Brace Jovanovich, Inc., 1969).

pists generally equate personality growth with personal creativity, but we often limit it to a certain very limited type of verbal creativity. Why do we diminish the written word or the picture?

When clients have asked me if they could keep a journal or diary along with their sessions, I have usually agreed for I knew they had something to say they weren't telling me. Over the years, my experience has been that the written and pictorial word does not interfere with the mainstream of therapy. For certain clients, it even facilitates it.

Obviously, not every client can keep a journal, write a poem, or start a novel; but those who cannot, surely can paint something, or mold clay, or smear. Some of our greatest artists expressed their mental conflicts through their art. This is how they were able to remain more or less intact people. I apply some of the same principles to my clients as an adjunct to therapy. Because the written word and the picture are the most available adjunctive media, I want to concentrate on them, although they are merely prototypes for still others.

The written and pictorial communication is as much the client as he is himself. Kafka and Henry Miller can only be Kafka and Henry Miller, and no one else. Artistic productions have two psychological aspects. First, the creation of a work is itself a healing process. Second, the product can be analyzed for psychological meaning, and for insight into the character of the artist, much like a Rorschach Test.

NONVERBAL MODALITIES

The written word is the medium most frequently used as an adjunctive healing procedure, because language is our currency, but it is not the only form. There are also painting, drawing, sculpting, ceramic work, and other plastic media. Among the art forms which may be used are:

1. Journals
2. Diaries
3. Notebooks
4. Letters
5. Autobiographies
6. Poetry
7. Short stories
8. Novels
9. Plays
10. Oral tape recordings
11. Video tape recordings
12. Drawings
13. Paintings
14. Sculptures
15. Ceramic work
16. Metal working

IMAGES AND SYMBOLS

Knapp[3] notes that manifest systems of communication have shadowy and silent counterparts which are little recognized.

> The cardinal vehicle of this inner language can be called images, a term with many connotations. I use as core definition: "a representation . . . or imitation of sensible experience, with or without accompanying feelings, the reproduction or imagination of sensations of sight, touch, or hearing, etc."
>
> Images may translate themselves directly into outer expressive patterns, such as emotional display, pantomime, or the endless variety of art forms. . . . These vary widely in duration, clarity, and intensity. They may be fleeting or sustained over long periods of time. They may be simple and precise, the focus of sharp attention, even part of the most highly developed thought, as is true of a scientific diagram. As mental contents, however, they are more often elusive, and unclear. They may be vivid and evoke a marked response, or they may lurk in the background, dim and almost unnoticed.
>
> "Bleached" in this way, playing an inconspicuous role, the image may still be crucial for one's thought or action that is in the center of the mental stage. Planning a route to be taken or searching for a name in the past, we scan rapidly vague inner maps or collections of dimly recollected contexts, from which we select and articulate precise details. All of this generally happens rapidly outside of explicit awareness.

Images acquire meaning and become organized into symbols which are the vehicles of metaphoric communication. These symbols permit men to abridge the actual motor operation itself, as in language, so that mental life becomes compact and facilitative.

Some symbols are directly tied to events, like the symbolic archetype of the sun (its rise and fall), but most are discursive. A point to point relationship between symbol and event is rarely discovered but may be assigned. This is also true of words, which are symbols tied to action, and mathematical notations which stand for logical and measuring operations.

We are only interested in symbolization as it operates in written and pictorial productions. As vehicles they convey cognitive as well as emotional messages. That is, a painting of Mother releases certain feelings about Mother, through the symbol which represents her. The symbol of the snake comes to represent evil, the snake's dirty work, as well as the phobias associated with snakes and snake-like things in our culture. Life would be impractical and dull if only the snake, and not its symbol, provided the stimulus for evil. Life is symbolization and neurosis is a disorder of symbols and images.

In therapy, it is difficult to discover the repressed symbolism of the person because the process itself has so much of the socially negative built into it. Writing an autobiography or painting a picture breaks the social barrier and reduces the censorship symbols since the product itself is more justifiable as some kind of work of art. People paint gladly, even eagerly, as a hobby, but paint with less enthusiasm as psychoanalysis. An artistic

[3]P. H. Knapp, "Image, symbol, and person," *Arch. Gen. Psychiat.*, 1969, *21*, 392–406.

activity, as ancillary therapy, however, combines the structure of science with the openness of art. How the artistry is actually and expressly coupled to the science is the problem of the therapist.

The unconscious symbolizes things the conscious rejects. A message is an unbelievably complex event which conveys meaning on several levels simultaneously. The hallmark of mental efficiency is not the quantity of symbols but their phenomenal quality. The beauty of a dream is its appositeness for the needs of the dreamer at the moment rather than any of its substantive structure. In therapy we improve the quality of the symbol-making function, and we further release those symbols already blocked and repressed. Interpreting a symbol gives it freedom, but it reduces its capacity to do harm as well.

My theoretical position on symbolization is closer to Jung's than to Freud's. Jung demonstrated that there are universal symbols, which he calls archetypes, and individual symbols peculiar to the time, place, and person. Thought, feeling, and perception are combinations of the two in special matrices. Symbols carry affects and through therapy these symbols can become existential rather than oppressive. In the case of one patient named Renee,[4] an apple came to be a first overture from a subjectively murderous mother who had to be experienced as a good mother, and in no other way. Eckhardt[5] describes how this feels in somewhat general language.

> Change is not premised on insight or on a "know thyself," but on reviving in the patient a sense of being a living organism: a sense of constant change in spite of continuity, on his knowing that maturity of adjustment is not a state of affairs but our ability to find a path when we have lost it, or our ability to heal wounds received and given. Change includes our appreciation that we need to care for what we cherish or desire to come about, otherwise it will deteriorate. Above all there needs to be a meaningful appreciation that, while we are interdependent in our relation to the world (a better word would be "inter-responsive"), this idea includes the premise that the world is also in a state of responsiveness to us.

The vehicles for "being a living organism" are the symbols, images, and affects which give quality and meaning to an otherwise stultified, fixated, and meaningless existence—a neurosis. It is not the dream, picture, or diary which changes one but the fact of having done these things. Clients resist adjunctive procedures much more than they do therapeutic verbalizations because they are genuinely afraid that they will suddenly be precipitated into "wellness"—a condition they are ambivalent about. A client of mine, with severely repressed affect, located considerable amounts of instinctual energy after only six drawings. His surprise and chagrin led him to interrupt therapy; but he will surely return when ready for more affect. A description of his treatment would make a useful contribution to the literature on the

[4]M. A. Sechahaye, *Autobiography of a Schizophrenic Girl* (New York: Grune and Stratton, 1956.) Also *Symbolic Realization* (New York: International University Press, 1951).
[5]M. H. Eckhardt, "Therapeutic perspectives," *Contem. Psychoan.*, 1969, 6, 1–12.

deficiencies of current methods of diagnosing affect and the problem treating clients who lack it.

JOURNALS AND DIARIES

A journal or diary is an intimate communication meant only for the Self. The Self reflects uniquely on itself in this way. For this reason, diaries usually have locks, and journals are usually published posthumously. But each writer has a secret Other for whom he is, indeed, writing. In marital counseling I discovered diaries were invariably found by the spouse from whom they were carefully hidden. This was the unconscious intention, of course. I often considered the consequent upset which prevailed therapeutic. Only the Self can cure itself. While self-analysis is often a fruitless procedure, therapy which does not permit the person his aloneness, working-through in his own special way, is defeating.

ADVANTAGES AND DISADVANTAGES

I have earlier summarized the advantages of written communications and I want to restate them here.[6]

(1) The preparation of a "written production" such as a diary, autobiography, short story, poem, letter, etc., by a client is an expressive and creative act. It both analyzes and synthesizes emotion in a deeply personal way and as such, works counter to repressive and regressing forces in the personality. It is catharsis in the best sense. It heals through its major symbolism—not unlike Greek drama —and because the unexpressible can often be expressed.

(2) The content of the "written production" provides materials for analysis similar to dreams, fantasies, projective tests, and other imaginative productions. The language of the 'written production' is also a source of parapraxes, as are slips of the tongue, forgetting, etc.

(3) "Written productions" further interval therapy by providing *rehearsal* of therapeutic hours. In this way the development of insight and cognition is encouraged. Above all, if the psychotherapist is the respondent of the "written production", his presence in interval-therapy is given a tangible, imaginal form.

(4) A "written production" usually has a wider social base than an individual therapy session. In this sense, it is more outer-directed for it involves family, peer groups, authority figures, etc., in greater quantities than in the sessions. Since society is the place where the client ultimately makes his life, "written productions" permit him a wider social integration of analytic material.

(5) My impression has been that, under certain circumstances, the time required for treatment may be eclipsed by judicious use of "written productions."

(6) Under emergency circumstances of separation of client and therapist, "written productions" have a place along with the telephone, stand-by colleagues, etc.

[6]Burton, "The Use of Written Production in Psychotherapy," pp. 13–14.

The disadvantages of written communications, I said, were the following:

(1) A "written production" displaces the emphasis from the interaction between the client and therapist to a solitary activity away from the therapist. In this way it is dissociating.

(2) Intellect is to some extent subsidized at the expense of affect, and the therapeutic currency becomes ideas instead of feelings.

(3) The therapist may be less inherently creative than his client and be unable to use the medium of "written productions." Conversely, not all clients have the capacity to use written productions.

(4) Writing may be a defense from the honesty of direct confrontation. In this sense it may serve as still another form of resistance.

(5) If a "written production" is helpful, there may be a tendency to assign more and more of the actual therapy to the interval, because of convenience, simplicity, and self-improvement. The theoretical point of absurdity is reached when the patient comes, to all intents and purposes, to be treating himself.

(6) The tone and structure of the psychotherapy may be insidiously altered in the ways explained above.

(7) "Written productions" are imaginal rather than actional. They focus on the interior of the person but externalizing may often be the need at certain stages of treatment. In this sense, introspection rather than integrative action may be promoted.

To this Ellis[7] adds, "The main disadvantages of this kind of written communication, I discovered, were that not as much material was covered when the patient and I were speaking; and, secondly, the patients seemed a little more reluctant to bring out certain aspects of their lives, such as their sex feelings and actions, when they had to write them down on paper than when they could speak them into my ears."

Raimy,[8] in summing-up the shortcomings of written communications, says expression of feeling may be markedly reduced in written material which would defeat the purpose of therapy.

Every candidate for interpersonal therapy has the potential for the use of written or painting communication. In practice, however, they are infrequently clients. The danger is that the verbal will be totally replaced by the nonverbal. Art therapy and bibliotherapy are not, after all, psychotherapy. I have never found them sufficient in and of themselves. If there is danger of diluting the main encounter stream, as happens with some clients, adjunctive therapies should not be used. Who are the clients to which these techniques *do* apply, and under what exact circumstances should they be used?

[7] A. Ellis, "Some Uses of the Printed, Written, and Recorded Word in Psychotherapy," in L. Pearson (ed.). *The Use of Written Communications in Psychotherapy* (Springfield: Charles C Thomas, 1965. p. 25).

[8] V. Raimy, "The Use of Written Communications in Psychotherapy: A Critique," in L. Pearson (ed.) *The Use of Written Communications in Psychotherapy*, 64.

CLIENT INDICATIONS FOR ADJUNCTIVE THERAPY

A. High-Energy Level Clients

Clients come to interpersonal therapy with varying degrees of libidinal energy at their disposal. The range extends from the depressed to the hypomanic. Also, many life styles involve eager and active pursuit and stasis or inactivity exacerbates conflict in people with such styles. These clients have to be doing something. They feel dissatisfied with even four hours of therapy a week—a rare possibility—and need some collateral work in the interval between the hours to feel full.

B. Gifted Clients

Some clients are extraordinarily gifted in general or special intelligence or in selective capacities. They feel their intelligence should not be left out of their treatment. If the therapist fails to acknowledge their gifts, or even to use them in some way, they may eventually discontinue therapy with the feeling they were not basically understood. Some of our greatest artists have reported their psychoanalytic experiences this way. Permitting them to use customary modes of expression as an adjunct to therapy meets a variety of motivational needs and can be curative. When things are seriously blocked in free association, one of my clients brings her cello and improvises for the hour. We then easily move on.

C. Poor Verbalizers

A professor as a client doesn't usually have any trouble with verbalization. His major communication investment is words. But there are clients who are not skilled with words, who are parsimonious and even suspicious of them. People who make their livings by being instrumental instead of verbal are often oriented this way. Adolescents are not sure of their words and prefer the graphic, and the sensorially handicapped need not be excluded from interpersonal therapy because of their handicap. Adjunctive techniques can carry the day in these situations.

D. The Schizoid Client

Schizoid or schizophrenic clients cannot be dumped into a sensitive verbal encounter precipitously. They react by coding their messages even more vigorously than is customary because words are dangerous to them. They are also fearful of their own feelings and of a possible cataclysmic release of these feelings. Permitting clients like this to work along by themselves with some adjunctive mode like sculpting may make the difference in whether or not they can accept therapeutic help.[9]

[9] I have described the treatment of one such client in the following: A. Burton, "The Quest for the Golden Mean: A study in Schizophrenia," in A. Burton (ed.) *Psychotherapy of the Psychoses* (New York: Basic Books, 1961).

E. The Depressed Client

Sometimes clients have insufficient life energy to mobilize their ego for therapy. In extreme cases, this is called depressive psychosis; but total energy blockage is not rare in any therapeutic process. Quite often such an impasse is frightening for the client and it leaves the therapist at wits end as to how to get things moving again. Sometimes, the use of electro-convulsive and medicative therapy by psychiatrists is made necessary by this state.

These clients need to symbolize their guilt rather than speak it. Crucifixion symbols, rebirth images, and peace signs are common in their artistic work which helps them. Adjunctive media again can make or break their interpersonal therapy in times of great stress.

F. Character-Disordered Clients

I have found that people with character and anti-social disorders suffer from a lack of success as few others do. They have very few achievements to point to which receive social recognition in any way. Their childhood is replete with examples of recognition consistently withheld from them or confounded. A drawing or painting they do is a recognition of a socially-approved task and proof they are part of the mainstream. Many have become respected artists and sell their work. In verbal therapy their personality forces them to be deceptive and resistive, but this is not so true in their artistic communications.

WHEN TO APPLY ADJUNCTIVE THERAPY

The proper use of written and painting communication depends a great deal on timing. The problem is something similiar to deciding when dream analysis is to be introduced into therapy proper. I have, in this sense, seen dream analysis which has been more of a hindrance than a help because of its slavish and persistent use at the wrong time. Written and artistic communications function in the same way, and they are elastic forms. They can be introduced and removed at short notice without harm. Here are some suggestions as to when they might be appropriate in interpersonal therapy.

A. Opening or Closing Phases

Written and artistic communications are never indicated in the first third of interpersonal therapy, and only rarely so in the middle part. They are best applied in the latter stages of the process where the final synthesis of image, symbol, idea and affect must occur. They require an interpersonal encounter, and a certain amount of preanalytic work, as a background, before the client will undertake them, and before they can be meaningfully incorporated into therapy.

B. Symbolic Fixations

Many clients bring archetypal fixations to interpersonal therapy. Their central problem may revolve around the animus-anima structure, mother, father, their relationship to terra firma, to the devil, to the hero, to the "wise old man," or to the shadow side of themselves. These universals are invariably expressed symbolically as myths and have cultural forms. Each person must, if he is to be healthy, come to terms with them. When, in therapy, the usual verbal techniques do not lead to archetypal expression and integration, adjunctive methods can be helpful.

C. Transference Regression

The client who needs a transference regression of a very deep kind can helpfully express oral, anal and other pre-genital needs through the "mass" or "mess" quality of paint, clay, and plastics. Since regress is child-being, play materials of this sort are indicated for adults on a regressed level.

D. Over-Aggressive Client

The client who becomes over-hostile and over-aggressive during inter-personal therapy is benefitted by adjunctive communication. Also, the therapist who becomes submerged in counter-hostility can clarify his own feelings through the client's paintings or sculpture. It may be helpful to paint, draw, or sculpt along with client under these circumstances.

E. Total Blocking in Therapy

When therapy is totally blocked, when a consultant does not help, when one is thoroughly disgusted or fed up with the client and himself, having the client write, paint, or sculpt will, almost without fail, provide the answer in the fantasy communication, and allow therapy to proceed on schedule.

So far I have failed to specify how I get my clients to write, paint, or sculpt, and I want to do this now.

First, asking a client to communicate through a painting is not like administering a Rorschach Test to him. There may be a hundred ways of successfully doing the former, but only one prescribed way for the latter. Since the artistic medium is, itself, inherently unstructured, its methodology should always follow this pattern.

I prefer a medium which gives the client the greatest possibilities for expression. This is why I prefer painting to drawing, for example. The client usually selects his own medium and his own form of expression; but if he is a trained artist, I suggest he try a medium he has never before worked with. I limit the cost of materials and suggest the least expensive ones. For written communications, more facility is needed than for painting and this is harder to get into. Notebooks, journals, diaries, among written productions are most helpful because they are most personal. The client may want to write and paint at the same time, but in practice both cannot be done successfully. If the client has strong aspirations to be a writer, even if he has never written, I suggest writing. If he aspires to be a painter or sculptor, I offer that. Whatever the clients prefer, I approve of. Some clients are sure of their interests and know immediately what they want but others have to be urged into some activity.

I try to keep the instructions I give them to a minimum. I say,

> It would be helpful to you and your therapy if you could do some painting (writing, sculpting) for me. We are, of course, not interested in artistic production but merely as an adjunct to your treatment. It often helps to express oneself in this way and any kind of painting is satisfactory. Please get an easel, water (or oil) colors, brushes and paper. You may paint as much as you like but bring only the first one to therapy. Remember, they do not have to be finished products, even a gob of paint thrown on the paper or some hatched lines will do. Try to paint when you are off by yourself. Allow the images to flow freely through your mind and select your theme or no-theme from what seems important to you at the moment. It is usually not a good idea to invite critical comments from your family or from spectators.

The client brings the painting to a regular therapy session and we look at it together. I ask for free associations to it, its meaning, and then do a "testing of the limits." I refrain from making diagnostic judgments or comments about the painting but I may offer an interpretation in relation to the problems currently before us in therapy, particularly if we are having severe hangups. Clients often press hard for comments, as they do with their dreams, but the purpose of the pictorial communication is somewhat different from that of a dream.

Other approaches can be used and wide improvisation is possible. For example, the client can be asked to portray specific feelings. "Paint that murderous feeling; let's see what it looks like on paper." "Paint the loving feeling you have for him."[10] Specific people, or groups of people, or certain objects can be suggested as subjects. A client with latent homosexual feelings painted a series of women. Starting from a gross blob he came finally to portray women of identity. Sometimes color, space, or time are the problems related to the client's personality and these are focused upon.

I rarely ask for more than ten paintings. The client may continue to paint after this but he does not bring them. Sometimes, only three or four paintings are needed, but the client may paint a number of times during the course of a long-term therapy.

In relationship to psychotherapy, the Jungian school has done most to interpret the part symbols play in the human psyche. I can only mention a few common symbols which I have regularly found in the paintings and drawings of my clients.[11]

Animals are frequently depicted in painting and sculpture. Much of man's mythology and culture involves animals. Representations of the demon

---

[10]A recent article on art therapy gives a number of ways painting can be used in group art therapy. Some of their techniques are also adaptable to our situation. Cf., J. M. Denny, and A. C. Fagen. "Group art therapy with university students: A comparative case analysis," *Psychotherapy*, 1970, 7, 164–168.

[11]The reader is referred to the following for a more detailed description of Jungian conceptions of the symbol: C. G. Jung, (ed.). *Man and His Symbols* (New York: Doubleday, 1964).

and of God often assume this form. Animals represent instinct, passion, power, violence, the unconscious, and nature. Even today the study of man is felt by some to be possible only through animals as, for example, in ethology. For some, animals are still pristine while man is corrupted. Animals have no guilt and no neurosis and do not fear death. Animals, we believe, survive eternally as species, but man may die. Thus animals are totemic, demonically palliating, reincarnative, and so forth.

In therapeutic painting and sculpture, the number and kind of animals portrayed, their pose and spatial characteristics, their functions, are all inter-preted against a mythological-instinctual background and against the inter-current needs of the client. This gives the therapist some better idea of the instinctual aspects of the client, and of how he meets them than the spoken word does.

Geometrical forms are commonly found in our paintings and sculpture, as they are in modern art. Jung found that the mandala, intricate combina-tions of angles and circles, are universal in Eastern and Western art. Jaffee[12] explains them this way:

> In the visual art of India and the Far East, the four- or eight-rayed circle is the usual pattern of the religious images that serve as instruments of medi-tation. . . . As a rule, these mandalas represent the cosmos in its relation to divine powers.
>
> But a great many of the eastern meditation figures are purely geometrical in design; these are called Yantras. Aside from the circle, a very common yantra motif is formed by two interpenetrating triangles, one point-upward, the other point-downward. Traditionally, this shape symbolizes the union of Shiva and Shakti, the male and female divinities, a subject that also appears in sculpture in countless variations. In terms of psychological symbolism, it ex-presses the union of opposites—the union of the personal, temporal world of the ego with the non-personal, timeless world of the non-ego . . . The two interpenetrating triangles have a symbolic meaning similar to that of the more common circular mandala. They represent the wholeness of the psyche or Self, of which consciousness is just as much a part as the unconscious.

The circle and square are recurrent motifs and some modern painters, Klee and Mondrian specifically, portray feeling in this way primarily. Jungians believe the circle represents the psyche, and the square (and rectangle) the earthbound matter, body, and reality. Circles and squares together are the relationship of body to mind, soul to matter, and so forth.

These are merely illustrations of the way analysis of non-linguistic forms can proceed in therapy. It is not intended, however, that the learner will go this far in adjunctive therapy unless he is so inclined by will, training, and interest. Expression of the symbol alone, without tight analysis is often suffi-cient to achieve therapeutic effects.

A diary may be written for years, not necessarily as a part of therapy. Written communications are clumsier to handle than painting or sculpting. Also, they are usually available in greater abundance which can be a handi-

---

[12]A. Jaffe, "Symbolism in the Visual Arts," in C. G. Jung (ed.) *Man and His Symbols.*

cap. As a rule, none of the client's productions should be taken home by the therapist since he rarely gets to them. They should be studied in the office and I often use my break between clients for reading the productions or studying the paintings. (Sometimes I just never get around to them but I know that the client's doing them is more important than my studying them.)

I make no attempt to analyze every detail of the written communication or the painting. This cannot, and possibly need not, be done. After all, this is not art diagnosis or art therapy. Casting the communication in the verbal mold defeats the adjunctive mode and most of the ego-synthesizing which goes on when one writes, paints, or sculpts. Analysis must not totally divorce the art from the adjunctive medium.

For the most involved and difficult clients, adjunctive therapy may be the difference between success and failure. The learner will want to try it and test it for himself and come to his own conclusions about its efficacy. Again, there is a danger of overdoing adjunctive therapy since it generates so much enthusiasm.

USEFUL
POLYADIC VARIATIONS

X

Interpersonal psychotherapy recognizes the important contributions made to therapeutic practice by group methods. It does not consider group therapeutic approaches competitive with individual therapy but rather coordinate with it. They are often an asset. Steinzor[1] believes the dyad is itself a group of two, so that the classical distinction between individual and group therapy is, perhaps, overstated. Some therapists routinely ask their clients, at some stage in their treatment, to participate in a group the therapist leads. Others are more cautious with such collateral treatment and, without forbidding it, do not encourage it. Still others find it obstructs therapy and seriously depletes the energies they feel should be applied to the primary therapeutic relationship.

The purpose of this chapter is to make clear when a group experience may be curatively justified in interpersonal psychotherapy, and the major forms such experience might be expected to take. *Classical group therapy, family therapy, the basic encounter group,* and *transactional analysis (Berne)* are singled out for discussion from among literally a hundred other possible group approaches. All therapeutic group approaches have common theoretical substrates, so these examples should suffice. As I see it, no psychotherapist is completely trained until he has had some experience with therapy in groups. With this background, interpersonal psychotherapy can seldom become parochial, inbred, or totally abstract.

Interpersonal psychotherapy finds that group therapeutic experiences can be particularly helpful in several areas of treatment. Dyadic therapy can, of course, accomplish the same ends, but they are often facilitated and achieved more economically through the dynamics of group action. Groups can sometimes be harmful, depending on a host of factors. It has to be left to the individual therapist to decide when and where a group experience should or should not enter interpersonal psychotherapy. The following situations offer an invitation to a group process of one kind or another:

[1]B. Steinzor, "On n+1 Person Groups," in A. Burton (Ed.), *Encounter. Theory and Practice of Encounter Groups* (San Francisco: Jossey-Bass Publishing Co., 1969).

ACTING-OUT

Classical forms of individual psychotherapy, including psychoanalysis, set severe limits on acting-out. Acting-out is considered extreme resistance—a flight from treatment. Psychotherapy calls for thinking about and symbolizing the wish and impulse, not acting on them directly—at least not until a certain preparation in therapy makes the behavior less risky. Acting-out is, therefore, universally recognized as impulsion, lack of control, displacement, and denial.

I have earlier said[2] that acting-out, and what I call living-out, do not necessarily interfere with treatment, but may be necessary parts of it. I have been concerned with what seems to be a phobia among psychotherapists about acting-out, and the urgent need for passivity and quietism on the part of our clients. Of course, acting- and living-out can, and often do, interfere with the orderly process of interpersonal therapy. Sometimes they even lead to termination of therapy. But group experiences reveal that acting-out and living-out are not as damaging as has been supposed. Some clients need to act- and live-out, or they cannot come to a final conclusion of their treatment. Such behavior need not be catastrophic—suicidal, homicidal, criminal, or immoral—if clients are given an opportunity to express elemental and increasing gradients of living in an accepting atmosphere. The interpersonal psychotherapist cannot always provide a setting for acting-out in this way. He may be fearful of it, or unable to control it. This is where participation in a group can help. More acting-out and living-out is possible in groups, and they are much less destructive in a group situation than in an individual one. Indeed, a group therapeutic situation is, by definition, living-out. Growth in groups cannot come without such living and acting. To act-out atrociously with the therapist alone is often to destroy the transferential relationship. Most certainly this will bring the family or community into the treatment in an untimely and awkward way. But it can almost never damage group therapy this much. Transference is not the central factor in the group as it is in the dyad. Groups protect their members from damage. They also reduce the members' need to go against authority and its mores by offering satisfactory alternatives. Groups are designed to encourage getting on from day to day and they are much less involved with classical dynamics and deep interpretations. The here-now, feeling and behavior, the intercurrent, is the currency of the group. The self and its conscious reflections, rather than unconscious conflict, tend to govern. Groups are less morally weighted. This is why group members act-out with each other without basically damaging their treatment. Clients with strong social needs and impulses, which they have to act on, are wisely referred to a coordinate group for a limited period of time so that the energy behind the impulse can be drained. Meanwhile, the client brings to interpersonal psychotherapy the meaning of the acting-out.

[2]A. Burton, *Modern Humanistic Psychotherapy.*

GROUP EGO

Every group I have been a part of impressed me with the strength of its Group Ego, a strength which went way beyond the sum of the individual egos. I do not know what a Group Ego is. At best it is a metapsychological construct, but it is certainly related to the force and behavior of collectives. It is not to be found through taking member by member as a summation of force. Suggestion, persuasion, reinforcement schedules, common goals, hope, idealization, leadership, and identified common suffering are all factors which have something to do with Group Ego, but they do not explain it. The Group's Ego draws forth the members' individual egos and helps reinforce them in some yet unknown way. In the union of similars there is strength, and collectives have changed the behavior of individuals as well as nations. This group principle has recently received great impetus from Synanon, Alcoholics Anonymous, Weight Watchers, and similar groups, which have demonstrated surprising effectiveness in altering habitual and refractory behavior. Possibly the Group Ego draws power from the identification of parts and wholes of members with each other. All this is done in a proto-magical or transformation-possible setting of hope, example, and impetus which the client less frequently finds in the dyadic situation. Most clients are eager to join a therapeutic group, or an encounter group, but they uniformly shy away from individual therapy. They feel easier throwing their lot in with common sufferers in an attempt to find a common solution instead of submitting the problem to authoritative or definitive resources.

Referral to a group is indicated when strong character elements resist transferential analysis and when insight and group work can proceed along with interpersonal psychotherapy without conflict.

INFORMATION GIVING

It is difficult, and often unwise, to give direct information in interpersonal psychotherapy if for no other reason than that the client doesn't truly want it. He accepts information more readily from a group, or in a group. Groups have tremendous linguistic traffic, and much of it is informational rather than symbolic. The neurotic person's ignorance of the basics of life is appalling and in paradoxical contradiction to his fine intelligence. Embattled married people, for example, often lack information about basic biology, personality structure, sexual function, economics, child rearing practices, community resources, and many other things. There is, perhaps, a selective disperception mechanism which operates to preserve our clients' social naivete. One does not need to be a well-informed person to be non-diseased or fulfilled, but a certain minimum of critical information is necessary for achieving intimacy and successful social living. Lack of information is apparently the reason the mentally deficient are never stellar social lights, in my experience.

The group pools and shares its personal and social knowledge, takes wider risks with it, and makes it more immediately relevant than does the dyad. The material of interpersonal psychotherapy is, of course, not irrelevant, but it is relevant on a deeper level, and perhaps less immediately instrumental than group therapy.

CONFRONTATION

Directive and explosive confrontation in dyadic therapy is difficult, sometimes unpleasant, and fortunately rare. In group therapy it is frequent, a part of the therapeutic currency, and easily surmountable. The marathon encounter is the best example today of directive confrontation for therapeutic purposes. Synanon is another outstanding example.

There is nothing special or unique in such confrontation, and justifying an encounter group merely on this basis seems specious. Confrontation takes place all the time in interpersonal psychotherapy, and therapy is, by definition, confrontation with the Self. But there are some clients—possibly even more of them than we know—who can never bring themselves to hostile accusation and showdown in the dyad but who still need the clarification and release which come from a toe-to-toe battle with another. The sudden burst of emotional energy—its life or death quality—seems to provide something the slow sustained release of affect in dyadic therapy does not provide. I have been astonished when clients I had seen individually for as long as 100 hours brought forth cathartic material in group encounters which I had not even begun to appreciate as part of their psyches in interpersonal psychotherapy. Ours is a process of gentle violence. Complexes need to burst their boundaries from time to time, and this form of confrontation is their phenomenological manifestation. There may also be neurophysiological equivalents involved, correlated with psychic outbursts and release, which involve the autonomic nervous system.

The group process lends itself admirably to directive confrontation. Total disclosure is not only accepted but expected. No individual disclosure can produce rejection no matter how bizarre or frightful it may seem. The group, as a microsociety, absorbs the hostility, pain, and gaucherie of confrontation with little damage. It supports the client, and even rewards him by recognition for the deed. In the dyad, confrontation becomes personalized, and the need to destroy is increased. No therapist welcomes explosions and the possibilities of injury or termination of treatment. The danger in dyadic direct confrontation is a documented fact.[3]

Referral to a coordinate group is advisable when the client's mobilized energy is not finding a proper outlet, when the transference is too great or too little for proper pacing of the client's advance from introspection to object libido, or when the social limitations of culture (as in the young) interfere with the orderly process of interpersonal psychotherapy.

SOCIAL TECHNIQUES

Clients, by definition, lack social graces and social "know how." Their neuroses inhibit them from doing the socially correct thing. Probably they

[3]W. Freeman, *The Psychiatrists* (New York: Grune & Stratton, 1968).

were not permitted to learn such matters in childhood, either because of a lack of a model or because permission of the family was not given. Clients have technical problems making dates as well as emotional problems. Often, they just don't know how to do it. One can go far in our society with proper social modes and courtesies, and in the face of the most extraordinary handicaps, but lack of social techniques adds to the burden of people's neuroses. Many clients can profit from modeling schools, service clubs, and similar social organizations. Through them, they learn social and facilitative customs they somehow missed along the line. The therapeutic group observes similar social amenities and members are not excused from these amenities because of their illness. The group reforms the barbarian and tutors him in better ways of gaining social ends.

The client soon finds accepted social techniques offer an orderly and more satisfying mode of self-expression, that this is the way society works, and that he should identify with it. He becomes more socialized as a result. Observations of therapeutic groups reveal that this form of tuition is an ever-lasting part of their work but a demeaned and overlooked one.

BODY TOUCHING

Almost two millenia of Judeo-Christian doctrine has created a modern-day dissociation between body and mind—with the body considered demonic and the mind considered saintly. Lowen[4] offers the best contemporary description of this malady but, his correctives need buttressing. Therapy brings with it a need to "touch" and "be touched," to be one with the Other. This is rarely permitted in dyadic therapy for legal, technical, and social reasons. But the client's need is still there, and symbolizing or analyzing it doesn't always suffice. Clients need to rediscover their bodies.

The therapeutic group, with its wider limits for risk taking, allows and even encourages touching and somehow removes the sexual-legal stigma. The encounter group, particularly, focuses on body awareness and response. Freud, while he regularly shook hands with his patients, and even stroked their foreheads on occasion, did us a disservice by indirectly sexualizing "touch" in psychotherapy. There are, actually, many kinds of "touching," and tactility, while sensual, need not be sexual. Non-verbal methods have been slighted in psychotherapy but they are now undergoing a renascence since we have come to understand that language can deceive while it enlightens. Tactility is more straightforward. Some people go through their entire lives seldom touching others, or only touching others in perverse ways. The therapeutic group approaches tend to correct this tactile deficiency and make body intimacy more open and possible. Many clients, somewhere in their treatment, feel themselves all over, or specialize in certain parts. This is the first time they have realized their body as such, strange as it sounds.

---

[4]A. Lowen, *The Betrayal of the Body* (New York: Macmillan Company, 1967). See also his *Love and Orgasm* (New York: Macmillan Co., 1965); and *Physical Dynamics of Character Structure* (New York: Grune & Stratton, 1958).

When the client's bodily needs are overriding, when his body image needs immediate bolstering, when his body demands direct nurturance, a coordinated group therapeutic approach can be helpful in achieving something that is done only with greater difficulty dyadically.

FOUR GROUP THERAPEUTIC APPROACHES

I come now to the four heuristic examples of therapeutic groups beginning with classical group therapy, that is, simultaneous therapy with more than one person at a time.

Group Therapy

Group therapy is the oldest form of polyadic therapy and has many styles, forms, and structures. It can have a single leader, multiple leaders, and even be leaderless. Group therapy can vary from the offering of didactic lectures to psychodrama to psychoanalysis to family therapy. These all involve therapy with more than two people at a time, but with identical goals and philosophical substrate of psychoanalysis proper, psychodrama, family therapy, and so forth. All group therapeutic approaches have their time and place, and all have a certain effectiveness. Any theory of healing can be applied to groups, and any setting, from the mental hospital to the community clinic, to private practice, is an adaptable one. Group therapy is usually well tolerated by clients and even refractory psychotics, sociopaths, and others respond to it in some fashion.

Group therapy is always less intensive and deep than dyadic therapy but it may be more socially relevant since it is collective. The emphasis is less on the historical regressed person and more on the current Self and its problems. It tends to emphasize the "wellness" of the person, what he can do, while dyadic therapy more or less focuses on the disabilities of the client and his consequent helplessness. Group therapy rejects labels for behavior, and action, rather than ideation, is the transaction. This does not mean there is no obsessive introspection in groups, but rather that the group is more hospitable to molar behavior than it is to continued inward looking. The group therapist is less able to dominate the group and project his own training biases and interests on it. In many groups, he simply becomes another member without extraordinary privilege. In this way he becomes part of the Group Ego and sets his own aside.

Yalom[5] sees the curative aspects of group therapy as falling into the following ten special categories.

1. Imparting of information
2. Instillation of hope
3. Universality

[5]I. D. Yalom, *The Theory and Practice of Group Therapy* (New York: Basic Books, Inc., 1970).

4. Altruism
5. The corrective recapitulation of the primary family group
6. Development of socializing techniques
7. Imitative behavior
8. Interpersonal learning
9. Group cohesiveness
10. Catharsis

This seems to me to be an excellent framework for exploring the topic.

Imparting Information I have already mentioned that group therapy is a source of information about the Self and Other, and about the society in which ones lives, in a way that differs from the dyadic model. I fully agree with Yalom that clients in group therapy "learn a great deal about psychic functioning, the meaning of symptoms, and the process of psychotherapy." This learning is more observational than reflective, more interactive than incorporative, more conscious than subconscious. Giving information in a way designed to encourage learning, or leading a group member to new information, is one of the primary purposes of any group. Even psychoanalytic group therapy, which more or less preserves the passive stance of psychoanalysis itself, gives more information in groups than psychoanalysis normally does. Learning in groups takes place essentially by passing information from a knowledgeable member to the one needing knowledge. It's a form of primitive and elementary social tutelage by example. The information need not come from the therapist, for the clients themselves have a surprising amount of knowledge at their disposal. The therapist's function is rather to see that what is exchanged is not misinformation, or unusable information. There is a trend today to reestablish the value of the cognitive and the group illustrates this very well.

Instilling Hope Hope as a concept is returning to therapy. Eric Erickson,[6] J. D. Frank,[7] and Melges and Bowlby,[8] among others, have recently written about it, and this is something of a departure from their earlier psychological conceptualizations. It seems ironic that something as self-evident as hope now has to be acknowledged as a factor in therapy. Despite their basic pessimism, therapists are a hopeful lot. Why else should they spend the major part of their waking time with people who, indeed, resist their cure? Both Freud and Jung were this kind of hopeful-pessimist. Full-time therapists have to fight constantly against their negative, depressed feelings in order to provide a beacon of hope for their clients. Without hope no treatment can succeed. I have found it helps occasionally, if the therapist can

[6]E. H. Erickson, *Insight and Responsibility* (New York: W. W. Norton and Co., 1964).
[7]J. D. Frank, "The role of hope in psychotherapy," *Intern. J. of Psychiat.*, 1968, *5*, 383–395.
[8]F. T. Melges, and J. Bowlby. "Types of hopelessness in psychopathological process," *Arch. Gen. Psychiat.*, 1969, *6*, 690–699.

write a poem, make excellent love, stay briefly in another culture, or himself master a crisis of some moment. The therapist must daily confirm the beauty of existence. This was Camus' message basically.

By some strange trick of fate, clients are sometimes more hopeful about themselves than their therapists, even though they may have no right to be. Perhaps this is because they cling to their illusions and fantasies and will not recognize clinical realities. Hope was ever thus! But we are a pathology-oriented profession. It is through pathology that we find our professional identities. One of the prime achievements of the therapeutic group is to offer its members hope by example and by word. (The sometime presence of an alumnus in the group is a hopeful charge unequalled by any other.) The group will not—cannot—accept the idea of incurable mental illness. It, perhaps, has a better sense of the normative than the therapist has. The fact that clients are in the group, and that they sustain their membership in the group, is immutable proof that they are hopeful. I have even seen manic-depressives, who felt totally worthless in their despair, react salubriously to the spirit of hope in group therapy when nothing else would work with them.

Universality By universality I mean we are all part of the human condition, and that anxiety, obsession, compulsion, depression, dissociation, denial, and somatizing, are in the public domain. Clients are always guarding "secrets" about their Furies. Masturbation, for example, was once in this category. Secrets use up energy, are a source of guilt, and build up the distances between people. They also have a way of growing, by accretion, to mountainous proportions. Every client believes his demons are unmatched by anyone else's. This may be an arrogant form of narcissism, but the client is confident and fearful of his distinction.

Group therapy allows the walled-off and secretive client to compare notes in a supportive climate. The first game played in the group is, "I am sicker than you are." Our clients have somehow gotten the notion, and we have possibly conveyed it to them, that every fibre of them is sick, and that they are incapacitated all over. Nothing is further from the truth. Group therapy demonstrates to the person that only part of him is sick, and it's not his symptoms that count but what he does with them. Psychic symptoms, by themselves, are not illness or incapacity. Only the response to these symptoms is sick. Clients cautiously compare "secrets" in the group and find that thoughts about incest, bestiality, murder, and cannibalism are not as unique as they had supposed. They find that the harboring of the "secret" is the illness, and I have seen tears and laughter when clients discovered this and were then able to go on to important life matters.

Altruism It is probably true that very few people get a chance to intimately help others in today's world, but everyone wants to or needs to. Philanthropy is automated. The motives which drive us to become therapists must also operate in clients to make them want to heal people. The impulse to offer nurturance, help the sick, and be a brother is deeply ingrained in the Judeo-Christian ethic. We still very much live by it. Group therapy offers the opportunity to express this need, to be a healer at the same time. If one can heal others, then one is not so sick after all! Certainly the healer must first heal himself as Aesculapius and Hippocrates knew so well.

Family Group Recapitulation　It has not seemed to me, in my group therapy work, that the group became a family surrogate with any great regularity. While certain members can—and do—serve as father- and mother-figures, or as siblings, this is only an *ad hoc* occurrence. Most groups do not take up family analysis on any consistent, deep level unless they are specifically directed this way. Family therapy, of course, has this as its special exemption and function.

Any group of people meeting regularly together, or related in some way, can be called a family because a certain familial structure exists in such gatherings. What distinguishes a client-family from the pedestrian family is the relevance of the family for life or death. The quality of its members' existence hangs upon it. I do not find this in ordinary group therapy, so that the family is not often a duplicate of the original, and only possibly a very mild surrogate.

Socializing Techniques　I have already mentioned the socializing aspects of groups in an earlier paragraph. It is only necessary to say that people with problems allow themselves very little opportunity for social learning. They fear rejection and failure in a terror-stricken, abject way. Under the aegis of the group, they can make mistakes in a more hospitable climate, and learn from them. Frustration is, for once, not socially reinforced. People in therapy are usually what we call middle class, and they pay much attention, in one way or another, to custom and manners. They were basically reared in a tradition of gentility and feel uncivilized without the courtesies. They have only to feel free to develop a humanistic approach to people and the group often makes this possible.

Imitative Behavior　The role of imitation as a causative explanation of behavior has been played down the past five decades. At one time it was the cornerstone of psychological theory, but today we speak rather of modeling, suggestion, persuasion, and more dynamic imitative concepts in place of raw copying. The notion of imitation dies hard.

It is often startling to see a client assume the postures, mannerisms, and even goals of his therapist. Of course, somewhere along the line, as I have said, he wants to become a therapist as well. Clients do imitate, model after, identify with, and introject their therapists. This is a fundamental psychological process, and may even make therapy possible to begin with. Most of it occurs on a level below conscious awareness, but some of it is deliberate. We want to—or have to—become like those we love or hate. In group therapy, modeling and introjection occurs less frequently and less intensively, but on a wider, more dispersed basis since more figures to introject and model on are available. There is a kind of perceptual sorting process which operates continuously. The client takes what he needs in the way of models from other group members and, at the same time, serves as a model for those who need him. This can occur on a piecemeal basis in place of total introjection of a personality.

Interpersonal Learning   This group factor is the general basis for this book and needs no specific elaboration. I want to say, however, that therapeutic groups justify themselves almost entirely on the basis of interpersonal learning, whereas dyadic therapy has this strength and more. Since all behavior is ultimately referrable to social collectives, and is validated there, group therapy is a major arena where the interpersonal details of a social microcosm can be explored and worked through. Of course, this happens in the therapeutic dyad as well, but the group is particularly well adapted for it and the dyad and polyad can be used together for greatest effectiveness. We tend, today, to use the concept of interpersonal learning as a better way of describing what happens when two people encounter each other for therapeutic purposes. Certainly both learn something from each other, and they apply this learning to still other dyads and polyads in their world.

Group Cohesiveness   The work of Alcoholics Anonymous, Synanon, Weight Watchers, and Parents Without Partners, is a testimonial to the effectiveness of a group cohesion factor which reinforces will and personality in group change. Indeed, their success is so amazing as to have been unpredictable. None of us could have foreseen the vast proliferation of such self-help organizations.

Psychiatry has probably underestimated the ambivalence and hostility its clients feel for it. This is something Freud understood best of all. The lampooning the profession receives in the public media indicates this ambivalence. One reason for it may be the distinctions therapists make between clients and themselves, sometimes unknowingly of course, giving the profession the appearance of a Brahmin or secret caste, as if its members were party to the forbidden aspects of life. An insight into this is given by Wheelis,[9] who, in fictional form, comments on his personal feelings toward his clients and his deep feelings about himself as analyst. Despite fine intentions, the rift between the two is startling. Freud, as far as I know, only infrequently commented publicly or in his letters about how he felt about specific patients. I gather, however, that at times he became rather exasperated with them, and thought them a dull, resistive, and sometimes cowardly lot. It is not easy to stop judging clients. Would they come to us if we didn't offer them a platform of power and privilege?

Very little of this social structuring can happen in group therapy for a true equality exists between group members. The group's cohesiveness factor is based on the fact that all clients are in the same boat together, and the boat has the same leak. If the therapist is a true member of a group, he is merely a part of it. Nothing communicates like common suffering. Helping someone is, in a sense, helping yourself, and loving someone is similarly loving yourself. The group focuses on the common suffering identity and

[9]His latest work is *The Desert* (New York: Basic Books, 1970).

doesn't need an historic power basis to implement change. This does not mean group members do not hate, fight, or want to destroy each other, but theirs is a hatred within a special loving and understanding context. This is the cohesiveness of belonging. The group, therefore, coheres or it stops being a therapeutic group.

Catharsis   Catharsis is, of course, the ages-old psychic principle which Freud made the keystone of his psychoanalytic treatment system. Repressions hide us from ourselves and we need to rid ourselves of them. Catharsis certainly functions in every therapeutic setting, and the question here is merely as to the difference between catharsis in the dyad and in the polyad.

Before a client can get rid of mental debris, he must first have an overriding need to expel it, as well as an opportunity to do so. No one defecates on a public highway unless he is *in extremis*. The combination of dyad and the polyad can provide an ideal setting for catharsis. It seems paradoxical but a person will often make a group confession when he cannot make an individual one. In the history of man, a host of psychoanalysts and priests have been deceived by this fact. Most religious conversion experiences take place in a group setting, where the "testimony" is a public confession and restitution is openly promised. This is the basis of Billy Graham's revival practice. His converts are legion and I sometimes envy him. I have, myself, seen my clients cathart in a group repressed material, or more relevant versions of it, which they could not, or would not, give me alone. I have wondered about this since rapport was dyadically at its maximum. The catharsis of the encounter (and sensitivity training group) is similar, and it always seems more heavily freighted with content than in my consulting room. Considerable pressure is placed on members to "make a clean breast of it . . . You will feel better if you do and you will be helping the rest of us." This form of disclosure and honesty becomes the basic morality of the encounter group. Clients who join are prepared for it although they may be similarly afraid to disclose themselves.

Resistance and covertness are easier in interpersonal psychotherapy. It is easier to keep things and events from the Self and from the therapist, because such secretiveness is the earliest growth model. None of us recalls much about our childhood. But why not? If childhood were a uniformly happy time, would we not know more? It is harder to regress with a group. If one wants to be an intrinsic member of the group, he cannot play the resistance game he played with his mother and plays with his therapist. Of course, the group catharsis is never as deep or as integrative as the interpersonal one. By itself it often does not cure. But it is an important beginning. The group quickly discovers repression and deals harshly with the deceiver, while we are more understanding and humanistic.

Most clients ask their therapist about joining a group, particularly since encounter groups have become so popular. The interpersonal psychotherapist should explain his concept and feelings about group approaches, their indications and counter-indications in his particular treatment forms. The client should not be brushed off, otherwise he will join a group without consultation—and he may do so even with consultation. Sometimes it may be the therapist who will bring up the idea of joining a group as possibly valuable and it should then be thoroughly aired.

Whether or not group therapy is advisable must be left to the judgment and intuition of the therapist. But the following criteria indicating potential usefulness of group experience may be helpful:

(a) If the insight attained is at a high level but the client is unable to make social use of it.

(b) If acting-out, or sociopathic propensities, appear suddenly in treatment and threaten to terminate long-standing therapy.

(c) If the client needs to learn actual social techniques and modes of recruiting and getting along with people.

(d) If the loneliness of the client is such that he needs people acutely, any and all people, to feel human membership and the dyad is not most helpful at the moment.

(e) If the client has overweening altruistic needs he is satisfying in the wrong way, or is unable to satisfy at all.

(f) If the client needs affectional body support of a kind which goes beyond the possibilities of interpersonal psychotherapy at the time.

(g) If the client needs to have family or other supportive or hindering members present in his therapy.

(h) If the client has an unusual number of ego-game behaviors which lend themselves to quick and commonplace scrutiny.

(i) If the client needs direct social information he cannot get in certain ways from the interpersonal psychotherapist.

I want to repeat, at the risk of being boring, that none of these indications, or all of them collectively, apply in dogmatic fashion. They must be weighed against the pros and cons of the individual interpersonal therapeutic situation itself. In my opinion, group therapy is often not determinative, merely facilitative in the cure, so group experiences will not suffice in and of themselves. There are also multiple therapist models which offer great advantages.

Conjoint Family Therapy

Conjoint family therapy arose from the pragmatic demonstration that families often undo the work of interpersonal psychotherapists. This is particularly dramatic and visible in the case of the psychotherapy of schizophrenic patients. Some important theoretical constructs for personality have grown out of this work. One such construct is that the family, and not the person, is the dynamic unit of health and illness and treatment is by family. (This includes the extended family as well.[10]) It also appears that some fami-

[10]N. W. Bell, "Extended family relations in disturbed and well families," *Fam.-Proc.*, 1962, *1*, 15–193.

lies have unconscious needs to designate "victims" from among their members, and to "sanctify" still others as a way of maintaining family stability.[11] The fate of the family depends on these designated individuals. Fathers, in family therapy, reveal a "passivity-within-aggressivity," which may lead to a new hypothesis of fatherhood, at least in some families. They are uniquely socially important and successful men. Mothers of these families are apparently the carrier wave of family communications—traffic managers, if you will—and the "noise" they sometimes make in the communication system consists of double-binds and similar garbled or contradictory messages. Achievement is simultaneously demanded and disapproved; affection is similarly demanded and disapproved; and so forth. In essence, the family pathogen is that the client cannot label critical family situations with any precision, nor can he respond directly to affective situations which affect his welfare. An example of a family in which this is beautifully demonstrated is given by Jackson and Yalom.[12] The basic technique of unraveling such family problems was developed by Virginia Satir[13] and others. But Bell[14] puts it this way.

> Different researchers have focused upon different aspects of the patterns of interaction, some emphasizing the persistent structural features, others the nature of communication process, still others the discordance between overt behavior and inner feelings. Common to all appears to be some conception that, as a group, the family must try to adapt to the discrepancies within and between individuals and reach some equilibrium.

It is difficult to describe how family therapy heals to someone who has never participated in it. To a considerable extent, it happens so quickly and so much takes place at once that it defies adequate notation. For these and other reasons family therapy is more intuitive than other therapies. If one had to wait for the intellect to guide its tactics the critical moment would be lost again and again. The therapist, often to his chagrin, gets highly involved as an *ad hoc* family member. Perhaps the best way to describe it is to offer Ackerman's[15] natural history of a family in homeostatic difficulty.

> *Disturbed families tend to break up into warring factions.*
> a. Each family member allies himself with one or the other of the factions.
> b. Each faction competes for dominance.
> c. Each faction represents a preferred family identity and value system relating to goals, role expectations, and role complementarity.

[11] Ackerman calls the latter "healers." But in my experience they are "children who can do no wrong" who are exempted in some way from the family paradoxes to which the others are subjected.

[12] D. Jackson, and I. D. Yalom. "Conjoint Family Therapy as an Aid in Intensive Psychotherapy," in Burton, A. (ed.), *Modern Psychotherapeutic Practice* (Palo Alto: Science and Behavior Books, 1965).

[13] V. Satir, *Conjoint Family Therapy* (Palo Alto: Science and Behavior Books, 1964).

[14] N. W. Bell, *Extended family relations in disturbed and well families, op. cit.*

[15] N. W. Ackerman, "Prejudice and Scapegoating in the Family," in G. H. Zuk and I. Boszormenyi-Nagy (eds.), *Family Therapy and Disturbed Families* (Palo Alto: Science and Behavior Books, 1967).

d. Each faction attaches specific meaning to individual differences and organizes around them specific devices of prejudicial scapegoating.

A leader emerges in each faction.

a. Each leader epitomizes the family identity and values of his faction.

A particular family member is chosen as the victim of the prejudicial attack.

a. Some individual quality of this member becomes a symbolic expression of a perceived threat to the family on the part of one of its factions.

A defensive counterattack is mobilized.

a. The scapegoat allies himself with another family member and asserts an opposed form of prejudice.

b. To the extent that this defensive alliance succeeds, the primary scapegoat minimizes his own injury at the expense of another. He may shift from the role of scapegoat to the role of persecutor.

c. To the extent that this defensive alliance fails, the primary scapegoat finds himself undefended and alone.

   (1) He becomes progressively more vulnerable and may suffer a breakdown.

   (2) He shifts to the role of healer; if this succeeds, he may nullify or reduce his vulnerability.

A member of the family unconsciously is selected as the "healer."

a. He provides the emotional antidote to the destructive effects of the prejudicial assault.

b. He may be motivated to accept this role because it offers the protection required for his own safety.

The health-sickness continuum is influenced by the shifting balance of the effective struggle between factions toward:

a. Entrenchment of valid values of family identity and equilibration of family functions that enhance genuine loyalty, sharing, and growth.

b. Entrenchment of progressive, irrational, competing prejudices, tightening of family organization, and constriction of roles that reduce emotional nourishment of all members.

Such a family sees a threat when one of its members enters therapy and it protectively attempts to undo the therapy if it can. Fortunately, this is not true of all families. We do not know in advance which family contains this kind of organization. Families with non-achievers, delinquents, and schizophrenics have been found to have such family homeostatic problems, but the structure certainly goes way beyond this and may even be a general principle. When is it useful to employ a family therapy model as an adjunct to interpersonal psychotherapy?[16]

Many times the client's inability to move from a plateau in therapy brings up the question of family threat or family undoing if he is successful. Under such circumstances, one may be forced to see other family members, at least for a single interview, or risk having the therapy go down the drain. There have also been therapeutic situations in which the client was forbidden to come and financial as well as emotional support was withdrawn. The therapist may suddenly be seen as an unsavory or malevolent character. At times like this, with the concurrence of the client, I may see the significant nurturing person, either alone or together with the client. This may

[16] I. W. Charney, "Integrated individual and family therapy," *Fam.-Proc.,* 1966, *5,* 179–197.

help, and sometimes results in the family member coming independently into interpersonal psychotherapy with me or with someone else.

Such family intervention should be rare. It is fraught with a great many hazards for the identified client. I employ it when it appears absolutely certain that family forces will keep the client from discovering or employing his capacity for growth and fulfillment. If this temporary bridge fails, I then ask for a conjoint family approach.

Sometimes one, two, or three conjoint sessions, spaced intensively or wide apart, are helpful. These meetings seem to satisfy certain needs as well as fears in the family and interpersonal therapy is then allowed to go on. I have found that family members are jealous of the attention the client gets, as well as fearing it, and they want to be heard as well. The identified client speaks unconsciously for them all, but they want to speak for themselves. When they are summoned, they come gladly on the basis of the help they might be able to give in understanding their "sick" family member. But once they come to the session, their Self becomes mobilized and they may usurp the client status.

There is then a danger that the client will feel he has once again been manipulated out of a position of favor and trust. Also, he is systematically "undone" in the presence of his therapist as "proof" of his illness and cupidity. While this process is fascinating to watch, and even participate in, it is the most subtly destructive thing I have ever witnessed. It mobilizes considerable anger and feelings of helplessness in the therapist.

Conjoint family therapy has such a varied stance, and interventions come so rapidly, and hostility and affection are so bold that the interpersonal therapist must be alert to maintain his therapeutic posture once he returns to the dyadic pattern. It is a contagious and exhilarating form of therapy. Conjoint family therapy is a kind of "off-limits" therapy to those classically trained. It takes considerable "getting used to," and this posture cannot be switched on and off at a moment's notice. It can become a therapeutic style.

If conjoint family therapy is indicated, and I would say it should not be in more than one out of ten cases on the average, should the therapist do it himself or refer the client to a family therapist? The client should not be referred because the earlier work will be essentially wasted and the referral may not be acceptable to the client. In my experience, it is better to blunder at first as a family therapist than to make such a referral, for the whole structure of the treatment is philosophically shifted.

Basic Encounter Group

The need to humanize business and industry, and the often startling findings of small group research following Lewin, gave birth to a form of group work called sensitivity training. I participated in such a group as a supervising psychologist, planning, directing, and evaluating the work of a moderately large staff of clinical psychologists. The purpose of the group was to sensitize top- and middle-level administration to their employees as people in order to promote efficiency and production. Much of this early work came from, and was stimulated by, the National Training Laboratory.[17]

The original N.T.L. workers proliferated so that every university school of industrial relations now has a sensitivity training and human relations specialist. A few are outstanding in this area.[18] Jack Gibb, one of the earliest workers, for example, has now evolved a TORI system of interpersonal relationships and offers seminars and marathons to industry and lay groups.[19]

Sensitivity training then "caught fire" as clinicians, educators and lay healers sought a quicker, more effective, and more palatable way to attain fulfillment. At first the goal was principally to become more aware of Self, to experience one's body more gracefully and perhaps pleasurably, and to be able to love more deeply and intensely. At this stage, it was not clear whether sensitivity training was therapy and whether or not the leader, the "group facilitator" as he was called, should be a clinically trained person or not. Psychiatrists[20] were mostly hostile or indifferent, so the field was left to the charismatic, persuasive practitioner with a good face-validity approach. Centers for this practice boomed, and weekend encounters became, if not helpful, at least fashionable or fun.

Still later, sensitivity training became basic encounter, and the impetus of Carl Rogers, George Bach, and Albert Ellis, among others, offered it a more clinical format. My own work with basic encounter groups led me to believe that the encounter group was a form of treatment, with specific indications and counter-indications.[21] I came to see the need for state certification of encounter group leaders who offered themselves to the public for a fee.[22]

It is not yet clear what part the basic encounter group will play in generic group therapies, but I believe encountering is not a vogue, that it has considerable growth power, and that it is a new cultural manifestation. The question is how and when it can be useful.

Descriptions of encounter group experiences are testimonial and incomplete. It is described by one investigator in the following way.[23]

> Human encounter is the sudden recognition that there is someone else in this world who is related to us in some fashion, someone with whom we can share our private world, someone who can share his world with us.

[17]L. P. Bradford, J. R. Gibb and K. D. Benner. *Group Theory and Laboratory Method* (New York: John Wiley and Sons, 1964).

[18]A recent work provides readings and excerpts from this area of investigation: R. T. Golembiewski, and A. Blumberg (eds.), *Sensitivity Training and the Laboratory Approach* (Itasca, Illinois: F. E. Peacock Publishers Inc., 1970).

[19]J. R. Gibb, and L. M. Gibb, "Role Freedom as a TORI Group," in A. Burton (ed.), *Encounter* (San Francisco: Jossey-Bass Publishing Co., 1969).

[20]See, for example, J. L. Kuehn, and F. M. Crinella, "Sensitivity training: Interpersonal 'overkill' and other problems," *Am. J. Psychiat.,* 1969, *126,* 840–845; and L. A. Gottschalk, and E. M. Patteson, "Psychiatric perspectives on T-groups and laboratory movement: An overview," *Am. J. Psychiat.,* 1969, *126,* 823–839

[21]Burton, A. *Encounter.*

[22]Presentation to the State of California, Psychology Examining Committee, Board of Medical Examiners, San Francisco, October 24, 1970.

[23]T. O'Banion, and A. O'Connell. *The Shared Journey: An Introduction to Encounter* (Englewood Cliffs, N.J.: Prentice-Hall, Inc., 1970).

Each group leader has a different set of positive findings and no clean and consistent theory of basic encounter is yet available. My experience, and that of others, indicates that encounter groups make up for some of the modern-day deficiencies of psychoanalytic psychotherapy, while adding their own particular fraction of growth induction. Therapeutic "morality" is different in the encounter group. Acting-out is permitted and encouraged; the body is returned to therapy and life; uncompromising honesty is the primary necessity; confrontation is demanded; trust and intimacy are shown to be non-injurious; social friendships are promoted, along with some of the other benefits common to all group therapies. With all of this, there is the motivational background—propelled by our changing culture—to become a fulfilled person—to not fall into the trap of the Fathers.

Many clients come to interpersonal therapy after having been in one or more encounter or marathon groups. Some clients have even served as the group facilitator for one or more such groups. Others participate clandestinely during treatment, particularly clients who are college students or young marrieds. What do they report? The testimony of such group members to their therapists is, by and large, uniformly favorable. Gendzel, a well-trained psychiatrist, says:

> There is no basis for claims of an important and enduring change in one's personality pattern from this one experience and the follow-up session. Our experience, however, indicates that participants became more aware of their feelings, experienced a sense of well-being, and gathered some insight that they carried back to the real world and applied toward more satisfactory functioning. For those in concurrent psychotherapy, the experience provided valuable material to be further explored in their therapy.[24]

Most people today have lost the model of health and joy and they do not know where to find it. A natural peak or euphoric experience is a rare thing, which is why the sexual orgasm is so sought after. Such people do not know what it is like to feel good, to be open to the world, to have contact without fear, to have no hidden agenda. Language has, over their lifetime, closed doors rather than opened them. Suddenly they find they can be freed of its confines, at least momentarily. The microcosm of a new subculture which accepts variegated dress, habit, age, race, sex, religion, size, handicap, and similar cultural stratifications, and totally rejects their delimiting aspects is a salutary and astonishing experience for anyone. Encounter is often the first community experience people have had. It comes as something of a shock to the system, and more than rarely the reaction is comic or psychotic, as well as releasing.

The basic encounter group rapidly precipitates emotion, displays it, and makes it demonstrably interpersonal. It is, at times, a mild form of group hysteria, but it has positive, beneficial effects. These benefits are, in my opinion, proportional to the ability and personality structure of the leader. They

---

[24]I. B. Gendzel, "Marathon group therapy and nonverbal methods," *Am. J. Psychiat.*, 1970, *127*, 62–66.

show little correlation with his encounter style or the media he uses to facilitate awareness and growth.

The interpersonal psychotherapist should, himself, sometimes experience an encounter group or marathon either as a lay member or as a leader. In this way he can best understand the process, know what his clients are talking about, and make referrals to encounter groups if he believes them helpful. He will, in this way, avoid proscribing them on the basis of incomplete information or prejudice. Encounter is formative group therapy and deserves study as part of the principles of group dynamics and group therapy.

I seldom comment on the encounter group experience my clients report to me. I do not make an issue of surreptitious participation. To do so is to enter a dialogue about the comparative merits of two approaches to fulfillment which are not antithetical. However, when I refer the client for such an experience, it becomes part of his therapy and subject to analysis. One of my clients has had at least six such experiences, and still seeks more. He came to me for help with his disabling symptoms, and for fulfillment he couldn't find in encounter groups. He will stop searching there when our interpersonal psychotherapy has progressed sufficiently so that he no longer needs such groups.

I refer clients for encounter group experiences when they are so blocked that they lack affect to continue in interpersonal psychotherapy, or when they lack motivation for self-discovery to begin with. If their hostile or loving structure requires rapid confrontation which might be dangerous in interpersonal psychotherapy, I refer them to such a group. But they must not be potentially psychotic and the group experience must be time-limited. Sometimes, in desperation, I refer them to an encounter group when I can find no basis in common humanity with the client. Of course, interpersonal psychotherapy proceeds along with the encounter experience and usually benefits from it.

Transactional Analysis

Transactional analysis is not a form of psychoanalysis at all. It is an examination of the client's ego behavior as it shows up in the minor social defenses and subterfuges of interpersonal relationships. Eric Berne,[25] its founder, and Thomas Harris,[26] its major acolyte, see basic awareness and honesty in social encounters as the road to mental health. But social behavior, in their thinking, always has a payoff. This, they think, is precisely where we get into difficulty as people. The payoff is often more than we have bargained for, and when the "due bill" is presented, we use what Berne calls "games" to get it paid. These games pervade the whole spectrum of life including sexual, economic, body, manners, marriage, and like forms of behaviors. The clever titles, "Rapo," "Wooden Leg," "Schlemiel," "If it Weren't for You," and others, with which Berne labeled these games, served to em-

[25]E. Berne, *Games People Play* (New York: Grove Press, 1964).
[26]T. Harris, *I'm OK—You're OK.* (New York: Harper & Row, 1970).

phasize their appositeness for every person and gave them popular social appeal.

According to Berne, the personality is made up of the "adult," "parent," and "child," analogues to Freud's ego, super-ego, and id, but different from them. A person relatively free of "game" behavior is an adult; one full of it, a "child." The "parent" is the moral authority, the guide, the conscience, and that, too, must be free of game behavior.

A transactional group is always ready to fire on its members who come to analysis. They must be bombarded by provocative stimuli provoking "game" behavior in the group and then awarded green, yellow or other stamps as payoff, a kind of illicit reward which substitutes for the hidden payoff. The group focuses and pressures for more "adult" behavior, shaming, coercing, and intellectualizing the client into it. Its purpose is confrontation with Self, as Synanon does, in order to bring better understanding of social or Self-behavior and more mature performance. In addition, many of the healing aspects common to group therapy are provided.

Transactional analysis seldom goes deeper than such superficial behavior, although it must not be presumed that these games are always conscious. Most of them are definitely preconscious, but very little attempt is made in transactional analysis to get at the dynamics of the unconscious. This is usually left to accompanying dyadic therapies if required.

As a useful adjunct to interpersonal therapy, transactional analysis would find a place in the latter stages of treatment. Traditional dyadic therapies pay little attention to such things as pastimes, rituals, conventions, games, and similar Self mechanisms on the social level. They struggle with the deeper levels of the personality. The assumption is that release from repression, the formation of insight, and greater risk-taking will by themselves reduce or eliminate such game behaviors. And they do, but sometimes not quickly enough, and not in all clients. In such instances, referral to a transactional group may be helpful.

TERMINATING
PSYCHOTHERAPY

IX

Terminating psychotherapy is probably the most difficult of all the operations the therapist is called on to perform. At least in the case of the longer-term therapy, an analogy might be made to a settled-in marriage which must be broken up. Any process in which the emotions are deeply involved, particularly the most intense form of emotion which includes both love of Brother (Agape) and love of Eros, can only be broken off with great difficulty. Therapy is no exception to this rule.

The end of therapy is often a quixotic thing. Ideally, in a psychoanalytic sense, it should accomplish the following things:

> . . . an abandonment by the patient of mendacity, a thorough analysis of the patient's character even in its expression in peculiarities of appearance or behavior, an inner freedom manifested by the patient's surer grip in acting and making decisions, adequate "working through" which is permitted by an attitude of timelessness in therapist and patient toward the duration of treatment, a conquest of fears of castration in the male patient manifested by feelings of equality in relating to the therapist, an acceptance of her role without resentment by female patients, and as an almost invariable occurrence a transformation in the nature of the patient's symptoms before the end.[1]

But things are rarely this way.

The discontinuance of a significant personal relationship, possibly the only one the client has, so far, been capable of, brings yearning for things that might have been, guilt for unexemplary behavior, and concern for the therapist's future welfare. The discovery that the relationship is finite often comes as a great blow to some clients who fantasy an ever-enduring one. One client has been in psychoanalysis for 21 years with three psychoanalysts. In such situations, separation anxiety and depression as mourning will intervene. These can be extremely serious and should not be taken lightly. They become worse if the therapist wants to be rid of the client but doesn't know how to manage it. Many clients suddenly regress just when they should be leaving therapy.

[1]M. Edelson, *Termination of Intensive Psychotherapy* (Springfield, Ill.: Charles C. Thomas Publishing Co., 1963), p. 6.

The fantasies of therapy are always ahead of its realities; giving these up is what makes separation so difficult. On another level, for certain middle-class, urban people, therapists make desirable friends and companions. They are decided assets at cocktail parties. Their capacity to bore is perhaps so much less than other people! Termination rules out their social presence on a very practical level. With rare exceptions, former clients or analysands do not become the friends of their therapists. The process, while it need not do so, prevents it.

People who come to therapy in some way select themselves because they have greater attachment needs than others. Their disengagement can, therefore, be expected to be more difficult than it would be for non-clients. There is considerable danger for the client, and possibly even for the therapist, in incorrect termination of therapy. Abandonment of someone who already feels terribly vulnerable, who has extreme feelings of loneliness, who sometimes wants to die, and who at last has found someone who deeply understands him, can result in the actual death of that client. He must be permitted a proper time for mourning if the separation is to be effective. The client basically buys constancy and duration of affection. If this wavers or is arbitrary, he feels his world has no stability whatsoever, even in the face of great early gains in his treatment.

A study of the literature on termination of therapy[2] reveals wide disagreement not only on how to terminate but the indication for it. Edelson,[3] for example, says,

> Successful terminations from which the answers to important questions might be induced are infrequent.

However, the following are cited from time to time in the literature as indications for termination leaving the client better off than when he came:

1. When the client has attained an insight into his situation which he did not have before therapy began.
2. When childhood amnesia has been reduced to the lowest possible denominator.
3. When there is nothing more to talk about in therapy.
4. When paranoid and depressive anxiety are reduced to reasonable levels.
5. When the client shows improved work capabilities.
6. When the client is free of neurotic misery.
7. When the client has a better sublimation.
8. When the client's adaptive patterns are altered in a healthy direction.
9. When the primary process has become secondary process.
10. When there is an increase of inner freedom.

[2]See, for example, S. K. Firestein, "Problems of termination in the analysis of adults," *J. Am. Psychoan. Assoc.*, 1969, *17*, 222–237. This is a fine summary of a symposium held by psychoanalysts on this topic.
[3]Edelson, *Termination of Intensive Psychotherapy*.

11. When the transference neurosis is completely resolved.
12. When the client is self-realized.
13. When the client has the information he needs.
14. When the client is more effective socially.
15. When the client improves his economic circumstances.

The question arises: Is there a final and universal point for termination of therapy, and particularly longer-term therapy involving pre-genital character referrents, Oedipal problems, and their analysis and synthesis? In my experience, therapy is never as clear-cut in its final phases as Sigmund Freud believed. In today's intimate world of "hot" media, with its unlimited possibilities for visual and auditory contact, and in the face of ubiquitous alienation, we may not be able to count on a "final" termination between client and therapist. "The problem of termination is not how to get the therapy stopped, or when to stop it, but how to terminate so that what has been happening keeps on going inside of the patient."[4]

In my own practice I have felt a final termination occurred only when one of my clients died of leukemia, and in another instance when the client went to prison for more than a life sentence. This does not mean clients do not terminate therapy, but only that death and imprisonment without parole seemed to sever the interpersonal bond in a more permanent way, without revival privileges. Regardless of how termination takes place, the parting must leave room for reinstatement of therapy if it should be required. There must be a basic feeling to the parting which says, "I am still interested in you, will always be, and I will be here if needed . . . Good luck to you on your venture."

On the other hand, planning for termination of treatment starts with the first hour—or at least it should. It is exceedingly difficult for any therapist to become involved in what might be a perpetual or everlastingly open-ended psychotherapy with anyone. Even an actual marriage can no longer be planned on this basis. One has to plan for its ending some day, which is a realistic and even biological thing. Therapy has a kind of inner organization, which, like life, carries it from beginning to end—so that there must be a psychological end to it.

In certain forms of therapy, for example, when the client is told that there are only twenty hours of therapy available to him, or when the therapist can only devote a limited number of hours to him, there is a time-limited aspect to the therapy. The evidence seems to indicate that where therapy is set up for a specific length of time, and must absolutely end at that time, treatment may be no less efficient or less helpful than when it is open-ended. Freud considered this a form of blackmail, but admitted that it worked in some cases. Ferenczi recommended it as a form of precipitation of mental work when the client's resistances could not be overcome.

Clients carry their therapists around with them as kinds of amulets,

[4]Edelson, *Termination of Intensive Psychotherapy.*

as mystical images or icons (they sometimes ask for a parting token), and these images are, from time to time, pulled out and refurbished in crises without making actual contact with the therapist. Jung said that in every culture extant, and of record, men who are about to die call for their mothers, even though they may have been dead for a great many years. Therapists are like mothers in this sense. All therapists find, and Freud did also to his chagrin, that their most successful and "cured" cases one day show up on their doorstep for further treatment. Can any treatment insure against future incapacity of the Self in the face of new and intense stress which may occur, and in view of biological surges and life stages which are the oscillations of the instincts in every person in growth? Is psychotherapy mental hygiene? Should it deliberately precipitate crises and resolve them so as to prevent something 20 years hence?

When is the client cured, or at least sufficiently improved, so that no further therapy is indicated in his lifetime? For Freud the supposed answer to this question was stated this way: "The implication is that by means of analysis it is possible to attain absolute psychical normality, and to be sure that it will be maintained, the supposition being that all of the patient's repressions have been lifted and every gap in his memory filled."[5] In another place he said, "Let us assume that what analysis achieves for neurotics is only what normal people accomplish for themselves without its help."[6] Therapy, according to this view, provides the means by which a person learns to cope with any crisis which comes up in a normative way, and to find help only within a nonprofessional framework. Like the mental hospital, therapy, once resorted to, is always there as a form of helpful regression— even though its function is to counter regression. Szasz and Leiter offer the interesting theory that, for most people, it is more advantageous to go to jail than to a psychiatric facility.

It is of course impossible to say when a client is cured. This varies with the client and the therapist and their particular vantage point. I might, for the moment, beg the question by asking: Who decides when the client is cured? Some authors, including Carl Rogers, claim the client himself decides when he is well. And I do accept the idea that the client has the final say as to whether or not he comes to therapy. But many clients will not, or cannot, leave therapy without the concurrence of their therapist—that is, unless the therapist also feels they are ready to take the necessary steps to terminate. It is really not up to the client alone, and Rogers is most certainly incorrect in this instance.

But mutuality of aims and goals in therapy, is, I find, quite rare. It quite often happens that the therapist feels the client is ready for breaking-off but the client demurs; or the client may feel he is ready for termination, but the therapist believes there may be more to do. I think it is a quite rare event, even though theory postulates it, that the therapist and client mutu-

---

[5]S. Freud, "Analysis Terminable and Interminable," in J. Strachey (ed.). *Collected Papers, Vol. V.* (New York: Basic Books, 1959). p. 320.
    [6]*Ibid.*, p. 327.

ally arrive at exactly the point where they feel therapy should be discontinued. Therapists have been known to suddenly "cure" their clients when fees were no longer forthcoming, when they are suddenly threatened by homosexual upsurges, or when they had someone more interesting waiting in the wings.

I like to think the question of cure is, in a sense, an artificial and abstract one because the conception of cure can never be clear. No client ever leaves therapy cured or so fulfilled that he can be said to have been totally renovated, to have a new character, or a new personality.

In part this is so, "because the ego treats recovery as a new danger and will not finalize it." What happens instead is that the client comes to feel differently about himself, about other people, and is socially more effective. He has more meaning and purpose in his life, has more hope and faith, and accomplishes more of the things mentioned in the chapter on aims of psychotherapy. Freud's final and pragmatic definition was: "The business of analysis is to secure the best possible psychological condition for the functioning of the ego; when this has been done, analysis has accomplished its task."[7]

The client, however, does these new things on a rather uneven level, with many setbacks and regressions. There are still many things he opts for that he cannot do effectively or even attempt at all. He may never be able to get around to them. Fulfillment is a qualitative rather than a quantitative concept.

We must understand that nobody stays in therapy until he has a perfect cure or a perfect solution to a problem. The client terminates therapy long before he is ready in an idealistic sense. But he is constrained to it, particularly if he has done no acting- or living-out during the therapy. He must attempt to get along by himself; to attempt new things, maybe even to be "shot down;" but he has to do it this way. It is the function of the therapist to prevent unnecessary pain in his client, but pain must not be prevented at the expense of keeping the client in therapy even if it is apparent that serious mistakes are going to be made. If the mistakes will involve possible danger to the client, risk of jail, or other extremist forms of behavior, we have an obligation to clarify, to analyze the need for termination, and then to allow the client to do what he has to do. Of course, we protect him, too.

It is a greater mistake to try to "sell" the client on further therapy. It may be his therapy at that point requires that he synthesize and integrate in the world what he has cognitively and affectively organized in his work. With the question of termination, we confront the entire meaning of psychotherapy itself. Of this meaning there is no certitude today. Rather there are varying certitudes, among various practitioners. I must conclude that the outcomes of psychotherapy fall somewhat short of what I would like. And the effort and expense involved are enormous. On the other hand, very few "normal" people who have never been to a therapist have, in my opinion, much to crow about. The absurdity of the human condition is their lot. The

---

[7]Freud, "Analysis Terminable and Interminable," p. 354.

misery of the world is their misery. Those who have had the benefits of therapy are an elite group. They have a certain social awareness which does not play into man's sadism and inhumaneness. Their guilt becomes a more socially proper one. They become more human if not yet perfect people. This funcion was, perhaps, formerly the province of the priests, but nowadays the priesthood is rarely credible, and promises of heaven and hell fall on the deaf ears of our clients.

If therapy proceeds satisfactorily, termination is not actually a problem. The whole therapeutic situation is, itself, an integral gestalt. In termination, as in the beginning and middle of therapy, the various problems which come up, fall together, jell, and are solved within the framework of the therapeutic relationship. Termination then occurs in such a natural way as to be almost imperceptible, that is, without major strain on client or therapist. If the therapy has had unusual problems—or if it has not been structured and carried through adequately, or if there are unconscious needs in the therapist or client that have not been worked through, termination becomes a major problematic situation. And I have known therapies which have taken years in the termination phase.

Lingering termination must be avoided. If ambivalence is carried this far, therapy has not been proceeding on a proper course and must be reassessed anyway. Such terminal ambivalence may be either the client's or the therapist's. It is, at any rate, the therapist's responsibility to resolve it. This can be done by carefully analyzing the reasons for the client's continuance, and by giving the client reassurance and support about his current capabilities. If the therapist is holding the client in thrall, he must come to understand why he does it and discuss it with his client. This may require that the therapist consult with an outside senior therapist.

Sometimes limits have to be set, and firm and gentle insistence are required for less frequent interviews. A trial away from therapy may be offered. I do not approve of setting this during a vacation or holiday. At this point, telephone calls become more frequent since the client is seeking reassurance. On rare occasions, I have said to the client, "You seem ready to try it alone, let's attempt it. I'll be here if you need me," and then offered no further appointments. I have only done this, of course, after weeks and months of anticipation and preparation. The confidence of the therapist in his client's ability to "make it" is critical at this time. No one must panic at setbacks. Both know that the world is now less closed and frightening, and that one must experience it directly sometime as well as just talking about it.

There are many kinds of termination. Most of them are what I call "loving terminations." That is, the client and the therapist come to an understanding and affectionate parting of the ways, agreeing that it is time for termination and they are in accord on most of the major achievements. Both are interested in what happens to the other; both wish each other well; and we might say the divorce is, if not a happy one, a helpful one.

But there are the terminations which I call "hateful," in which the divorce is noisy, made with objections, recriminations, and resentments. These kinds of termination occur more often than is acknowledged in the literature. When the client breaks off in this way the therapy need not be considered unsuccessful. It seems the outcome of many successful therapies are "hateful" because the client is expressing something, not necessarily connected with his fate, or with the process of therapy, but a kind of relief about the whole event, and even attempting his new feelings knowing that when he leaves in this way his therapist will still not judge him, will still love him for it. Strean[8] followed up some young clients who terminated this way and found that they were indeed helped.

There are other kinds of terminations as well. Termination may be countertransferential. The therapist may become bored with, or frightened by, his client and need to terminate what has become subconsciously painful for him. Or the therapy may have hung up on a plateau for such a long time that it is apparent to the therapist, if not to the client, that it is never going anywhere. Sometimes the therapist has other things he wants to do: research, writing a book, administration, or travel, and the client keeps him from it. Possibly fee rewards no longer motivate him as well.

Obversely, the client can get bored with his therapist, or can recognize an immutable plateau. He may want to try somebody else, or a new style of treatment. As, for example, the lady who said, "Well, I'd like to try Eric Berne for a while, or a basic encounter group." Some clients at this point even offer to sleep with the therapist as a reality way of making a change! Some clients have job transfers to other parts of the country and the question of a referral or "flying in" to see the therapist comes up. There are many situations in which both voluntary and involuntary surreptitious terminations take place.

Termination always requires understanding, and working-through the need for termination. If this is not done, the therapist is left with feelings of ineffectiveness, being unwanted, and possibly with guilt. The client may also have feelings of having run away from treatment when his greatest gains were obvious, or he may have matricidal or parricidal feelings toward his therapist, or genuinely and passionately love him.

I have said termination begins in the first hour, that it is a naturally evolving thing (even though it rarely turns out to be such), at least this should be our ideal. What is the termination-hour like, and what is the termination-structure in which the prelude or first signs of termination appear?

One of the signs of beginning termination, of that time when the client can even think of separation as a concept, is a certain restlessness and disengagement. If the client originally hangs on the therapist's every word; if involvement with the therapist is life itself; if the client feels this particular attachment is the only one that counts; or if he feels the therapist model is the Self-ideal, then with the beginnings of termination, all of these states become reduced in quality. The client may, for example, challenge an interpretation, may even indeed deny it. He may see for the first time painful realities about the therapist model, as he did with his father at adolescence,

[8]H. Strean, "Psychotherapy with children of psychotherapists," *Psychoan. Rev.,* 1969, *56,* 378–386.

that is, he may come to disillusionment. A client may miss an interview, or be late after having always been almost painfully present and prompt; he may make some generally pejorative remarks about therapy; or he may point out that certain of his friends have had bad results with it. One needs to watch carefully, not only for the signs of ego-strength which reveal the growing capacity of the client, but for these negative signs which indicate detachment and diminution of transference. Some therapists react negatively to these negative signs. This must occur either because they are unprepared for termination or unwilling to recognize its need.

The following are several brief examples of how termination was first announced:

1. A client, an educator of some local repute, asked the therapist to appear on a panel he was chairing in which some outstanding psychologists, and friends of the therapist were appearing.

2. A client who never in her life had given a party announced one and invited her therapist to come.

3. A client who in many years of therapy had never given her therapist a gift, one day showed up with a very handsome one.

4. A client who assiduously paid her bill suddenly fell into delinquency and one of her checks bounced.

5. A client who came to therapy while pregnant did not return after the child was delivered. It was understood that the new issue was the stopping point without this being stated.

6. A client leaped up and slapped her therapist one day.

7. A client announced that he could have charge of the Washington office if he wanted it.

8. A client who at one time called his therapist "omniscient and omnipotent," suddenly said "baloney!" to an interpretation one day.

How then do you terminate therapy? Assuming the client now reveals a subtle readiness to try it on his own, how does the therapist foster his growing independence? The principal way, of course, is to recognize the client's new-found ego-strength in the conduct of the interview. One is less supportive, interprets less, clarifies less, and accepts the client more as a viable partner. One talks more, laughs more, and reveals more personal things about himself than before. The prevalent attitude should be, "now you are no longer helpless, try it and see." Peer replaces authority or seer. Clients continually look to their therapists for clues as to their adequacy, and they are extremely sensitive to his evaluation. One must genuinely feel the client is capable, for nothing is as disastrous in therapy as saying, "go," without meaning it.

An important method for promoting termination is interview spacing.

The frequency of the interview should be gradually reduced. If this goes well, a future date may be set for termination. Rarely, the interviews may be increased and concentrated for a brief period of time to work something important through. In some instances, quarterly or annual interviews can be planned after termination if the client finds it necessary. If the fifty-minute hour is being used, then possibly shorter interview times can be given as tailing-off.

In situations of some desperation, I have mobilized the client by discussing my flagging interest in him as no longer "sick," and offered to "treat" him in a different way on a "well" basis. This forced him to face up to his growing strength. It told him my own growth possibilities in the therapeutic situation had diminished because his affect was now more appropriately directed toward other persons and objects. He was really not, in fact, a client anymore.

It is important for the therapist to publicly declare his termination-policy, so to speak, at an appropriate time in the treatment. Most clients fear termination, and sometimes even fear the wrath of the therapist should they try to break off. Some just fail to come back. When the client is beginning to show the earliest signs of termination, and particularly when the ego-strength to accomplish it is still lacking, I bring up the termination-policy.

The termination-policy is my general statement about the ends, meanings, and conclusions of psychotherapy. It often serves to reassure the client that termination is merely one integral part of the entire treatment process and can be handled nominally. I point out that therapy goes on outside the hour as well as in it, that life itself is the best therapist, that the considerable insights and gains one finds need to be applied in the world eventually; that trial and error is a part of every learning process; and that I am there to see the therapy through in all of its phases even including termination. I re-affirm the principle that therapy ought not to go on one hour longer than required. If I have any specific feelings about the termination of this particular client, I bring it out at this time. Since most clients never discover how their therapists feel about finalizing therapy, such statements set the general tone of termination possibilities for the treatment.

A word has to be said about the interminable client. There are a considerable number of clients who continue for years in therapy, pay their fees regularly, and insist that they are making gains, although it appears to the therapist that they have attained maximal help. Discussions of termination with them always end up with the plea that they still need help, or with a regression in their feelings or behavior. Should one see such a client as long as the client feels he is receiving help and continues to meet the conditions of treatment? In medicine it is not unusual to maintain life-long contact with a diabetic, a cardiac, or an allergic patient if medication and periodic review are necessary for maintenance of a reasonably healthy life. In therapy we may, for example, be giving the equivalent of digitalis for the heart in still another form. Are there some clients who need us more or less perpetually, as in general medicine, and do we take on this kind of task?

Freud said,

> We come across people, for instance, of whom we should say that they display a peculiar "adhesiveness of the libido." The process which their analysis sets in motion is so much slower than in other people because they apparently cannot make up their minds to detach libidinal cathexes from one object and displace them to another, although we can find no particular reasons for the cathectic fidelity.[9]

The differences between individuals in completing psychotherapy have not been sufficiently noted. Some people take one hundred hours to do what others do in ten; some take ten hours to do what others can do in one. Therapy is not a process which has equilinear units, nor can it be equated from case to case in terms of time. Some hurry; others do not. Each case has its own configuration, and the temporal aspects vary widely even when the area traversed is the same. Why should we expect that two cases of hysteria would respond in the same number of interviews?

The question of "terminable and interminable" involves questions of economy and motivation. Economy involves the basic scientific premise that the client is to be helped as quickly as possible, that he contribute commensurately to the earnings or production of the therapist, and that he not clog the therapeutic avenues for others in society who also need help. By motivation I mean that if the therapist no longer grows himself in his work, he tends to lose the challenge of the therapeutic encounter, and loses the desire to be with particular clients for these reasons. His efficiency drops if he forces himself against his motives. While therapy is sold like anything else, it is a service which takes more "heart," "soul," and "will" than other service. We cannot assume that the therapist can always be maximally motivated, or that he can constantly remain so with any particular client. We often dissimulate for economic and social reasons and more clients leave therapy because of a lessening of their therapist's motivation than is ever known.

Each therapeutic interview is scrutinized by the "third ear" and approved or disapproved for its quantum of growth-inducing property. If it does not add its increment, and if it is followed by successive negative-growth interviews, and the therapy therefore seems to be on a final plateau, then that therapy has to be terminated, or it will terminate itself. This is true even though some of these clients may go to other therapists.

The client's attachment to his therapist, to the therapeutic process, and even to the particular room in which therapy is done, has to be analyzed, interpreted, and worked through in a way which encourages the client to be independent. In successful therapy, the client finds someone outside of the therapeutic situation who can temporarily serve as a surrogate for the therapist himself. If the client can carry his therapeutic attachment conveniently and pleasurably along with him into the environment, therapy cannot become interminable. If the therapist can be with the client merely as a symbol, or in

[9]S. Freud, "Analysis Terminable and Interminable," p. 344.

thought only, therapy can be terminated. If the client cannot use this intermediate meaning process he may really be an interminable client. This is an impasse which is outrageously difficult to solve.

Problems with interminability are the therapist's problems, not the client's, although they are usually presented as client problems. There is an ever present temptation to have a client one "loves" (therapeutically loves) coming back and back because one needs him. This may be true, as well, for certain hostile clients. In these instances, the therapist has to demonstrate something to himself, or he may be meeting some covert need, or he may need the fees the client brings.

Countertransferences are ever present irrational dangers to therapy, even for therapists who have been "fully" analyzed. The therapist is particularly prone to guilt. If he becomes troubled or obsessed or irritable over a specific client, this is an indication that he should be looking to his countertransferences. Interminable psychotherapy represents the therapist's weaknesses—his positive or negative side projected on the client. Suicide, or suicide attempts, by therapists themselves, are a countertransference termination of their own lives. I have evaluated the effects of this on some clients. It is uniformly bad. It does not suffice professionally to say, "Oh well, he would be seeing Dr. Smith if he wasn't seeing me," as a way out of deserting a client. For some clients who cannot detach themselves, a general medical practitioner may serve interminably with greater economy and usefulness than a psychotherapist, and such a solution should be encouraged.

The problem in contrast with interminable therapy is too-early termination, which can come about surreptitiously, or because termination was unplanned-for. Sometimes nothing injurious happens in such premature terminations. The client may find that when his therapist is taken to the hospital and needs an emergency appendectomy, for example, he can manage quite well without him. Yet, there have been therapeutic situations in which a client, having been denied a single extra hour by his therapist, committed suicide.

The rule must always be that unplanned breaks, or unplanned termination involving illness, vacations, conventions, changing locale, and the like, must be budgeted for in some way. Clients worry about the absences of their therapists, fearing that they may die or be killed, or that they will not see them again because they, the clients, are not worthy of being seen. They worry about the therapist's health and his ups and downs.

Unplanned interruptions and terminations go much better if the therapeutic relationship is well established and the therapy is proceeding normally on course. This type of therapeutic relationship is secure because both participants have a major investment in seeing it through. Beyond this, it is necessary to prepare the client for the fact that the therapist will be absent both voluntarily and involuntarily. If the life-style of the therapist includes considerable recreation or professional travel, or if he's on the board of several professional organizations which meet regularly, or if he has a chronic physical illness or handicap which may force him to be away from therapy, all of these things should be outlined for the client with the statement that this is the way the therapist lives. The vast majority of clients recognize and accept this and can work within such a framework, even though they may not particularly like it.

Can psychological tests such as the Rorschach Test or Minnesota Multiphasic Personality Inventory help us know when the client is ready for termination? Should close relatives furnish collateral information about the functioning of the client away from the office? There is no question that tests provide us with important dynamic information and that, for example, when they are given seriatim, they reveal the client's state of being and growth. They have, however, two difficulties. One is that they are intrusive and tend to upset or change the therapeutic relationship. (For this reason, they are best given by another psychologist.) The second is that as therapy continues, one gets to know everything one needs to know about the client, and the needed answers are not to be found in any extraneous criterion but in complete understanding of the treatment situation itself. Also, findings on the Rorschach and the MMPI have to be dynamically and prognostically translated. Evidence indicates that the validity of such transformations are low. Diagnosis is not necessarily correlated with prognosis. Many psychotic or borderline-psychotic clients respond more healthily to some psychotherapy than some neurotics. Psychiatric rubrics are poor indicators of who profits from therapy, and how quickly they respond. Diagnosis is the strong point of psychological tests, and the tests are, therefore, of more limited help to therapists.

Relatives are also poor indicators of progress made—partly because they have a vested interest in client-maintenance, and a biased point of view. Despite this, any independent material which comes unsolicited to the therapist is grist for the termination mill. But termination is an internal and evolving process and is to be measured only by the signs inherent in the process itself.

Should social or other contact be made with clients who have terminated therapy for follow-up reasons? No one has yet invented a follow-up procedure that works uniformly. Unless a research program is involved, it is better to allow the client his privacy unless he takes the initial step of contacting you. Of course, one is always open to hearing from ex-clients, and one even wonders from time to time how things are going with them. It is one of the unfortunate aspects of psychotherapy as a profession that we have so little feedback on the work we do. But our not hearing from the client or about him probably means he is making it!

CONCLUDING
SCIENTIFIC POSTSCRIPT

XII

The attainment of status and proficiency as a psychotherapist, even achievement of that lordly state we might call authenticity, does not end the original "call" to become a psychotherapist, nor does it satisfy the requisites of being scientific. More is involved as the following paragraphs reveal.

THE MOTIVATIONAL CURVE

There is a burning-out and disillusioning process which takes place in psychotherapy. No therapist can maintain a high positive regard toward his clients enduringly. This regard fluctuates not only with the specific client but with each year or epoch of practice. In order to practice psychotherapy fully, however, it is necessary to be ever motivated to heal, and even occasionally to have a peak experience. Therapists need satisfaction as much as their clients.

Many psychotherapists unconsciously choose to become therapists because they have some unfinished personal business. Should this business soon become finished, the drive to be with neurotic people, to persevere with them, and to love them might slowly evaporate. This does manifestly happen with psychotherapists who do psychotherapy with chronic schizophrenics.[1] While some surgeons give up surgery and become psychiatrists, more psychiatrists give up psychotherapy and become specialists of another kind or merely do research, teaching or administration in psychiatry. The emotional demands on the psychotherapist are recognizably exorbitant, and possibly the most demanding of any of the psychological and medical specialties. To maintain such a high level of interest and involvement over decades is indeed a task.

There are certain things a therapist can do to maintain his motivation. First, he should have, if not a training analysis, at least some personal therapy —and this may need reinforcement over the years. The purpose is not only to give him an understanding as to what it means to be a client but to get to know his unconscious and his Self so that his dependency and countertransference on the client, or on a certain client, will be kept to a minimum.

[1]Burton, A. "The adoration of the patient and its disillusionment."

Therapists as human beings fall in love too and have their special covert needs for people. But this must not be an extraordinary neurotic need or love. Continual inner frustration in psychotherapy eventually leads to a hostile-sadistic therapeutic organization, or to abandonment of the field.

It seems sophomoric to say that a meaningful and satisfying family life helps with the motivational problem. Each full day of therapeutic load calls for a climax of relief—the opportunity to relax and talk to one's spouse in the social institution called home. Being with persons who are non-persons all day calls for a modicum of intimacy with a person who is already a person. Being natural and away from psychotherapy, removing oneself from one's office "self-presentation," is relieving. There are also children, Bach and Beethoven, gin and tonic, books, and so forth. Psychotherapists I have known have not had distinguished marriages, which, of course, constitutes a handicap.

Psychotherapists require non-vocational outlets of more than usual proportions. Freud liked to travel and hike. Jung visited far-off cultures, traveling to China and Africa when few white men went there. Frankl climbs mountains, and others drive racing cars, sail, or are amateur archeologists. It helps to take risks away from therapy and to employ the gross bodily musculature in diverse pursuits.

IMPROVISATION

It is possible to be a fully satisfactory and authentic psychotherapist while confining oneself totally to one style of therapy. Most psychoanalysts do not, in their lifetime, depart from the dyadic analytic form Freud set down. Psychotherapists in general find a metier and stick with it. But the advantages to a psychotherapist of multiple therapy, psychodrama, group therapy, encounter group work and other forms are not necessarily in their special efficiency, or the fact that they do indeed reach more clients. Their value lies even more in the imaginative elaboration of the healing principle which allows expansion of the therapist's psyche. The therapist is stimulated by the novelty, learns from it, and finds new ways of accomplishing old ends. These therapeutic forms inspire him to look more deeply into the personality in a quite different way than he was trained to do. They are also less arcane and lonely forms of therapy and do not feed upon themselves as much.

There is also the aspect of improvisation which leads a psychotherapist to work with a new set of clients who would never ordinarily reach him. This could be the grossly impoverished, various Blacks, the drug hipster, the youth commune, the aged, and similar others; as well as service in a suicide prevention center, in a crisis clinic, in a labor union psychiatric clinic, a Family Service agency, or something similar. Psychotherapy applied to humanity in such diverse social and political forms challenges the therapist's fundamental healing premises and forces constant revaluation of them. Improvisation is the fount of creativity every therapist needs.

NEW KNOWLEDGE

Psychotherapy is an endeavor in which the hazards of never acquiring any new learning are very great. It is difficult to read systematically, to even read at all, when there is always a new client waiting to be taken on, or a new crisis on the telephone, or when recreational needs produce occasional disgust or surfeit at anything psychotherapeutic. Psychotherapy, if permitted, can become merely instrumental healing. One goes reliably through the motions with client after client. The psychotherapist sooner or later comes to believe in the mythology of his magic and charisma, and begins to believe that he doesn't need to know more. After all, look how well his clients are doing! This is not necessarily personal cupidity. It's an inherent danger in a profession which lulls one by success and adulation with insufficient feedback built in.

A part of the information problem is how to narrow down the tremendous quantity of materials available. Here are some suggestions on this score. They have worked for me.

1. Subscribe to a current computer scanning service which selects and delivers reprints in your area of professional preoccupation.
2. Subscribe to a periodical which announces books "about to be published" for appropriate novels, non-fiction, poetry, biography related to psychotherapy or to your personal interest.
3. Subscribe to some underground newspaper, and to some "slick" magazine such as the British magazine *Encounter,* to keep abreast of politics, economics, and social science. Even if you peruse none of these regularly, an infrequent glance still makes them worthwhile.

RESEARCH

Paradoxically, psychotherapists who do research on psychotherapy rarely treat clients, and clinicians who treat clients rarely do research on treatment. The practical problems of doing both are, of course, obvious. It costs a great deal of money to do research, to give up fee-time for research, especially when the outcome of one's efforts may be minuscule. The therapist's office is, furthermore, not a laboratory and clients do not take well to being subjects. Most research is done by university personnel who justify their subsidies by research output and not by the number of cases treated. It seems to me this always gives their research findings an artificial quality. One feels, on reading it, that the researcher does not basically know the interpersonal situation.

This is yet an unresolved dilemma and other professions fall heir to it. Still, Freud changed the entire outlook of a culture as a clinician. Each psychotherapist should be required, at a minimum, to write up and publish one case history a year. He should, in addition, publish several scholarly papers on psychotherapy if empirical research is not feasible at a neighboring facility. The personal rewards are tremendous. This provides a bridge to the therapist's heritage and the wider function of the sciences which produce the Ph.D. and M.D. The possible shortcomings or irrelevancies of the degree for psychotherapeutic practice do not cancel the contract which was made in accepting it and practicing by it.

THERAPIST SATISFACTION

No profession with which I am familiar rises and falls as much on the basis of feelings as psychotherapy does. This is an unsatisfactory and sometimes unpleasant basis for evaluating the work of a profession. In my opinion, the feelings of the therapist have been disregarded in favor of the client's. Countertransference is classically considered more insidious than transference. What are the satisfactions a psychotherapist has a right to expect from his work? Are his fees, status, and power sufficient reward? I do not believe so. The fantasies of the psychotherapist are quite florid. How much should they be realized? Is the encounter group movement really in the vanguard in recognizing true equality of *all* members in the group? Is it true, as one famous psychotherapist told me, that one out of three psychotherapists acts-out with a client sooner or later?

I would urge every psychotherapist to have an annual "satisfaction check-up." This could be done by senior (and liberated) psychotherapists made available from professional panels. These check-ups would be extra-territorial and unrecorded. Their purpose would be to assure every psycho-therapist that he is getting his kicks.

FUTURE OF PSYCHOTHERAPY

I am optimistic about the future of psychotherapy. My study of Zen, meditation, yoga, and the like reveals nothing that can yet match psycho-therapy as a way to fulfillment and salvation. Psychotherapy places the person squarely on his own, responsible for his individual fate. It does not permit him to cop out through myth, illusion, or promise of an afterlife. It supplies a life crutch for as long as it is needed. And it provides necessary love to the unloved without guilt or fault. Above all, it confirms the values of civilization to an essentially uncivilized person. It allows beauty to shine forth—particularly the beauty of the encounter with another person. It helps recover lost humanity.

BIBLIOGRAPHY

1. ADLER, A. *The Individual Psychology of Alfred Adler.* New York: Basic Books, 1956.

    A basic exposition of Adler's social and ego theories, highly relevant to today's problems.

2. ACKERMAN, N. W. *Psychodynamics of Family Life.* New York: Basic Books, 1958.
    One of the leading authorities on family therapy interprets the internal aspects of family life and shows how to alter them.

3. ARBUCKLE, D. S. (ed.) *Counseling and Psychotherapy: An Overview.* New York: McGraw-Hill Co., 1967.

    A symposium incorporating a number of viewpoints on counseling and psychotherapy ranging from the existential to the rational-emotive.

4. BEIER, E. G. *Silent Language of Psychotherapy.* Chicago: Aldine, 1966.
    A rather heavy-handed review of psychotherapy and its manifestations.

5. BENJAMIN, A. *The Helping Interview.* Boston: Houghton Mifflin, 1969.
    A new and readable work on the structure of the interview and its working mechanisms.

6. BINSWANGER, L. "The Case of Ellen West," in *Existence*, ed. R. May. New York: Basic Books, 1968.

    A now classic case history which defines the existential-phenomenological approach to healing.

7. BUHLER, C. *Values in Psychotherapy.* New York: Free Press of Glencoe, 1962.
    An important discussion of a neglected and somewhat walled-off area of psychotherapy.

8. BURTON, A. *Modern Humanistic Psychotherapy.* San Francisco: Jossey-Bass Publishing Co., 1968.

    A number of essays setting the basis for a new humanistic approach to psychotherapy.

9. BURTON, A. (ed.) *Modern Psychotherapeutic Practice.* Palo Alto: Science and Behavior Books, 1965.

    A collection of case histories demonstrating the work of psychotherapists with diverse points of view.

10. BURTON, A. (ed.) *Psychotherapy of the Psychoses.* New York: Basic Books, 1961.
    A pioneering work on how to do psychotherapy with psychotic—mostly schizophrenic—patients.

11. CARKHUFF, R. R. and B. G. BERENSON. *Beyond Counseling and Therapy.* New York: Holt, Rinehart, and Winston, 1967.

    An avant-garde symposium discussing most of the social and philosophical issues usually left out of books on psychotherapy.

12. COLBY, K. *A Primer of Psychotherapy.* New York: Ronald & Co., 1951.
    A basic and readable "how to do it book," now somewhat ancient and overly psychoanalytic in scope.

13. ELLIS, A. *The Theory and Practice of Rational-Emotive Psychotherapy.* New York: Lyle Stuart, 1964.
    A basic exposition of Albert Ellis' intellectual approach to healing the neurosis.

14. FRANK, J. D. *Persuasion and Healing.* Baltimore: Johns Hopkins Press, 1961.
    An insightful discussion of what helps in psychotherapy by a scholar who has given much thought to this subject.

15. FREUD, S. *An Outline of Psychoanalysis.* New York: Norton, 1949.
    One of Freud's many works which outlines his ideas as to what produces neuroses and how they can be altered.

16. FROMM-REICHMANN, F. *Principles of Intensive Psychotherapy.* Chicago: University of Chicago Press, 1950.
    A most insightful book on psychotherapy by a therapist's therapist.

17. GLASSER, W. *Reality Therapy. A New Approach to Psychiatry.* New York: Harper & Row, 1965.
    Somewhat arrogant and over-arching, but an important point of view on treatment of character disorders and related problems.

18. GLOVER, E. *The Technique of Psychoanalysis.* New York: International Univ. Press, 1955.
    The single most useful book on the psychoanalytic technique for treating the neurosis.

19. HARPER, R. A. *Psychoanalysis and Psychotherapy: 36 Systems.* Englewood Cliffs, N. J.: Prentice-Hall, Inc., 1959.
    Briefly describes the various systems of psychotherapy extant: a kind of cafeteria offering.

20. HORNEY, K. *New Ways in Psychoanalysis.* New York: Norton, 1945.
    Horney is now more of historical rather than contemporary interest, but she was one of the first to recognize the social and cultural aspects of the neurosis and of psychotherapy.

21. JUNG, C. G. *The Practice of Psychotherapy.* New York: Pantheon, 1954.
    Jung's technique of psychotherapy is difficult to pin down, but this book is as good as any for defining his method.

22. LAING, R. *The Divided Self.* London: Tavistock Publications, 1960.
    A highly original exposition of the nature of Self and the vicissitudes of putting it back together.

23. PATTERSON, C. H. *Counseling and Psychotherapy.* New York: Harper & Row, 1959.
    A light review of counseling theory and procedures from a psychological, rather than psychoanalytic, point of view.

24. RANK, O. *Will Therapy and Truth and Reality.* New York: Alfred A. Knopf, 1945.
    Rank heavily influenced the practice of psychiatric social work, but his theories seem less important today.

25. ROGERS, C. R. *Client-Centered Therapy.* Boston: Houghton Mifflin, 1951.
    Rogers' second basic work which established client-centered therapy as a flourishing therapeutic entity.

26. ROGERS, C. R. *Counseling and Psychotherapy*. Boston: Houghton Mifflin, 1942.
    A classic still to be read; a new point of view regarding the client and the therapist, now somewhat ancient but still applicable.

27. ROSEN, J. N. *Direct Analysis*. New York: Grune & Stratton, 1953.
    Possibly the most directive of all approaches to psychotherapy, but important for treating schizophrenia.

28. SATIR, V. *Conjoint Family Therapy. A Guide to Theory and Technique*. Palo Alto: Science and Behavior Press, 1964.
    The Jackson group's "bible" of family therapy.

29. SECHEHAYE, M. *Symbolic Realization*. New York: International Universities Press, 1951.
    Describes the process by which schizophrenia can be healed through the central use of its symbols.

30. SINGER, E. *Key Concepts in Psychotherapy*. New York: Random House, 1965.
    A fairly recent systematic discussion of the problems of psychotherapy and their resolution.

31. SNYDER, W. U. and J. B. Snyder. *The Psychotherapy Relationship*. New York: Macmillan, 1961.
    A learning approach to the psychotherapeutic relationship.

32. STEINZOR, B. *The Healing Partnership. The Patient as Colleague in Psychotherapy*. New York: Harper & Row, 1967.
    A point of view which makes the client an equal partner in his own healing.

33. STIERLIN, H. *Conflict and Reconciliation. A Study in Human Relations and Schizophrenia*. New York: Doubleday, 1969.
    A small, but valuable, book on what therapy is all about. Every page ought to be treasured.

34. SULLIVAN, H. S. *The Collected Works of Harry Stack Sullivan*. New York: Norton, 1956.
    Hard reading; but Sullivan is the man who gave credence and substance to the interpersonal point of view in psychiatry.

35. TRUAX, C. B. and R. R. CARKHUFF. *An Introduction to Counseling and Psychotherapy: Training and Practice*. Chicago: Aldine, 1966.
    Concepts of counseling and psychotherapy based more on experimental findings than on practice.

36. WOLBERG, L. *The Technique of Psychotherapy*. New York: Grune & Stratton, 1954.
    An encyclopedic compendium on psychotherapy—the basic reference work.

37. WIENER, D. N. *A Practical Guide to Psychotherapy*. New York: Harper & Row, 1968.
    Discusses many of the issues treated in this book; valuable for a complementary point of view.

38. WHITAKER, C. A. and T. P. MALONE. *The Roots of Psychotherapy*. New York: Blakiston, 1953.
    An important conceptual work on psychotherapy which, for some reason, never gained recognition.

39. ZUKER, H. *Problems of Psychotherapy*. New York: Free Press, 1967.
    An elementary treatment of some of the problems in psychotherapy.

INDEX